STUDIES FROM TEN LITERATURES

STUDIES FROM TEN LITERATURES

BY

ERNEST BOYD

Essay Index Reprint Series

BOOKS FOR LIBRARIES PRESS, INC.
Freeport, New York

First Published 1925
Reprinted 1968

LIBRARY OF CONGRESS CATALOG CARD NUMBER:

68-20287

TO

HELEN BYRNE AND HAMILTON FISH ARMSTRONG
IN TOKEN OF A
FRIENDSHIP WHICH IS PART OF THE CIRCUMSTANCES
OUT OF WHICH THIS BOOK AROSE

CONTENTS

FRANCE

SPAIN

ITALY

PORTUGAL

SWITZERLAND

FRANCE

FLAUBERT AND FRENCH REALISM

THE connotations of the word "realism" in French literature are varied. In its later developments realistic literature presented a considerable problem, and a constant source of irritation to the guardians of the academic portals to Fame. Wherefore, these gentlemen exercised a remarkable ingenuity in the art of evasion and denial, which is responsible very largely for the diversity of opinion as to what realism is, and when it made its appearance in France. When challenged by modern realism they evaded the issue by asserting that it was not modern, and by denying that it was realistic. Thus, as every text-book will show, it was seriously argued that "the real French realists" were Racine, Molière, Boileau, La Bruyère, and Lesage. The rise of the Classical School in 1660 was described as a reaction against the Romantic period of the preceding half-century. Then followed a didactic era, when theses and theories were the essential, and finally, after an interval of sterility, there came, with Chateaubriand, a renaissance of the imagination. The Romantic movement was born, and it dominated the literary scene until about the middle of the nineteenth century.

It is at this point that we encounter realism as it is understood to-day. Balzac, who died in 1850, is accepted by all parties to the controversy as the precursor of the movement which was to crystallize in the work of Flaubert, the Goncourt brothers, Emile Zola, and the Naturalists. Balzac has been called "a realist in the observation of material facts," but "a Romanticist in his invention of plot

3

and incident," and this dualism in his work accounts, I think, for the strange unanimity of such irreconcilable adversaries as Brunetière and Zola in greeting him as the founder of the Realistic movement. The mandarins claimed him joyfully, because he served admirably to becloud the issue which the Goncourts, Flaubert, and Zola were trying to force to a decision. Zola and his disciples were glad to invoke a venerable name when fighting for their literary lives against a criticism which never ceased to decry them until they died or renounced their heresies.

Balzac, therefore, is the first name associated in modern French literature with realism, and his work provided material for the species of argument which, as I have said, involves the whole subject in a maze of qualified statements and contradictions. His successor Flaubert, after his death in 1880, was also drawn into the debate for the same purpose; namely, to support the thesis of the conservative critics that the modern realists were neither realistic nor modern. Both writers were powerfully influenced by the Romantic movement, and thus lent themselves to such interpretations as were placed upon them by the conflicting groups of their admirers. Flaubert, however, seemed more definitely to belong to the new school, for several reasons. In the first place, he did set himself deliberately to repress and finally to dominate that exuberant Romantic imagination which he shared with his age. He conceived *Madame Bovary* in a thoroughly realistic fashion and accomplished his task in strenuous obedience to a theory which was to become the dogma of Naturalism a generation later. In the second place, unlike Balzac, he enjoyed a clash with the official moralists, and at the outset of his career he acquired the halo without which, I suspect, no modern realist is authentic in the eyes of the average reader. When Flaubert was indicted for the immorality of *Madame Bovary* he was irrevocably committed to the company—since so numerous—of those writers euphemistically called in English "unpleasant."

Although the term "realism" does not, as is often supposed, date from the publication of that work, Flaubert is generally accepted as the father of the realistic novel. It was after a dinner given in his honor by Maupassant, Zola, Huysmans, and Octave Mirbeau, in 1877, that the "Naturalistic" school was created by the French press. The fame of Flaubert is definitely associated with Realism and Naturalism, and, as these are precisely the elements in contemporary American literature which are cultivated by the younger novelists, it is interesting to glance back at the chapter in French literature which began with *Madame Bovary* in 1857.

It was a year in which the unsuspecting Flaubert had every reason to believe that he could go on quietly writing for himself, as he had been doing ever since his return from the East. Labiche's comedies and the melodramas of Dumas *fils*, kept the theatre public busy; at the opera the first performance of Weber's *Oberon* occupied the attention of music-lovers, while the reception of Augier at the French Academy and the death of Alfred de Musset provided the literary world with excitement, varied by the thrills of legal scandals, the trial of Baudelaire for *Les Fleurs du Mal*, and Victor Hugo's attempted injunction against *Rigoletto*, on the ground that it was stolen from *Le Roi s'amuse*. Paris had obviously plenty of things to attend to without troubling over the first novel of Gustave Flaubert, whose name was utterly unknown to more than a small circle when he began to issue *Madame Bovary* as a serial in *La Revue de Paris*.

Unfortunately, that review was in bad odor politically with the authorities, and they made the novel a pretext for harassing the editors. Flaubert was, however, more fortunate than Baudelaire, a few months later, for he was acquitted, in consideration of the serious artistic purpose which clearly inspired his work. The trial, as is the custom in these affairs, merely served as an enormous advertisement for the new author, of which his publisher reaped the immediate benefit, for Flaubert had received only five hundred francs for the rights to the book during five years. So great was the success of the scandal that a newspaper at once offered him fifty centimes a line for his next novel, clearly a substantial advance upon the terms he had received for his first work. All the interests of the crowd were driven into the background by *Madame Bovary*; no vaudeville show was complete without its song on the subject, and burlesque playlets were written with Emma Bovary as the central figure. The reviewers had naturally jumped into the fray and the furious and eternal battle was waged with great vigor, only Sainte-Beuve, Barbey d'Aurevilly, Baudelaire, and a few of the more discriminating realizing the true value and the literary significance of *Madame Bovary*. The press as a whole gave preference to Ernest Feydeau's *Fanny*, a novel which appeared about the same time and presented a certain superficial resemblance to Flaubert's in its treatment of a similar theme, but is long since forgotten.

All the circumstances were propitious for a further exploitation of public curiosity, but Flaubert returned to his home near Rouen and gave no heed to popular clamor for five years, when he published *Salammbô*. In the interval all sorts of rumors had been in circulation; the author's first book was flying backward and forward like a shuttle-cock between the camps

of the Realists and their opponents, and the general
expectation was that Flaubert would either aggra-
vate his former offenses, or offer some sort of *amende
honorable*. Flaubert did neither; he simply flabber-
gasted both his friends and his enemies by publishing
this lengthy novel of Carthaginian life. Sainte-Beuve,
even, called for a lexicon with which to decipher this
mass of exotic words and archæological terms; the
learned experts denounced the pretensions of this
novelist turned historian, and the inaccuracies of detail were solemnly exposed. In the main there was
agreement on one point: the book was dull, though
some suspected, and tried to prove, that indecencies
were concealed beneath its soporific weight. The
dulness and latent obscenity of *Salammbô* were the
leading counts in the popular indictment of the book,
for Flaubert was now a public personage and had to
pay the penalty. Once more his name and his work
were bandied about in the couplets of vaudeville
singers, and an elaborate burlesque, *Folammbô, ou
les Cocasseries carthaginoises*, was produced at the
Palais-Royal Theatre, in which Hamilcar became
Arriv'tar, and by dint of much punning of this type
the whole story was turned into ridicule, precisely
in such a manner as to preserve the legend of the
author's manifold indecencies. It is remarkable
how the cheap humor of this parody summed up the
general tendency of contemporary criticism toward
Salammbô, into which Flaubert had poured all his
romanticism, his love of the fabulous Orient, of color
and sound and primitive passion.

The author himself considered this book to be an
even more definite manifestation of his theory of
art than *Madame Bovary*, and it was upon his theory,
the doctrine of "impersonal" literature, that the
whole reaction against the Romantic Movement took
its stand. The Romanticists were entirely personal

and subjective; the Realists sought for an objective, dispassionate notation of life, from which the author's personality and his sentiments are eliminated. What is the explanation of this misunderstanding between the master and his disciples? To ask this is to raise the whole problem of Flaubert's realism, for, it has often been pointed out, his works are apparently realistic and romantic alternately. After *Madame Bovary* came *Salammbô*, and then *L'Education sentimentale*, which was followed by *La Tentation de Saint-Antoine*; after which came the unfinished *Bouvard et Pécuchet*. If the author of these works was hailed and denounced as the begetter of the realistic novel, if the Goncourts and Maupassant and Zola elected him as master, later criticism is disposed to regard him rather differently, and to refuse to allow him to be claimed either by the Realists or the Romanticists. He seems at bottom to have belonged to the latter rather than the former, but his romanticism was not based upon that horror of reality which is the true mark of the French Romantic school.

Thus in his works of sheer imagination, *Salammbô* and *La Tentation*, the desire for reality, for verisimilitude, for the suppression of his own personality, leads him to write his romance as Zola documented himself for his records of the Second Empire. In his realistic novels, on the other hand, he took refuge from the despotism of facts by transferring his romanticism to his characters, to Frédéric in *L'Education sentimentale*, to Emma in *Madame Bovary*, and, above all, by allowing himself the freest play in the beauty of his words, in the wonderful rhythm of his phrases, so that a story of provincial adultery, the most hackneyed theme in fiction, takes on the glamour of Chateaubriand's adventures in mythical regions of tropical beauty. As his correspondence reveals, Flaubert's romantic imagination was never more powerfully stimulated than when he was engaged upon a work of realism, but when he turned to a work of imagination, then his scrupulous concern for reality insisted upon satisfaction.

This Romanticist who had no fear of reality was destined to live just long enough to see the rise of a literary generation which cultivated that fearlessness to a point where the Realist dominated everything else. In 1877 he was the guest at a dinner-party from which came the six authors, Emile Zola, Guy de Maupassant, J. K. Huysmans, Henry Céard, Léon Hennique, and Paul Alexis, who launched the Naturalistic movement with *Les Soirées de Médan*, which was published the year of Flaubert's death. Looking over the work of this group, not to mention the deservedly forgotten host of their imitators, it is difficult to connect them with Flaubert. That scrupulous artist, who could spend five days over the writing of one page, whose style is one of the delights of French literature, was surely the strangest progenitor for that brood of Naturalists. The Goncourts still preserved their cult of the "exact word," of the "rare epithet," but these writers cultivated the commonplace in both style and matter. Their virtues are seen in the work of Maupassant and in that sardonic little masterpiece of Henry Céard's, *Une Belle Journée*, but who even remembers Léon Hennique and Paul Alexis, "the shadow of Zola," as he was called?

In the pleasant process of progressing backward, in which the younger American novelists are just now engaged, the oblivion which has descended upon Flaubert's succession seems to be ignored, or, at least, to suggest no disquieting reflections. There is a drift in contemporary fiction which takes the novel back to France of the eighties and late seventies, but not to the fifties, when Flaubert expressed the only durable reaction against Romanticism. All literature is the history of the reaction of one generation against the idols of another, and *Madame Bovary* marked the end of the Romantic movement. It was the work of the transition and is therefore characterized by that hesitation between two schools which is the essence of Flaubert. The modern Realists, like his immediate successors, have emphasized only one element in the movement of which he was the leader, and their preoccupation with the mere details of actuality will as surely condemn them to neglect as it has condemned the voluminous literature of the Naturalistic school. With the exception of Baudelaire, no other French writer in modern times has exercised so powerful an influence as Flaubert with so small a volume of published work. During his lifetime only five books of his were published, yet they endure, while the twenty volumes of Zola's Rougon-Macquart series and the sixteen other volumes of his miscellaneous fiction have fallen into increasing disrepute, together with most of the "polygraphy" of that period. *Madame Bovary* shocked the bourgeoisie in accordance with all the rules of Naturalistic procedure; it evoked and reconstructed the life of a provincial town with the superb skill of the creative genius who is master of detail, in a fashion which only makes the labored piling up of facts seem intolerable in his successors. Yet it lives, after all these years, as photographic realism never lives after the external circumstances of the time have changed. It lives because of that dual element in the genius of Gustave Flaubert, which enabled him to see the dream and the reality which together make up the sum of human existence, and to express both with the sensitive beauty of a great artist.

Flaubert having been acquitted, in due course

his sins were forgiven, and he became a respectable figure, to be cited by the orthodox, together with Balzac, as an example of what decent realism should be. In this country, where French literature is simultaneously suspected by the moralists of outrageous licentiousness and credited by ingenuous youths with an ideal tolerance of the freedom of the artist, the fortunes of the realistic school from this point onward are instructive. Balzac having been canonized, and Flaubert being accepted for his romanticism tempered by realism, it might be imagined that the course of true literature ran smooth. It did not, however, for there continued an extraordinary confusion as to what a Realist really was. Brunetière actually discussed Rhoda Broughton in the same category as Flaubert, Zola, and Maupassant, while Dickens, George Eliot, and George Sand were—and still are—cited in every well-behaved French literary manual in discussions of realism.

In the circumstances, it is not surprising that, when a generation arose with a literature corresponding exactly to what the outside world now understands by French realism, the battle of *Madame Bovary* was resumed with intense vigor. The protagonist of this struggle was, of course, Emile Zola, whose name and influence have loomed larger in America, England, and Germany than those of any of his predecessors or contemporaries in the Realistic movement. Nevertheless, amongst both will be found men who never wrote worse than he, and several whose craftsmanship was vastly superior to his.

Let us begin with his own avatars. As early as 1847 there was Champfleury's *Chien-Caillou*, which was the first stone to be thrown at Romanticism by the actual pioneers in the campaign subsequently led by Zola. These pioneers were three gentlemen, of whom I need name only one, since his fame in this connection has survived him, Edmond Duranty, whose best novel, *La Cause du Beau Guillaume*, has been republished in Paris. During the early years of the Second Empire Duranty and his friends published a periodical whose title, *Le Réalisme*, was in itself a manifesto. When the first of its six numbers appeared, in 1856, Flaubert had not yet published *Madame Bovary*, and the very name of realism was something challenging, heretical, diabolical. Duranty had little to offer except his belief that a new literary epoch was imminent, that Champfleury was its precursor, and that romanticism was anathema.

When Zola was a young and unknown employee at the publisher Hachette's he came in contact with Duranty, who published *La Cause du Beau Guillaume* with that firm in 1862, at a time when Zola himself had not even issued his *Contes à Ninon*. Later Zola paid a brief tribute to this interesting and neglected figure in the history of modern French fiction, citing from *Le Réalisme* the formula which so largely anticipated the programme of the Naturalists: "Realism aims at an exact, complete, and honest reproduction of the social environment, of the age in which the author lives, because such studies are justified by reason, by the demands made by public interest and understanding, and because they are free from falsehood and deception. This reproduction should be as simple as possible so that all may understand it." Zola accepts this definition of purpose, merely extending it to include all classes of society, for he contends that Duranty's realism was too much restricted to the middle classes. Champfleury, however, was not a writer of sufficient stature to bear the brunt of such a programme, and by one of those ironies of literary history which are so delightful, Flaubert's *Madame Bovary* received only a brief and not very appreciatory notice in *Le Réalisme*, which thus died without being aware that it had witnessed the first serious breach in the ramparts it had attempted to storm.

Although Zola's earliest fiction was too unorthodox for Hachette, who refused one of the stories in the *Contes à Ninon*, and although his first novel, *La Confession de Claude*, in 1865, outraged the pruderies of the Empire, he had not yet produced the great work which was to place him at the head of the Realists, now christened Naturalists, in accordance with his scientific theories. That work was *L'Assommoir*, published in 1877, and the first big success of the twenty volumes of the Rougon-Macquart series. This is a date in Zola's evolution, but in the history of French realism that date was anticipated by Edmond and Jules de Goncourt in 1865, when their *Germinie Lacerteux* appeared. They were the real successors of Flaubert, and they had actually formulated the whole doctrine of Naturalism when they wrote, in 1864: "The novel of to-day is composed from documents, received by word of mouth or taken direct from nature, just as history is composed from written documents. Historians write narratives of the past, novelists narratives of the present."

Germinie Lacerteux contained a preface which is regarded as a document of historic importance, not only because it emphasizes the revolutionary character of the novel itself, but also because it lays down the theory of Naturalism. "The public like novels that are untrue. This is a true novel. They like books which seem to take them into society: this work comes from the streets. This is a clinical study of love. The public like harmless and comforting stories, adventures that end happily, ideas which disturb neither their digestion nor their peace of mind. Nowadays, when the novel has assumed the studies and the duties of science, it may claim the liberty and frankness of science." When this manifesto appeared Zola was an obscure journalist, and in a provincial paper he wrote one of the earliest of the few favorable reviews which the book received. The comments were, in the main, exceedingly violent in their hostility. "Putrid literature," cried one pundit, while a notorious pornographer described the book as "sculptured slime." Flaubert, however, was enthusiastic, and declared that "the great question of realism was never so frankly propounded." Sainte-Beuve realized that a new æsthetic was needed to criticise the new literature.

However, he kept this opinion and his appreciation of the book for the private consumption of his friends, following the precedent he had set for himself in the more delicate affair of *Les Fleurs du Mal*. The result is that, to this day, the Goncourts are viewed with a cold eye in academic circles. Even in Professor Saintsbury's enormous and catholic survey of the French novel they receive a few intolerant paragraphs, in which indignation takes the place of criticism and historical perspective. Zola himself, for some reason, escapes with milder censure, although his debt to the Goncourt brothers is obvious, the difference between the authors of *Germinie Lacerteux* and the author of *L'Assommoir* being that the former were artists, whereas the latter was a reporter. The Goncourts had a style and an æsthetic. Zola's style consisted in his having none, and for an æsthetic he substituted a scientific superstition.

Needless to say, it was Zola, not Edmond de Goncourt, who enjoyed the popular fame which for some years was the reward of the realistic novelists. To the end Goncourt, who outlived his brother Jules by a whole generation, was the object of an incredible vendetta. It seemed as if neither the mob nor its masters could pardon him for being a perfect man of

letters, happily independent of the exigencies of his
critics or his potential patrons. Zola, on the other
hand, threw himself into the struggle which the Goncourts disdained. The critics wildly denounced each
book of the Rougon-Macquart series as it appeared,
as they had begun, in 1868, by fulminating against
his earliest novel of importance, *Thérèse Raquin*.
Alphonse Daudet was kindly treated, as the tame
Realist who managed to be so much more gentleman-
like than his terrible friends and literary confrères,
Zola, Huysmans, Paul Alexis, Henry Céard, and the
Goncourts. But the strange fact remained that Zola's
readers surpassed those of Daudet in number, and
the sales of such books as *Nana* and *La Débâcle*
were rivalled only by those of the estimable George
Ohnet.

Everything tended to constitute Zola the leader and
spokesman of what was now known as Naturalism.
He came forward with his flock around him in 1880,
when the celebrated collection of stories, *Les Soirées
de Médan*, was published under the ægis of the
master. In addition to that of Zola, some of the five
other names in that volume are still remembered,
such as Huysmans and Maupassant; Léon Hennique
and Paul Alexis are forgotten, though George Moore
retold the one story of Alexis, *La Fin de Lucie
Pellegrin*, which deserves to survive. Henry Céard,
who was a member of the Academy Goncourt, and
until his death on August 16, 1924, one of the few
remaining members of the original Goncourt circle,
has never had the fame outside his own country to
which that sardonic little masterpiece, *Une Belle
Journée*, entitles him. It was issued here in an English translation just as he died, leaving Léon Hennique as the last survivor of the Médan group.

If only because, with *Boule de Suif*, it introduced
Maupassant, *Les Soirées de Médan* contained enough

to justify its existence, and to impose the new generation of Realists upon the attention of public and
critics alike. It presented six writers who were to
play a considerable part in current French literature
for a decade or more, and of whom two, Maupassant
and Huysmans, outlived the merely transient fame
attaching to the work of a challenging school. Moreover, the arrival of recruits was not delayed, and
soon to those names were added Camille Lemonnier,
Octave Mirbeau, J. H. Rosny, Paul Adam, Lucien
Descaves, and the brothers Margueritte, to mention
a few which will be familiar to the general reader of
to-day. These writers all gravitated around Zola,
and the formula of the experimental novel, with its
scientific observation of facts, its exact documentation, its objective study of social environment, seemed
to be assured of success.

England and Germany were translating Zola,
George Moore in London, and Michael Georg Conrad
in Munich were imitating him, and the upholders of
morals and traditions at home and abroad were up
in arms against this literary Antichrist. Not only
did the professors like Brunetière recoil in terror, but
critics as urbane as Lemaître and Anatole France
were troubled. France, in particular, was desperately aggrieved by the lack of patriotism in Abel
Hermant (now repentant and in turn the censor of
that venerable radical), and deeply offended by the
salaciousness and indecencies of such works as La
Terre. All that suburban moralists abhor in the
younger generation in America to-day was duly
abhorred and castigated in Zola and his followers
during the last quarter of the nineteenth century.
With a virtuous indignation worthy of a contemporary Society of Authors holding its skirts aloof
from a Dreiser or a Cabell, a group of schismatics
in the ranks of Naturalism turned upon Zola, and

provided us with one of the best jokes in the history of French literature.

In *Le Figaro* of the 18th August, 1887, shortly after the publication of *La Terre*, there appeared "The Manifesto of the Five." The signatories were Paul Bonnetain, J. H. Rosny, Lucien Descaves, Paul Margueritte, and Gustave Guiches, and they solemnly recorded their sternest disapproval of the master, whom they had weighed in the balance both of morals and æsthetics and found wanting. In order to appreciate the charm of their virtuous censure of Zola, one must know that Bonnetain had acquired fame as the author of a novel whose theme was onanism, J. H. Rosny had in that very year published *L'Immolation*, a novel of incest, Paul Margueritte was the author of a Lesbian masterpiece, entitled *Tous Quatre*, while neither Guiches nor Descaves could have been translated without considerable bowdlerization. However, they proceeded to a formal indictment of their literary progenitor, accusing him of having lowered the standard of Naturalism, of catering to large sales by deliberate obscenities, of being a morbid and impotent hypochondriac, incapable of taking a sane and healthy view of mankind. They freely referred to Zola's physiological weaknesses and expressed the utmost horror at the crudeness of *La Terre*.

At the same time they did not ignore the literary side of their brief for the prosecution. His experimental novels based on documentation are described as the work of a man "armed with faked documents picked up at third hand, full of Hugoesque bombast . . . and lapsing into perpetual repetition and stereotyped phrases." The observation in *La Terre* is "superficial, its technic old-fashioned, and the narrative is vulgar and commonplace, while the filthiness is exaggerated . . . the Master has descended to the lowest depths of dirtiness." Therefore, they conclude, "we energetically repudiate this imposture on real literature . . . we repudiate these rhetorical mouthpieces, these gigantic, superhuman, and incredible figures, devoid of all subtlety, projected brutally, in heavy masses, upon scenes viewed in chance glimpses from the windows of express-trains . . . we refuse to be parties to a shameful degeneration."

Thus ended a glorious adventure in realism, perhaps the greatest deliberate effort of the school in any country to impose its æsthetic and to alter the course of literary evolution by violent effort. The Five formulated in their literary criticism the substance of our judgment to-day on the work of Zola and his disciples. The scientific notation of life is an illusion, and when an illusory theory is added to an execrable style, the result is a foregone conclusion. It was left, however, to writers not one whit less improper, in the moralists' sense, than those they attacked, to break the spell of Naturalism, not by producing "realistic" novels in the manner of Rhoda Broughton, but by throwing over the preposterous convention which was the real offense of Zola against literature. The names that will survive from that period, between the death of Balzac and the decline of Zola in the last years of the 'nineties, are those of writers like Flaubert, the Goncourts, and Maupassant, whose genius transcended the limitations of the realistic dogma.

Yet, it is still on moral and not upon æsthetic grounds that realism is impugned. In English-speaking countries the term is synonymous, in the popular mind, with literature that is unpleasant and more or less obscene. To such an extent is this convention accepted, even unconsciously, by those who theoretically know better, that a French work which is not avowedly realistic, which treats of psychological and spiritual rather than physical and material conditions, may with impunity emulate the strangest aberrations of the much-decried Naturalists. Marcel Proust's astonishing epic of sexual inversion, though not lacking in the crudest details, receives tributes of admiration from English and American critics who indorsed the purely political vendetta which resulted in the condemnation of Victor Margueritte's *La Garçonne.* The latter is nothing more than a typical volume amongst many which have recently far exceeded its frankness in describing the sexual life of a certain type of woman. Let us recall that time, more than thirty years ago, when Paul Margueritte was seized with a moral fervor ostensibly as genuine, and inherently as ridiculous, as that of which the surviving brother is now the victim. These incidents have only the remotest concern with literature.

At the present time realism in French literature is in abeyance. Its exponents are chiefly the survivors of the Naturalistic period: Céard, Victor Margueritte, Lucien Descaves, and Paul Adam, to whom must be added the isolated creator of *Jean Christophe.* The younger men who may be counted as the continuators of the realistic tradition are not numerous, for they are separated from their literary forebears by the Symbolist generation, whose fiction cannot be called realistic, although Anglo-Saxon virtue would blush at the charming impudicity of Henri de Régnier's novels, were he not protected by that unwritten law in favor of those who have no specific purpose in exhibiting "human documents." A few names deserve mention among the contemporary Realists, Gaston Chérau, with his *Champi-Tortu;* Léon Werth with *La Maison Blanche;* Roger Martin du Gard with *Les Thibault.*

Realism, as it has thus evolved, more closely approximates to the English variety; it has shed its exuberances and modified its crudities, for it is no longer bemused by the pseudo-science of Zola. Such excesses as used to interrupt the easy flow of French fiction are disappearing, to make way for the very different experiments of impressionists like Jean Giraudoux and the fantastic adventures of Francis Carco, André Salmon, and Pierre MacOrlan. Such incidents as the expulsion of Victor Margueritte from the order of the Legion of Honor have no literary significance. Only extreme innocence of the character of the works which have simultaneously passed unnoticed can account for the foreign comment upon *La Garçonne*. No legal proceedings, it will be noticed, were instituted. We are far from the heroic period of Flaubert or even Zola. Realism, in that peculiar Anglo-Saxon connotation of the word, is a dead issue in France. That is why French critics who are aware of the real import of Proust's *A la Recherche du Temps Perdu* have wasted no inappropriate zeal in repudiating Victor Margueritte. *Ils en ont vu bien d'autres!*

ANATOLE FRANCE

"'Sylvestre Bonnard' a masterpiece? I agree. A masterpiece of platitudinousness. . . . It is the dullest and most colorless of all my books. I did it to win a prize and I did it so well—or rather so badly —that I won the prize." Thus Anatole France described that work which, in Lafcadio Hearn's translation, first introduced him to the English-speaking world, in 1891. Just ten years previously the same book had established him for the first time with the general reading public in France. Anatole France was then thirty-seven years old, but was practically unknown when the French Academy crowned *The Crime of Sylvestre Bonnard*, which was to become the most renowned and universally popular of all his works. France did not easily or quickly achieve the fame which was his so long that one is inclined to think of him as having never known the drudgery and obscurity of literary apprenticeship. He died in his eightieth year, after a career extending over a period dating back to 1868, when his first book, a critical study of Alfred de Vigny, was published, but he actually made his début at the precocious age of fifteen or thereabout with *The Legend of Sainte Radegonde*, a schoolboy theme published by his father, the bookseller of the Quai Voltaire, whose shop was the appropriate cradle of Anatole France's genius. We next hear of him as a contributor to an obscure periodical, *La Gazette Rimée*, for which he wrote two savage political satires in verse on the régime of the Third Empire, thereby hastening the early death of the review in question and almost delivering himself into the none too gentle hands of the imperial authorities. He then edited a bibliographical journal, which lasted but a few numbers, and an *Encyclopædia of the French Revolution*, finally finding a place with the famous publisher Lemerre, who intrusted him with the task of editing and writing prefaces for various classics and reading manuscripts. In 1873 Lemerre published his *Poèmes Dorés*, and in 1876 his *Noces Corinthiennes*, which were until recently, when those scattered prefaces were collected, the only works of this youthful period which their author acknowledged. In 1874 he became the assistant of Leconte de Lisle in the Senate Library, and from 1886 to 1891 he wrote those book reviews for *Le Temps* which have been preserved under the title of *On Life and Letters*. He was elected to the French Academy in 1896, and in 1921 he received the Nobel Prize for Literature. Such are the few dates in this peaceful life, so harmonious and so glorious, and so uneventful in the ordinary sense of the word.

Neither that volume of collected poems nor that dramatic epic, written under the benign and orthodox impulse of the Parnassian movement, created any stir, and *Jocasta* and *The Famished Cat*, two now familiar novelettes which appeared in 1879, added little or nothing to his fame. In 1881 he was as obscure as it is possible for an author to be after some fifteen years of regular literary practice. The award of the Academy changed all that, and *The Crime of Sylvestre Bonnard* and its author became suddenly famous. Then began a forty-year period of rich creative activity which has seen the emergence of a genius so exquisite and so national that the whole world recognizes a peculiar appropriateness in the adoption of the pseudonym "France" by the once unknown Anatole François Thibault. His work sums up the whole intellectual tradition of his country, and the essential strains of the French genius are found in his books, from the fabliaux, Rabelais and Molière, to Voltaire, Diderot, and the Encyclopædists, from Balzac and Stendhal to Renan. The spirit of his race lives in him, the urbane and thoroughly civilized tradition of Montaigne, which is, in the last analysis, the distinctive contribution of France to European literature.

No greater contrast could be found than that which is furnished by a comparison of Anatole France with that other great veteran from the same age of literary giants, the Danish critic Georg Brandes. France, characteristically, knew no language—no modern language—other than his own. He had, therefore, the national self-sufficiency, that suggestion of provincialism which the French betray the moment one escapes from the superficial cosmopolitanism of Paris. Brandes is "the good European" in the fullest meaning of Nietzsche's term; he is the interpreter of international values, the creator of a national literature, who has achieved his purpose by the very catholicity of his interests, by his instinctive disregard for the parochial and narrowly national. One could not imagine Anatole France discovering an obscure and erratic German professor and proclaiming the advent of Nietzsche, as Brandes did. In the four volumes of the Frenchman's critical writings there is hardly an allusion to any of the writers who were struggling in the early '90s for recognition. He denounced Zola and the Naturalists with all the fervor of his bitterest adversary, Brunetière. Yet Brandes, the internationalist, the fighter for freedom of ideas, and France, the classicist, the smiling sceptic, are at one in their fundamental philosophy, which is that of intellectual liberty, the belief that the mind alone can be free and that all other forms of liberation are an illusion.

The imposing series of Anatole France's work is conditioned by an even more imposing list of works, Latin and Greek and the French classics, which he has tirelessly read and annotated, and upon which he has meditated until their very essence has become part of himself. He was born in an atmosphere of books and his own creative impulse is rooted in books, through which he approaches life, life reflected and refracted, but never deflected, through literature, for he has frequented only the best company, as the professors who delight in tracing his borrowings have incidentally demonstrated. When the Dreyfus affair dragged him out of his study into the public arena he took his political refuge in the obvious shelter of radical libertarianism, with a complete absence of all that subtlety which normally distinguishes his ideas. But the case was not one where subtlety was demanded; it stirred that deep-seated belief in liberty which lay at the bottom of his scepticism as it lay beneath that of Montaigne and Voltaire. The petty æsthetes just fresh from the classroom and the anti-Semitic politicians of French literature have made great play with Anatole France's socialism, as if he were some soap-box revolutionary and not the author of thirty volumes, not one of which contains his few contributions to the literature of French radicalism. They are, however, just a little embarrassed by the necessity of explaining away that masterpiece of sardonic humor, *The Gods Are Athirst*, and the terrible satire at the end of *Penguin Island*, in order to preserve the fiction of Anatole France the naïve Socialist.

France's socialism, like his endless pursuit of ideas, has not escaped the scrutiny of that alert and scintillating intelligence of his, whose play is an enchantment never to be forgotten, the lure which draws one unfailingly to his books. He has none of the ingenuous rationalist's faith in reason. "I hate science," cries the Abbé Coignard, "because I have loved her too much, like the voluptuaries who reproach women with not having realized the dreams which they cherished of them." As an intelligent sceptic, France has explored the extreme limits of doubt and despair, and he regards mankind with a mixture of tenderness and contempt; there is pity in his scepticism and his irony is friendly. That irony runs through all his work like a golden thread, and whether the scene be ancient or modern, real or imaginary, one always finds in some disguise the interlocutor whose hand may be what it will, but the voice is the voice of France. In *Thaïs* the Epicurean Nikias warns Paphnutius of the fearful vengeance of Eros, the unconquerable, whose victory comes just when the lovely Byzantine sinner's conversion is accomplished. *The Sign of the Reine Pédauque* and its sequel, *The Opinions of Jérôme Coignard*, expound the irresistible philosophy of the famous Abbé, who is, next to M. Bergeret, the most delightful creation of the author's and his most authentic mouthpiece.

The Abbé Coignard, it will be remembered, restrained his scepticism only where "the truths of religion" are concerned; M. Bergeret supplies that omission. In *The Gods Are Athirst* France is the sage Brotteaux who is condemned to death because of his irreverence toward the great revolutionists, for, as he says elsewhere: "Robespierre believed in virtue and he inaugurated the Terror; Marat believed in justice and demanded 200,000 heads." In *The Red Lily* his views are doubly represented by the writer Paul Vence, who declares that "irony and pity must be the judges and witnesses of mankind," and by the sculptor Dechartre. He is the theatre doctor, Trublet, in *A Mummer's Tale*, that diverting excursion into the world of the comedians. The very titles of his stories, *Balthasar, Clio, Mother of Pearl, The Well of St. Clare, The Merrie Tales of Jacques Tournebroche, The Seven Wives of Bluebeard,* indicate the range of Anatole France's deft skill in exploring the various scenes of the great human comedy. Here are holy legends and Bible stories in the manner of Renan, Renaissance tales and rococo anecdotes, and even adventures in the supernatural world. "I am not credulous," says France in the *Reine Pédauque.* "I have rather a remarkable tendency to doubt, which makes me mistrust reason. . . . To everything that is strange I say: Why not, and this 'why not' tempts me to believe."

It was the Dreyfus affair which aroused Anatole France from that state of detached irony which is fascinating, but which might, in the long run, have become sterile. Between 1897 and 1901 he wrote the four volumes of contemporary history, *The Elm Tree on the Mall, The Wicker-Work Woman, The Amethyst Ring,* and *M. Bergeret in Paris,* and revealed himself as a satirist of incomparable skill, whose nearest antecedent was the Voltaire of *Candide.* Like all great satire, it transcended the immediate aim of the author. This analysis of private and political intrigue, of royalist plots, of anti-Semitic fanaticism and clerical wire-pulling, this picture of a republic suppressing republican demonstrations by armed force, is something more than a topical skit. The mere title, "Contemporary History," with which the four books are bracketed, seems in retrospect to have been an ironical thrust at the future. With *Penguin Island* he returns to the charge, tracing, this time, the whole history of France with that sharp pen; the Dreyfus scandal in the "case of the 80,000 bundles of hay"; the growth of civilization from that point when woman first discovered the effectiveness of clothing, and concluding with the disillusioned vision of the future, with its eternal recurrence of tyranny and revolution, or war and catastrophe. *The White Stone* is more utopian, but in *The Revolt of the Angels* he makes his final and disconcerting comment on the history of man. It is a history of human folly, related by the gardener Nectaire, an old comrade in arms of Lucifer, and is an admirable satire on anarchy.

This book appeared just before the war and has a strangely prophetic flavor now. It was Anatole France's last glance at contemporary events, for after that he lived in the memories of his childhood, adding to the three earlier fragments of autobiography, *My Friend's Book*, *Pierre Nozière*, and *The Aspirations of Jean Servien*, two supremely charming books, *Little Pierre* and *The Bloom of Life*. There is a grace and ease in the writing of these pages from an almost mythical past which must surprise even the most ardent of France's admirers, for it seems that age could not dim the magic of that style nor alter the sureness of every touch. In this patriarchal figure was surely a mortal beloved of the gods, who endowed him with an intelligence Hellenic in its subtlety, a Latin sense of realism and a pity that is Christian. As a French critic has said:

Give Montaigne more sympathy for the world which he judges, take the essence of Voltaire and the general attitude of Renan. Then combine Renan, Voltaire, and Montaigne, and cap them with the literary art of Racine and Bossuet. Transfer all these qualities to a personality that is original and profound. There is a man alive among us who answers to this astonishing definition, Anatole France. He is the glittering summit dominating a plain of mediocrity that grows flatter and flatter.

Ever since the Dreyfus case dragged Anatole France into the political arena, his socialism had made him abhorrent to all conservative Frenchmen, but at the time of his death he had survived long enough to encounter another sort of unpopularity, which will seem surprising to those who think of him as a consecrated name and an already established classic of modern French literature. He had lived long enough to become the *bête noire* of all the smart young men who are building up a French literature based largely upon maudlin Catholicism, eccentric syntax and typography, and a strange combination of homosexualism and sport-mysticism. These aggressive youths, led by a generation masticating the cud of stale controversies dating from the Dreyfus affair and the separation of church and state, constitute to-day a well-organized opposition to Anatole France and all that he represented. By some mental process, known only to themselves, these young prodigies adored the tub-thumping jingoism of Maurice Barrès; the Socialist platitudes of Anatole France excited their contempt. The one was credited with political genius, the other with senile demagoguery. Obviously neither should be judged by political tests, but while there is always an excuse amongst the younger generation for Barrès the chauvinist, there is none for France the Socialist.

This triumph of Bergsonian intuition was, of course, in the act of development before the war, an event which came appropriately to test the protestations of mystic patriotism and anti-rationalism which marked the literature of the generation which was to be practically exterminated before peace was declared. But their successors, the writers who were not articulate in 1914, always under the safe tuition of the sheltered survivors of the Dreyfus pogrom, carry on the proud tradition which consists in "conspuing" Anatole France. He, it will be remembered, volunteered for active service, whereas Barrès talked and wrote the war to the bitterest end. They are

adept pupils of that school of abuse of which Léon
Daudet is the laureate. As witness Philippe Soupault:

Anatole France's name falls from my pen like a blot. All
his books, or at least all those that I forced myself to read,
pursued me for some weeks like nightmares. I ceased to write
myself. This rose-water scepticism, this cheap perfection of
style, represents to me all that is worst in literature. I fled in
terror.

An older commentator, the celebrated caricatur-
ist, André Rouveyre, a great friend of Guillaume
Apollinaire, wrote shortly before the celebration of
France's eightieth birthday:

The most significant representative of those writers who have
paraded the greatest vanity and ostentatiously displayed their
own superiority is undoubtedly Anatole France. . . . He is
the last and most perfect type of what seems to us most out of
date. He is the witty trifler, with a set, beatific smile, the elas-
tic man whose curves are soft, the image of instability, both
because of his poverty of original ideas and systematically: a
rhetorician to the marrow of his bones, whose Nirvana is vague
and inexpressive. . . . His great official renown has made him
impressive, but is not connected with any genuine, positive,
human action, precisely because the talent of an Anatole France
is made up entirely of scholastic acquisitions, with nothing original which might contain the profound spiritual fire of this
epoch. The time has passed for such feeble, servile copyists.

Both these quotations are typical, including the
muddy, redundant style of Rouveyre, which is not
altogether preserved in translation. They will suffice
as specimens of a certain criticism which, if remotely
traceable to the politics of the Dreyfus case, has now
evolved into a semblance of something more important than politics. It is not mere royalism, for
Rouveyre is no *Camelot du Roy*, and Charles Maurras,
the only intelligent royalist in France, is not only
a lifelong admirer of Anatole France, but is actually
the writer whose mind is most nearly allied to his,
the one person, in fact, who should succeed to his

chair in the French Academy. It is an attitude engendered by æsthetic Catholicism and dadaism, using the latter term in its most general sense to describe incoherent writing, disordered thinking, and
a total lack of all humor and urbanity—the Fascist
spirit in literature, which corresponds in Europe to
Ku Klux Kriticism in America.

The chief exponent of the Neo-Catholic revolt
against Anatole France is that mediæval inquisitor of
letters, Henri Massis, editor of *La Revue Universelle*,
and literary critic. Massis's pursuit of demons is
not limited to France, for it extends to André Gide
and the *Nouvelle Revue Française* group, which is
remote from Anatole France and includes some of
his least sympathetic critics. Gide as a Protestant,
of course, is even more hateful to Massis than the
pagan Anatole France. Thus he accuses the former
of "demoniality," but the latter is an "inhuman
humanist," a pitiful victim of the superstition that
Greek civilization was beautiful and that Christianity drove the joy of life and beauty out of the
hearts of men. Being older and more educated than
the irrepressible Monsieur Soupault, Henri Massis
makes no effort to be unnecessarily ludicrous by
denying Anatole France's supreme qualities as a
master of French prose. In fact, when he dismisses
him with Voltaire as a wretched man who misused
his gifts, one hardly feels it necessary to continue
the discussion. It is better, I should say, to be dismissed with Voltaire than to be classed with Claudel.
Æsthetic Catholicism has its reasons which reason
cannot understand. It is interesting to note that
Charles Péguy, one of the few authentic Catholics in
the front rank of French literature, had no doubt as
to the importance of Anatole France, who gave
Crainquebille and other contributions to the *Cahiers
de la Quinzaine*, that enduring achievement of
Péguy's editorial genius.

The unpopularity of Anatole France, in other words, is neither a political nor a religious question, although both elements enter into it. He did not shock the deep, elemental Catholicism in Péguy nor has the monarchical Maurras ever allowed himself to misunderstand the real significance of the Dreyfusard who created M. Bergeret and Jérôme Coignard. But neither of these writers is an obscurantist, and political and æsthetic obscurantism are the order of the day. Anatole France disturbed the two groups, so they coalesce in defense of all the aborted literature to which his own luminous French is the retort courteous, and of all the faded dogmas to which his clarity and wit meant destruction. His career itself was a negation of the hasty, half-baked, modern method of forcing a way that has not been prepared into literature. It is forgotten, as a rule, that he was nearly forty when he wrote *Le Crime de Sylvestre Bonnard*, his first contact with the general reading public and his first success. Even his first book of verse was not published until he was within a year of thirty.

That long apprenticeship, that gradual maturity are often overlooked by critics like Ortega y Gasset, who accuse him of a monotonous perfection that has never advanced beyond its earliest culminating point. If he had only rushed in where nowadays nobody fears to tread, his rawest efforts would not only serve to measure publicly his progress, but would serve to earn him immediate laurels as a genius. By so doing, of course, he would have sacrificed all that ease and balance and dignity, that deft assurance in his ideas and in his craft, which are his enchantment. He would have fumbled and groped, and thus escaped the hatred and mistrust which superior men excite in their inferiors.

THE PROTESTANT BARRÈS: ANDRÉ GIDE

In the happy 'nineties, when André Gide's first book, *Les Cahiers d'André Walter*, appeared anonymously, the initiated, who knew who the author was, nicknamed him "the Protestant Barrès." No more remarkable first book has come out of France in his generation except that of Maurice Barrès, *Sous l'Œil des Barbares*, which had preceded Gide's by three years. Hence the analogy suggested between these two writers, the antithesis of each other, each of whom was to become a leader of the younger generation, according to the taste and temperament of their disciples.

Having rapidly transformed himself from the interesting and stimulating individualist of those early novels of *Le Culte du Moi* into a one hundred per cent Nationalist patriot, a French Babbitt, so to speak, Maurice Barrès very naturally loomed more prominently in the public eye and in the public prints than André Gide. To his literary influence, based upon a style which survived even the cheapest claptrap of his later years, he added the mob prestige of the chauvinist, politician. Unlike Barrès, Gide has been prominently associated since the war with the movement of that handful of people in France who understand how civilized men should treat their conquered adversaries; having remained silent during the conflict, he was one of the first to propose an intelligent intellectual understanding with Germany. But here again he was unlike Barrès, for he made no effort to reach the masses. He might have shared the humanitarian lime-light with Romain

Rolland, or the radical amplifier of Barbusse. Characteristically he appealed only to the few, who, after all, decide what really matters and determine all enduring values.

The inconsequential fame of politicians is such that Barrès is at least a name, I imagine, to many people in this country who have never heard of Gide. So far as translation is concerned, neither author has hitherto been adequately represented. Lady Rothermere translated Gide's *Prometheus Ill-Bound* a few years ago, and *Colette Badudoche* brought Barrès into English on the wave of war-time sentiment; but, to all intents and purposes, the two literary leaders of contemporary France exist only for those who read them in the original. There has been no perceptible excitement since André Gide's *La Porte Etroite* appeared in the excellent translation of Mrs. Dorothy Bussy as *Strait is the Gate*, nor even that minimum of appreciative attention to which a first-rate work of modern fiction is entitled. The translation has been made under the author's supervision, for he knows English well, and has translated Conrad and Tagore. It so adequately reflects the sober charm of the French that it will be quite unnecessary to cite it as an excuse for whatever neglect may be the fate of Gide in America.

His reception here contrasts sharply with that accorded to him in Germany, where *La Porte Etroite*, *L'Immoraliste*, *Paludes*, and four other works of lesser importance have long since been translated. In English there is one adequate study of him, in Edmund Gosse's *Portraits and Sketches*, as against several in German. He receives a perfunctory paragraph in Professors Cunliffe and de Bacourt's *French Literature during the Last Half-Century*, and is not mentioned at all in the recent history of Professors Nitze and Darzan. A brief article reviewing *L'Im-*

moraliste and *La Porte Etroite*, in Madame Duclaux's *Twentieth-Century French Writers*, completes, I think, the meagre comment of the English-speaking world upon André Gide.

In France his name is one with which to conjure up controversy so violent that it is a proof, at least, of Gide's challenging originality. One of his most aggressive opponents, Henri Béraud, has collected into a volume entitled *La Croisade des Longues Figures* the results of many months' campaigning against André Gide and the *Nouvelle Revue Française* in the French press. In the second volume of his *Jugements* Henri Massis, the conservative critic, has delivered a virulent indictment of Gide, in which, with characteristic mediæval piety, he accuses him of sorcery and of casting demoniacal spells. Even the lamb-like Henri de Régnier, whose continual literary ecstasies in *Le Figaro* are one of the unconscious delights of that journal, departs from all his rules to declare that he cannot read André Gide, whose "best books have in them something dull, feeble, and factitiously sober," whose talent is "due to the desire to display it rather than to its actual possession." Thus, while his adversaries do furiously rage, *Strait is the Gate* causes not a ripple in our own literary duck-pond.

In 1909, when *La Porte Etroite* had just been published, Edmund Gosse thought that Gide was "the most interesting man of letters under the age of fifty," and said that "his mind is more closely attuned to English ideas, or what once were English ideas, than that of any other living writer of France." From which he assumed that the writings of André Gide should have a special interest for English-speaking readers. Whether that assumption is sound, this translation of "one of the most beautiful works which have been printed in English for a long time"

—to quote Mr. Gosse—will prove. Curiously enough, while those of us who know and appreciate Gide have been complaining of his neglect, the essence of Henri Béraud's charge against the author is that he and his friends of the *Nouvelle Revue Française* monopolize foreign attention and, with the assistance of French propaganda funds, have foisted themselves upon us at the expense of really important French writers. "Even in Belfast," exclaims M. Béraud, "where there are fewer books read than in any other city in the world, there is a French book-shop, containing chiefly cooking-books and the works of MM. Claudel, Suarès, and André Gide."

Béraud has also discovered in the works of André Gide "eight barbarisms, thirty solecisms, two misconstructions, several instances of amphibology, misspellings, some mistakes in the agreement of tenses, irregular usages of verbs, a vicious ellipse by change of number, divers superfluous negatives, several pleonasms, and certain succulent imbecilities." In company with Gide's more serious critics he also finds that he is a Puritan, a Calvinist, a Huguenot, and, generally speaking, one of those depressing, scoundrelly Protestants, whom all French "integral nationalist" patriots classify with Jews and Freemasons as enemies of France. Remy de Gourmont and Gide crossed pens on this issue of puritanism in the early days of the *Nouvelle Revue Française*, when Gide charged Gourmont with a deep hatred of modesty, and of Christianity the root of all modesty. Gide repudiated Calvin, but could not obliterate the imprint of his Protestantism.

The great Protestant names in French literary history are for the most part Swiss, and in modern French literature there are only two Protestant writers of note, Pierre Loti and André Gide. In the former there is no trace of his religious origins, which were never, I suspect, very deep, but Gide's Protestantism is a vital part of his work. As Mr. Gosse says, it enables us "to discover what the importance of a Huguenot training can be in the development of a mind which has wholly delivered itself from the Huguenot bondage." Those who naturally believe that puritanism is the special privilege—or affliction —of Anglo-Saxon Christendom, should study its manifestations in the works both critical and imaginative of André Gide.

They are of an immense and elusive variety, which makes classification and enumeration difficult: the early sentimental and æsthetic meditations, *Les Cahiers d'André Walter* and *Les Nourritures Terrestres;* their sequels, in a sense, *Prétextes* and *Nouveaux Prétextes*, two most original volumes of literary criticism, to which may be added his recent monograph on Dostoevsky and the brochures on Wilde and Charles Louis Philippe; the plays, *Le Roi Candaule* and *Saül;* the philosophic dialogues and stories belonging to his Symbolist period, or written in that mood, *Le Voyage d'Urien* and the six "treatises" now collected in *Le Retour de l'Enfant prodigue;* finally miscellaneous volumes of travel sketches and impressions of the assize courts. From this variegated background his novels stand out, but he refuses to call them by that name. Those which best correspond to the ordinary meaning of the term are the four *récits*: *L'Immoraliste, La Porte Etroite, Isabelle,* and *La Symphonie pastorale;* then come the three *soties: Paludes, La Prométhée mal enchainé,* and *Les Caves du Vatican;* upon these the claims of André Gide must finally rest.

With the exception of *Paludes*, a truly delightful satire on the introspective intellectual, which has a peculiar aptness to-day, although written in 1895, the group of fantasias which Gide has classified with

the mediæval farces of his own country are not so
perfect achievements as the four "narratives," to
which he refuses the title of novels. *Les Caves du
Vatican*, which appeared just on the eve of the Great
War, is a curious compound of detective fiction, social satire, fantastic comedy, and picaresque adventure. It has had a vogue with readers who seem
utterly indifferent to the author's earlier and more
characteristic work. Had *La Symphonie pastorale*
not come later to show Gide once more in his true
vein, as the analyst of the Protestant soul, one might
have concluded that he had set out in his maturity
to follow a course which had tempted him in his
youth. As it is, this strange, turbulent book, full of
the disorder of an era on the point of closing, stands
out as an exceptional work, another example of Gide's
astonishing versatility. That versatility had a surprise in store for us in *Isabelle*, also, the story immediately preceding *Les Caves du Vatican*. It is a
tale, in the manner of Barbey d'Aurevilly, of the mystery lurking in an old château where a young student
comes to consult certain old manuscripts, and stum-
bles upon a passionate drama, involving the ruin of
a noble family.

By common consent, *L'Immoraliste* and *La Porte
Etroite* are Gide's masterpieces. Here he has studied
those cases of conscience which are peculiarly the
product of Protestant morality, the psychology of
those who are bound and shackled by that very
freedom of religious thought which once seemed to
be the very essence of all liberty. The emancipated
Huguenot in Gide is attracted by those problems
which postulate for their statement and solution
experiences such as he himself must have known.
His "Immoralist," for example, is the paragon of
God-fearing virtue, who has turned away from life and
love to find a substitute for living in books and ideas.

His virtues are all negative, and thus he passes for an exemplary character. He becomes immoral when, as a result of a serious illness, he creeps back from the edge of death with the realization that his ideals are false. Henceforth he will seek life in all its most vital and energetic manifestations; spontaneity and vigor are now more to him than the cautious qualities which he had once so sadly overestimated. He divests himself of everything that constituted his former self. His wife's illness and death leave him unmoved, pity is gone out of him, and his craving for the strong and full-blooded sends him off in search of adventures amongst thieves and poachers and drunkards. All his inhibitions are released, all his values are transvalued, and he is carried away on the dark stream of primitive life.

Strait is the Gate is another study of asceticism, "a searching analysis," as Mr. Gosse calls it, "of the incompleteness and narrowness of the moral psychology of Protestantism." Alissa Bucolin, the child of a Creole mother and a respectable Huguenot banker in Havre, is possessed by that dual heritage and finally destroyed by it. Her inverted romanticism, like her neurotic beauty, may be traced to that languorous, exotic figure so ill adapted to the staid Protestant society of the provinces, whose lovers and nervous crisis leave their indelible impressions upon the minds of the grave young Huguenot children whose story is told. These are Alissa, her younger sister and brother, Juliette and Robert, and Jerome, her cousin, whom she is to marry, according to the family understanding. A childish adventure of Jerome's with his amorous aunt Bucolin, and, one day, the revelation to Alissa of her mother's far from spiritual loves, drive deep into these little puritan souls the conviction of sin and shame. At church the preacher's fulminations against those who seek the broad path leading to destruction are recognized as references to the wickedness of the wild creature from Martinique, who has run away with one of her lovers. Jerome and Alissa decide that the strait gate and the narrow way shall be their goal.

Alissa's love for Jerome is to her mind the chief obstacle to salvation, and it is in a sort of ascetic ecstasy that she sets out to kill this emotion, so contaminated, as she has seen, by things of the earth earthy. Juliette also loves Jerome, and Alissa tries at first to profit by this opportunity to sacrifice herself in favor of her sister. But Juliette defeats her by marrying an elderly wine-grower, whom she does not love particularly, but with whom she leads an active and happy domestic life. To Alissa this is further proof of the treacherous insignificance of human passion, and renunciation becomes more and more the ideal. Jerome, meanwhile, has gone off to study in Paris, he has done his military service and has travelled. Life has opened out before him and he has gradually freed himself from the dogmas and superstitions of his youth; his faith, never so profound as Alissa's, cannot live without hers, and she denies him that support with truly pious severity; he must seek his own salvation. But his love for Alissa survives every change; he returns home determined to have their betrothal announced. Alissa repulses him for the last time, and when she goes into decline and dies, he learns from her diary how she wrestled against what an Irish bishop once called "The degrading passion of love," and died without surrender or victory.

André Gide has written nothing so harmonious and so finished as this variation upon one of the great themes of tragedy, renunciation in pursuit of perfection. He is in the great tradition of Pascal and Corneille when he here combines a spiritual purity of classic style with the heroic tension of a mystic soul's torturing quest and the tortuous self-questionings of exalted piety. Alissa Bucolin is the portrait of a Protestant saint, drawn with a sympathy and insight as profound as the author's disapproval of the aberration he has studied. This holiness is truly Protestant in its bleak, self-sufficient humility, its self-reliant dependence upon personal conviction and conscience. It is analyzed with a truly Huguenot simplicity, which Edmund Gosse contrasts with "a consecrated Huysmans vaporing about the ecstasies of St. Lydwine of Schiedam." Alissa's diary has already supplied pages which have an honorable place in anthologies of the best modern French prose.

Strait is the Gate is deservedly the book which made André Gide famous; it is one of the great classics of French fiction since the death of Flaubert. It is not only a study of puritanism, in the authentic lineage of Gosse's *Father and Son*, it is a fine picture of an unfamiliar corner of French provincial life, full of remarkable character drawing and lively incidents and observations. As the author of that widely different but kindred work has said of Gide: "There is something northern about his genius, which loves to cultivate caprices and the twilight hours. . . . He is allied with such tender individualists of the close of the nineteenth century as Shorthouse and Pater." His influence in France to-day is such that he may well mark the transition to a new orientation of the French mind.

THE SIAMESE TWINS OF FRENCH LITERA-
TURE: JÉRÔME AND JEAN THARAUD

THE partnership of Jérôme and Jean Tharaud is
unique in a literature which presents, nevertheless,
an extraordinary number of instances of collaboration between brothers. Beginning with Edmond
and Jules de Goncourt, modern French literature can
show a series of similar collaborators: Paul and Victor
Margueritte, whose series of Zolaesque novels dealing with the war of 1870 were translated into English
in the 'nineties; "J. H. Rosny," the joint signature
of two Belgians, Joseph and Séraphin Boëx, who
have been introduced to the American public with a
novel entitled *The Giant Cat*; and Marius-Ary Leblond, the authors of several remarkable studies of
French colonial life, whose tale of the sea, *L'Ophélia*,
has reaffirmed the high opinion held of them ever
since they were the almost successful candidates for
the Goncourt Prize in 1904.

It happens that the Goncourt Academy has been
associated with several of these literary partnerships,
as seems natural in view of the collaboration of its
founders. The brothers "J. H. Rosny" are members
of the Academy, and one of the earliest awards made
by the Goncourt foundation was to Jérôme and Jean
Tharaud, when, a couple of years after the unsuc-
cessful candidature of Marius-Ary Leblond, their
first important work, *Dingley, l'illustre Ecrivain*, received the Goncourt Prize for 1906. At that time
they had published very little, and chiefly in Charles
Péguy's famous *Cahiers de la Quinzaine*, where the
original version of *Dingley* appeared in 1902. Their

first works of fiction, *Le Coltineur débile* and *La Lumière*, two collections of short stories, were published by Péguy in 1898 and 1900, before the *Cahiers* were formerly launched. In the latter appeared also *Bar Cochebas*, one of their earliest studies of the clash between Jews and Christians, *Les Frères Ennemis*, analysis of the struggle between Calvinism and Catholicism, and *Les Hobereaux*, a picture of country life revealing the latent enmity that flares up between the peasant and the lord of the soil.

Jérôme Tharaud was born in 1874, and Jean three years later. The elder brother, at the age of twenty, was assistant professor of French in a college at Buda Pesth, where he not only learned enough Hungarian to translate a volume *Magyar Tales*, but acquired that interest in "the East End of Europe" which has provided the material for so many of their later works. Their fame, or perhaps I should say their popularity, rests upon these later works, beginning in 1912 with *La Fête Arabe*. This book opens the series in which the authors have tried to decipher the secrets of race and religion in the two great human groups outside of Christianity: Judaism and Islam. Both these interests are typically illustrated by the two books, *The Shadow of the Cross* and *The Long Walk of Samba Diouf*, which introduced the Tharaud brothers to the English-speaking public.

They have been called "the Siamese Twins" of French fiction because their separate identities have been more completely merged than those of any other similar collaborators. Edmond and Jules de Goncourt wrote separately as well as together; the partnership of Paul and Victor Margueritte was dissolved, and each maintained his own reputation apart from the other, the same being true of "J. H. Rosny." Jérôme and Jean Tharaud, on the other hand, are inseparable and indistinguishable; even their letters are signed with the initials J. J. Jérôme is bald, and always speaks first, in a voice that is rather piercing. He was a pupil of Romain Rolland at the Ecole Normale, and dedicated *Dingley, l'illustre Ecrivain* to him. Jean, whose real name is Charles, has a calm, deep voice and plenty of hair; at one time he was on the point of entering the Inland Revenue Department as an inspector. These meagre data are all that exist as a clew to the identity of the two brothers, who are never seen alone, and whose references to their work make it impossible to decide what is the share of each.

Their manner of collaborating has been described as a joint revery upon a single theme. They pool their impressions and ideas, develop and control them, and then group them about a central idea. Their first concern is that each shall see with the other's eyes, so that their reactions may be identical. They do not always gather their impressions together, and it is in the course of describing and explaining to each other that their minds interlock, so to speak, and work as one upon a given theme. When the material has taken shape in these prolonged conversations and discussions, one of the brothers dictates while the other writes, interrupting from time to time to make additions. The first manuscript thus obtained is revised and polished by each in turn until order emerges from chaos. Certain of their stories have been rewritten fifteen or twenty times. Even the published versions vary from one edition to another, notably *Dingley*, which has had five revised editions, the changes in the second, which was submitted to the Goncourt Academy, making it a very different work from that originally published in *Les Cahiers de la Quinzaine*.

This method of work, this incessant recopying, is not peculiar to the Tharauds, for it is also the method of Anatole France, as it was of Pierre Loti. What is peculiar is the unity into which their writing merges, so that it is impossible to discover the joining of two styles. In their solid and uniform construction no trace can be discovered of the juxtaposition of two minds. In the work of the Goncourts the situation was the reverse, as was their system of collaboration. They used to assign to each other definite parts of a narrative, and then make a mosaic in which, however cunningly joined, the contributions of each of them were clearly identified. Unlike the Goncourts, Jérôme and Jean Tharaud never make notes, relying entirely upon whatever facts and impressions their minds have retained. Their strength lies, consequently, in description, in the recording of intellectual conflicts, in the notation of external life. Introspection and psychological analysis require the isolation of a single mind. The Tharauds always work together.

For this reason their writings have tended more and more to become a form of inspired reporting, of journalism that is literature. Strictly speaking, they have written no novels since 1911, when *Dingley* had a worthy successor in *La Maîtresse Servante*. The former is a remarkable study of British imperialism during the South African War, with Kipling as its obvious protagonist, under the name of "Dingley, the celebrated author," who sets out for the Transvaal with the plan of a novel whose hero is a London loafer named Barr, recruited while drunk in a public-house, and transfigured by the heroism of war. The book is an analysis of the jingo spirit of England during that period, full of the atmosphere of that strange and tawdry adventure, and giving, at the same time, by the device of a story within a story, the Kiplingesque view of the situation. *The Serving Mistress*, on the other hand, is their finest portrayal of domestic French manners, the only substantial work, in a long list of exotic volumes, which does for provincial French life what the authors have since done for other peoples and countries. It is the story of a woman sacrificed by the egotism of a country squire and the cruelty of his mother, a powerful evocation of harsh pride and the narrow existence of the old landed families; "a sombre little masterpiece," as Maurice Barrès called it.

The Tharaud brothers acted as the secretaries of Barrès for some years, and his influence is not only discernible in their style, but in the later trend of their ideas. When they began to write of Dalmatia, Algeria, Morocco, Galicia, and the Ukraine, they were concerned only with the intrinsic interest of the problems presented by the Jewish and Islamic people. In *La Fête Arabe* they drew a striking picture of a French settlement in Algeria gradually losing all its charm when the railway is built, and the old French culture is submerged in a flood of adventurers from the shores of the Mediterranean, bringing gin, absinthe, and shoddy wares. *La Bataille de Scutari et d'Albanie* was an excellent record of an aspect of the Balkan war with its marvellous painting of the primitive life of the Montenegrins. *La Tragédie de Ravaillac* was a vivid reconstruction of the life and times of the murderer of the French King Henri IV, whose bias in favor of the Huguenots led to his death at the hands of this fanatic. Then came the great studies of Jewish life in eastern Europe.

The Shadow of the Cross is generally regarded as the best of a series which includes *Un Royaume de Dieu*, the story of a Jewish community in Poland in flight before the menace of a pogrom, and *When Israel is King*, to mention another work that has been translated. It is a picture of the Jews in Hun-

gary and the Bela Kun revolution. It is not really
a novel; an anecdote serves as its point of departure—
the anguish, the hopes, and the death of a Jewish
child who has looked at a crucifix—but this is merely
a pretext for an amazing panorama of Jewish life
and customs in a Carpathian village, the conflict
of century-old tradition, of an ancient civilization,
with the hostile conditions of modern times. The
mentality, the religious ceremonies, the social customs of these Hungarian Jews are noted with a vivid
pen, and the teeming life of the race is characterized
with a sure hand, making a work that is colorful
and fascinating, unique in its patient sympathy for
manners and beliefs that have their roots in all that
is most remote from Christendom. It is unspoiled
by the propagandist and anti-Semitic note which is
clearly discernible in *When Israel is King*.

The Tharauds are irresistibly attracted by the
restless and wandering races, the nomads who still
resist the advance of Western civilization. The Jews
first caught their imagination as a result of their
youthful acquaintance with Hungary, where they
met the sad figure of Bar Cochebas, the Jewish
student whose whole existence is disrupted by the
impact of Western ideas and education. Then they
turned to Islam, evoking in *Rabat ou les Heures
Marocaines* and *Marrakech ou les Seigneurs de l'Atlas*
the clash between the Mussulman order, the old Moor-
ish culture, and the Christian invaders. Here, however, we come upon the latest phase of their evolution, in which they have become more and more
conscious mouthpieces of official French colonialism,
invested with a journalistic mission in the suite of
some general or high functionary of the Republic.
Thus *Le Chemin de Damas*, dedicated to General
Gouraud, trails off from the cedars of Lebanon, the
tomb of Henrietta Renan, the Queen of Palmyra,

and other poetic themes suggested by the "road to Damascus," into the dissertations on British policy in Arabia, Emir Feysal, and the mission of France in the East.

The Long Walk of Samba Diouf is a good illustration of this other side to the interest of the brothers Tharaud in the exotic. Samba Diouf is a Senegalese peasant who sets off to a distant part of the country to receive the legacy of a flock. On the way he is recruited for the French army, and finds himself in France, and eventually at Verdun, where he helps to make history. The contrast between two worlds is skilfully drawn in this dramatic confrontation: on the one hand, the simple existence of an African native; on the other, the European cataclysm, and the coming together of the two in the person of the adventurous Samba Diouf. Naturally, upon the vexed question of the employment of colored troops in Europe, the Tharauds are silent. Their Senegalese Frenchman is no race-conscious heretic, and is accepted as naturally as are the colored deputies in the French Chamber. Although naturally written earlier, the book came after Rene Maran's *Batouala* and was regarded as the retort courteous to that protest against the white man. As the whole truth concerning the French negro's attitude toward France, it obviously leaves much to be desired. The Tharauds are now thoroughly orthodox in their opinions about the actual, or potential, colonies of France. But they still have that insight into strange and exotic manners, that eye for remote landscapes, which has been the enduring feature of their writing.

In a literature which, perhaps more than any other, has developed its fiction around the theme of sex-love, Jérôme and Jean Tharaud have never written a love-story. They are entirely uninterested in what they contemptuously call "the story about the gentleman and the lady." That is probably why they are attracted by Eastern life, in which woman is relegated to an utterly subordinate position. Having no other preoccupation, they have been free to turn their gaze upon the spectacle of the world at large. Hence the variety of their work, and its diversity within the appearance of a certain similarity. They have gone into the most obscure quarters of Europe and found there the material for poetry and drama as poignant as any inspired by the passion of man and woman. Since the death of Pierre Loti, they are the greatest French scene-painters in words, sensitive to color and beauty, and possessing an unrivalled faculty of preserving all the freshness of the sights which their eyes have seen.

Twenty-five years have passed since Jérôme and Jean Tharaud met Charles Péguy at the Ecole Normale and joined him in the efforts which finally resulted in the publication of the famous *Cahiers de la Quinzaine*. It was to their rooms Péguy brought the stock of books, including their own *Coltineur débile*, which he rescued from the collapse of his first publishing experiment. It was there that his camp-bed was stretched and where he edited that remarkable periodical in which much of the best work of the Tharauds appeared. The roll-call of Péguy's contributors is a brilliant one. Jaurès and Anatole France were, of course, established authors, but the names of those since famous, but then obscure, are significant: Romain Rolland, Julien Benda, André Spire, François Porché, André Suarès, and Pierre Hamp. In this remarkable group Jérôme and Jean Tharaud stand out with stature undiminished, not only another great tribute to the vision and sagacity of Péguy, but a test of their own high standing to-day in contemporary French literature.

PROUST IN ENGLISH

WHEN one looks over the names of the French authors who have been introduced to English and American readers during the last three years of intensive cultivation of Continental European literature, the list is an imposing one: Jean Giraudoux, Jean and Jérôme Tharaud, Charles Louis Philippe, Ernest Pérochon, C. F. Ramuz, Paul Morand, Edouard Estaunié, Marcel Proust, and Louis Hémon —to mention the best. Of all these, only two can be said to have aroused enthusiasm, Marcel Proust, with *Swann's Way*, and Louis Hémon, with *Maria Chapdelaine*, and each has attracted so different an an audience that probably few of the devotees of Proust's esoteric and exotic art can also be counted amongst the admirers of Hémon's idyllic simplicity. Both authors have "arrived," but the one has been the delight of Stendhal's happy few, whereas the other has achieved a wide popular success.

In the case of Proust, the necessarily limited appeal of his work has called forth a veritable cult, which is not without its unconscious humors, and whose development is rather interesting to those who have watched its growth from the beginning. *Du Côté de chez Swann* was first published in Paris by Bernard Grasset toward the end of 1913, in one volume, bound in the traditional yellow, and costing the now mythical sum of three francs and fifty centimes. At that time the author had published nothing except a collection of sketches, *Les Plaisirs et les Jours*, for which Anatole France had written a preface, in 1896, and he had translated two of Ruskin's works.

Like so many incidents relating to Proust and his works, there is more in this esteemed preface than meets the eye. It has, for one thing, the distinction of not being by Anatole France at all. In the first years of the eighteen-nineties there was a salon in Paris at the house of Madame Arman de Caillavet. The chief ornament of that salon was a shy and timid gentleman who had written a great deal of classical poetry, a couple of short stories, a novel of the kind known to Americans as "glad," and some very conservative critical articles in *Le Temps*—a certain Parnassian poet named Anatole France. His *Thaïs* had captured Madame de Caillavet, and she decided that he was one of those people who needed the guiding hand of a loving woman. Under his influence France began to work seriously, and so that there might be no mistake about it, a study was installed for him in her house on the second floor. Being, however, a punctilious gentleman, Anatole France never failed to put on his hat before coming down-stairs when there was company. In this fashion he preserved the illusion that there was an illusion that he had come in from the street.

During those years Anatole France wrote most of the books which have made him famous; Madame de Caillavet also wrote, and their admiration for each other's writings was mutual. He signed the preface which she wrote for Proust's first book, and allowed her to perform several similar services for him— but he signed only her prefaces, not her novels—*Le Roman d'une Demoiselle de Modes*, for instance. This would seem to indicate that as a writer of prefaces she more nearly reproduced the Master's voice than as a writer of fiction. Her preface to *Les Plaisirs et les Jours* adorns even the new edition of that baroque tome, "ornamented and perfumed by the flowers strewn by Madeleine Lemaire's divine hand," to quote the mellifluous prose of the introduction, the reference being to the endless pictures, tail-pieces, and vignettes of flowers, drawn by Madeleine Lemaire, for which Proust's sketches obviously served as a makeweight. The new edition has none of these relics of early Victorian art, but the elegant reference to the non-existent roses is retained. The dedication also survives, "To my friend Willie Heath," an English boy who was to have shared with Edgar Aubert of Geneva the honor of this delicate attention. His stern Calvinistic parents, however, being presumably better informed of Paris gossip, forbade the publication of his name. Thus the innocent son of perfidious Albion alone was thus immortalized. In such cases there is much to be said for the "splendid isolation" of Old England in those high and far-off days of Fashoda and the Dreyfus case.

Du Côté de chez Swann was reviewed in the ordinary course of events and was favorably noticed, but without any of that dithyrambic enthusiasm which coincided with certain facts which assume in retrospect a peculiar significance. The facts are these: two months before the war broke out, the *Nouvelle Revue Française* published two extracts from the *third* volume of *A la Recherche du Temps Perdu*, which would seem to indicate that Proust's *second* volume, *A l'Ombre des Jeunes Filles en Fleurs*, which was announced by Grasset, was not in the hands of the other firm. Then came the war hiatus, the *Nouvelle Revue Française* suspended publication, but re-issued *Swann's Way* in book form in 1919. In 1919 the second volume, *A l'Ombre des Jeunes Filles en Fleurs*, appeared, with the imprint of the *Nouvelle Revue Française*, and was awarded the Goncourt Prize. Thereupon the *Nouvelle Revue Française*, which had published *Du Côté de chez Swann* at seven francs and fifty centimes, and *A l'Ombre des Jeunes Filles* at the same price, reissued both works, dividing them into two volumes each and raising them to ten francs and twelve francs fifty respectively.

When the *Nouvelle Revue Française* received *Swann's Way* from the original publisher for review, it was not noticed by either André Gide or Albert Thibaudet, who were then reviewing all the books of outstanding importance. It was noticed with other miscellaneous fiction, and recommended in terms of very moderate enthusiasm. But once Proust had become the property of an enterprising firm, with a very influential review at its disposal, and his books had been doubled in price in response to the publicity of the Goncourt Prize, then Marcel Proust suddenly emerged as the greatest genius of our time. When he died, in 1922, he was at once elevated to the position of an idol—an idol so jealously guarded that the huge tribute to him, printed in the *Nouvelle Revue Française* in January, 1922, did not contain one word from such critics outside the charmed circle as Paul Souday, who actually saluted *Du Côté de chez Swann* with great enthusiasm and at length on its first appearance under the auspices of another firm.

Needless to say, this astute advertising soon accomplished its purpose by creating a branch of the cult in London, where the first edition of *Du Côté de chez Swann* passed unnoticed by those who subsequently announced themselves as belonging to the illuminati. In the excess of enthusiasm an English translation of *A la Recherche du Temps Perdu* was arranged, and then some one made the belated discovery that the essential theme of that work is such that it cannot be published in English without a degree of bowdlerization which would seriously mutilate it. *Swann's Way* was issued and then *Within a Budding Grove*, but the problem of *Sodome et*

Gomorrhe is unsolved, except that the American publishers of the first volume have prudently withdrawn from the scene, leaving the English translator to extricate himself and the London publisher as best he can. The humors of that problem were curiously illustrated in the English tribute which Mr. Scott Moncrieff brought together in emulation of the French tribute after Proust's death. The contributors included Joseph Conrad, Arnold Bennett, George Saintsbury, J. Middleton Murry, Arthur Symons, Clive Bell, and A. B. Walkley, among others of less importance. Most of them shy away from the dangerous topic of Proust's own morbid personality and close their eyes to the obvious implications of a work which, had it been written by Wilde, would certainly not have secured the suffrage of such a group of Englishmen. Mr. Walkley, who, unlike several of his colleagues, actually does seem to have read Proust through, has recorded his utter abhorrence of the character of M. de Charlus, the central figure of *Sodome et Gomorrhe*, which is very much as if one were to declare one's undying enthusiasm for Dickens's *Pickwick Papers*, but repudiate as intolerable Mr. Pickwick or Sam Weller. Mr. Clive Bell is more intelligent when he hints obliquely that Proust is inconceivable in English, while Mr. Bennett comes out boldly with the blunt statement that sexual inversion is "an unpromising subject according to British notions," and that, while Proust undoubtedly had genius, he never learned how to write. The other prominent names in the tribute are obviously here, for the most part, for decorative purposes. George Saintsbury, for instance, who has denounced the Goncourts, Zola, and Maupassant as obscene, has admittedly not done more than just dip into Proust—in the English version, moreover—and is innocent of what he is committed to. Those who have most thoroughly studied Proust are not names with which one could conjure up a public for him in England. The volume was, in short, a masterpiece of literary *snobisme*, and an appropriate comment upon the whole cult of Proust by people who show no signs of having read him, and most of whom would be horrified if they had.

So far in English we have only the first and second parts of *A la Recherche du Temps Perdu*, that immense work which has now reached eleven volumes in French, with several further volumes in preparation. The mere dimensions of such a work as this are sufficient to inspire respect, and to arouse curiosity in that section of the public which likes to talk about books rather than read them. To the French mind particularly *Remembrance of Things Past*, as the rather free English title of the whole runs, has seemed little short of portentous, rivalling the six thousand pages of Honoré d'Urfé's *L'Astrée*, hitherto regarded as establishing the record in French literature. The result is that there has been much more enthusiasm displayed over Marcel Proust than knowledge of his work.

To what Mr. Philip Guedalla calls the "Marcel Wave" we undoubtedly owe the existence of the two first parts of *Remembrance of Things Past*, and to the translation there has been extended the same welcome by proxy as to the original. Mr. Scott Moncrieff certainly undertook an ambitious, lengthy, and difficult task, which deserves credit, if only as a test of patience, skill, and endurance. But *Swann's Way* and *Within a Budding Grove* have been greeted as much more than that. Largely, as I suspect, by hearsay, they have been extolled as masterpieces, and it is confidently asserted that no such translator from the French has been seen in England in recent times. Having dipped here and there into the last

two volumes for purposes of comparison, I am not
so sure that this version of Proust is anything more
than an ordinarily competent piece of translation.

In the first place, the translator has apparently
decided to make the English Proust an exercise in
the manner of Henry James. For this reason, almost every paragraph is studded with words between inverted commas, which do not require this
Jacobean emphasis and do not so appear in French.
James does suggest English analogies for Proust's
method, but so does Meredith, and in neither case
is there the remotest resemblance in style, even when
allowance is made for the fundamental difference
between French and English. In the second place,
Mr. Scott Moncrieff is guilty of actual blunders,
which are rather elementary in many cases, and indicate, at best, an unfamiliarity with the fine shades
of French speech and manners. There is so much
haphazard praise and blame of translations, by critics
who carefully refrain from producing evidence for
what they say, that a few specific examples are desirable at this point.

On page 1 *"vulgaire esbrouffeur"* is incorrectly
rendered as "impossible vulgarian," while the force
of calling a person *"puant"* is lost in the too literary
form of "pestilent fellow." On page 2 *"la plus
grossière goujaterie"* is mistranslated as "the crudest
and coarsest form of snobbishness." The choice of
"Mistress" as a rendering of Mme. Verdurin's title
"La Patronne" is open to the strongest objections.
On page 34 "agitators," "mischief-makers," and
"men who make trouble" are utterly fantastic mis-
readings of *"agités," "brouillons,"* and *"faiseurs
d'embarras."* When the cook is described as *"éco-
nome,"* she appears in English "an economist." The
word *"poncif"* has consistently baffled Mr. Moncrieff, who thinks it means "typical." *"Décavés*

crapuleux" does not mean "alcoholic wasters," nor
is a person who is said to be "*d'un vaseux*" "too
sticky for words." "Detrimental" is a strange rendering of our old friend "*fin de siècle.*" If Mr. Moncrieff ever tells a very chic Parisienne, whose latest
creation makes "*un effet bœuf,*" that it is a "bovine
effect," unless she realizes that he does not know
French, she will be insulted. If she further decides
to "*faire la punaise,*" she will be amazed to hear that
she has "put her foot in it." When Bloch said that
Legrandin was "*très bien,*" he meant something
quite different from "he's a bit of all right." Mr.
Scott Moncrieff's misfortunes with "*barbante,*" "*bar-
bifiant,*" and "*raseurs*" are worthy of a place in a
collection of schoolboys' "howlers." The slang meaning of "*ostrogoth,*" the force of "*youpin,*" and the
simple meaning of "*belles madames*"—for it is certainly not "pretty ladies"—also escape him; nor is
"*sorbet*" an "iced drink."

The English version of Proust, then, is not the
world's greatest translation, nor is Proust himself,
for that matter, the greatest French prose-writer of
the age. He is, however, a fascinating and interesting chronicler and psychologist, with no sense of
form, repetitious and careless, yet the author of a
work which promises to be for its epoch what Saint-
Simon's *Memoirs* were for the age of Louis XIV.
There is no more delightful section than *Within a
Budding Grove*, with its memorable portrait of Ber-
gotte, the marvellous satiric sketch of the diplomatist
M. de Norpois, its picture of the Swann ménage as
seen by a child, and the remarkable analysis of the
boy's love and jealousy of the little girl, Gilberte.
Here, too, one meets, for the first time, the two important characters, Monsieur de Charlus and Alber-
tine, who are the male and female elements in the
Sodom and Gomorrah for which all these lengthy

preliminaries are a preparation. Saint-Loup is also introduced, the aristocratic counter-weight to Swann, that amazing portrait of a Jew in society, drawn by a writer who was himself partly Jewish. Arnold Bennett has declared that this portion of Proust's work marks the beginning of a decline, "a fearful fall," and with a candor emulated by none of Mr. Scott Moncrieff's group he adds: "As volume followed volume the pearls were strung more and more sparsely on the serpentine string." With this view a considerable section of French opinion is in agreement, although Mr. Bennett's boredom begins somewhat earlier than usual. The point where interest wavers is rather in the third part, *Le Côté de Guermantes*—a fact so well recognized by the artful publishers that they introduced a fragment of *Sodome et Gomorrhe* into the second volume of the French edition, where it has no justification except as an inducement to wearied readers to hope for the worst. Whether the work of Marcel Proust in English can progress beyond *The Guermantes Way*—minus the device of the French publisher—is extremely doubtful.

SPAIN

DON MIGUEL DE UNAMUNO

WHEN the military dictatorship of General Primo de Rivera was established in Spain in the autumn of 1923, one of the first intellectuals to suffer from the heavy hand of His Excellency was Don Miguel de Unamuno. Eventually the publication of a letter intended for private circulation led to his deportation to Lanzarote, in the Canary Islands. The affair aroused much excitement in Europe, particularly in the neighboring Latin countries, and this typical achievement of the Fascist or Ku Klux spirit led to violent protestations. The situation to those who know what Unamuno represents was very much as if the French Government had exiled Anatole France because he disapproved of the Ruhr policy, or the Italians Croce if he failed to do reverence to Mussolini. It was actually much more preposterous, for Unamuno has been all his life a liberal of the most orthodox type and has never inveighed against the Spanish powers that be one-half so sharply as Shaw has against the English, France against the French, or, to come nearer home, Mencken against the American. As one of the French critics who helped in drawing up the protest on Unamuno's behalf points out, "General Primo de Rivera has just done what the Tsarist government never dared to do to Tolstoy."

In a statement of protest published in various French papers Romain Rolland described Unamuno as "the greatest glory not only of Spain but of all the Iberian countries. It is a shameful mockery to see a government which describes itself as patriotic

61

depriving the country of the most precious ornament in its crown. . . . Miguel de Unamuno is an intellectual hero, a tragic and passionate thinker . . . for thirty years his heroic Quixotism has broken a lance against all the meanness and injustice of the social order. His sombre and ardent flame lights up the heavy shades in which the Spanish people are stifling. . . . As the heralds of Europe's conscience we cry aloud our indignation." D'Annunzio also expressed himself characteristically. He vindicated the inviolability of mind and of style against the Beast triumphant, and declared that "the entrails of Spain's horses gored in the arena seem less sinister to us than the sanguinary brains of her stupid leaders. We must brand this subordinate general, this petty, picaresque tyrant, marking him with a red-hot iron bearing the figure of the Flaubertian 'καταβλέπας.'" In terms less flamboyant than d'Annunzio's and pitched in a less tragic key than Rolland's, a host of intellectuals, varying in importance, associated themselves with this protest—André Gide, Séverine, Jean de Pierrefeu, Elie Faure, Gaston Chérau, André Spire, to mention a few that will be familiar over here. Francis de Miomandre found perhaps the best parallel for Unamuno's case by suggesting as an analogy the deportation of Bergson.

The comparison is sound, for the reason that in no other country in the world could a writer of Unamuno's caliber have come into conflict with the authorities. He is the vice-rector of Salamanca University and a professor of Greek there. His works comprise novels, short stories, poems, travel sketches, and essays, in addition to his two chief philosophical studies, *El Sintimiento trágico de la vida* and *La Vida de Don Quijote y Sancho*. Of all these only *The Tragic Sense of Life* has appeared in English, and little attention was paid to it. A volume of his essays,

however, is in preparation.   That first book appeared
in French before the war, and more recently a
volume of *Pages Choisies*, containing an excellent
brief selection from his essays, has been published in
Paris, also *L'Essence de l'Espagne*, a fine translation of the five essays known as *En torno al Casti-
cismo*, which, together with *The Tragic Sentiment of
Life*, give the quintessence of Unamuno's philosophy.   In addition to these already ample activities, the author is a ceaseless contributor to the
reviews and newspapers of articles in which he
endeavors to shake Spain, both governors and governed, from the lethargic and torpid acquiescence
into which it relapses between the revolutionary outbreaks that have punctuated its history in modern
times.

Remy de Gourmont has paid tribute to Unamuno;
Havelock Ellis has praised him; in that excellent
volume *A Picture of Modern Spain*, J. B. Trend,
the most discerning and sympathetic of English critics of Spanish life and letters, notes his significance;
John dos Passos greets him in *Rosinante to the Road
Again*, and a whole generation of Spanish writers
look to him as master.   His name was not very widely
known in this country, although he occupies a position in contemporary Spanish thought comparable
to that of Croce in Italy, though no other parallel
can be drawn between them.   Unamuno is what
Charles Kingsley might have called "a muscular
Christian," for the two men are rather alike, in spite
of the typical Protestantism of the Englishman and
the untypical but profound Catholicism of the Spaniard.   Both have made religion the basis of their
individualism and their social theories.

Miguel de Unamuno is a humanist and a Hellenist,
and the influence of his classical studies is deeply
imprinted upon his style with its Latin lucidity and

Socratic subtleties. As befits a true Hellenist, Unamuno is both an artist and a philosopher, and if *The Tragic Sense of Life* is the only formal exposition of his philosophy, his teachings are scattered through the seven volumes of *Ensayos* and that charming book *La Vida de Don Quijote y Sancho*, which many hold to be his masterpiece. Don Miguel is a philologist by profession and a philosopher by vocation, but he is also a poet and a novelist; he is of the true lineage of Cervantes.

His most recent book, *Andanzas y Visiones Españolas*, is a volume of travel sketches, making a companion book to the earlier collection *Por Tierras de España y Portugal*. In the preface he explains the genesis of the work rather curiously when he says that these *Walks and Visions* are to make up for the lack of descriptive passages in his novels. "Those who follow my work and who have read my novels will have noticed that, except in the first, *Paz en la Guerra*, I have avoided descriptions of landscapes and even definite settings of time and place and local color. . . . I obeyed my desire to give the stories the greatest possible intensity and dramatic character by reducing them, where possible, to dialogue and the narrative of action and feeling—the latter in dialogue form—and by avoiding what the dramatists call asides. I might easily have put into my novels the descriptions of lands and houses, of mountains, valleys, and villages which I have collected here, but I did not do so in order to lighten them. Whoever reads a novel, like a playgoer in a theatre, is held by the development of the argument, by the interplay of the actions and passions of the characters, and is strongly inclined to skip the descriptions of landscapes, however beautiful they may be."

This, I think, is the first time a novelist has ever

frankly faced what is commonly known to be a fact among readers of fiction, and Unamuno's method of meeting the difficulty is, to say the least, original. It is not, however, likely to become popular, for where would most of our fiction be if the "padding" were removed? In his own case it has resulted in this interesting volume, whose scenes move from Santiago and Coimbra to the Balearic Isles. The Spanish countryside is seen here from the highly personal standpoint of the author, whose vision is always sensitive and never commonplace. Some of the essays are in verse and are fine examples of Unamuno the poet.

In the light of his theories of novel-writing Unamuno's novels are of peculiar interest. They are five in number, *Paz en la Guerra, Amor y Pedagogía, El Espejo de la Muerte, Niebla, Abel Sánchez, La Tía Tula*, and *Tres Novelas Ejemplares*. The first of these to meet with any success was *Niebla*, which has the distinction of anticipating the method of Pirandello in his *Six Characters in Search of an Author*. The fable is exceedingly simple: the contrast between the intelligence of a dog and the stupidity of men. The dog, guided by his instincts, unfailingly finds his way through life, but man, confused by his illusions, his desires, and his dreams, cannot thread his way through the labyrinth of existence. Augusto Pérez, coming down the street on a rainy day, falls in love at first sight with a girl who is passing. An accident provides him with an excuse to be introduced to her parents, and he asks for her hand in marriage. The girl, however, is unwilling, because she loves Mauricio, but the latter, a good-for-nothing creature, wants her to accept what is an advantageous proposal. Eugenia grows indignant at his villainous suggestions and they part. Meanwhile Augusto has centred his facile heart upon a little dressmaker,

Rosario. Finally, after much manœuvring, it is arranged that Mauricio shall have Rosario, and Eugenia and Augusto become engaged. Then Augusto becomes jealous of Mauricio, has a row with Eugenia on the head of it, peace is made, and the wedding is fixed. On the eve of the ceremony Eugenia runs off with Mauricio; all the possible permutations have been exhausted. The farce is at an end. But is it a farce or a tragedy?

The conventions demanded that a coherent end should be written. Augusto might, in the traditional manner, kill the eloping couple and commit suicide. Instead, like Pirandello's characters, he goes in search of the author. He comes to Salamanca to see Unamuno, and tells him he is determined to commit suicide. But the author points out that this is impossible, since no person exists in reality as Augusto. He is almost resigned to go on living in the fantasy of his creator when he dies of overeating. The doctors examine him but they are unable to determine whether it was indigestion, apoplexy, or mental strain that killed him. Even death, like everything else, escapes from definition and defies the human reason. All that remains is the dog, and the book closes upon a sage discourse by this animal upon the absurdity of human passions. The book is a curious and original piece of work. There is no narrative, for the story unfolds in dialogues and soliloquies, not because Unamuno believes that character is revealed by speech, but for the contrary reason. Speech, he holds, is a social convention and therefore artificial and insincere. "Man lies in so far as he speaks, and he lies to himself when he talks to himself, that is, when he thinks deliberately and consciously." Unamuno's theory is that we speak first, then think what we say, then do what we think.

The same paradoxical, sceptical note is discernible

in *Abel Sánchez*, ironically described as a "story of passion." As in *Niebla*, the form is as rigid as a geometrical figure, and the incidents develop as though moved by a mechanism. Here again two couples are confronted: Abel Sánchez, the painter; Joaquín Monegro, the doctor; their wives and children. The artist, whose eyes are fixed on the surface of things, because his art is concerned with the appearance and color of life, is an easy-going person, easy to get on with, sympathetic, successful. The doctor, on the other hand, whose studies have forced him to look for the secret ills, the internal weaknesses, of humanity, is as complicated, as sad, as profound as the painter is simple, good-humored, and superficial. He is suspected of envying and hating his popular friend. What is called hate is merely the antithesis between happiness and grief, wealth and poverty, and has no psychological basis. It is there just as shade is inseparable from light. In the Biblical drama Abel is the victim, but it is Cain who deserves sympathy and pity. In this novel Unamuno shows us the paradoxical play of human destiny, which delights in representing the human soul in absurd and contradictory postures. The narrative is rigorously suppressed, and the story is told in short dialogues, ironical, logical, full of incisive observation. Unamuno has turned the art of fiction back to the technic of the Platonic dialogue.

The Tragic Sentiment of Life is a work which comes in direct line from the literature of the Spanish mystics. It is the reply of a Spaniard of to-day to self-sufficient radicalism, and in it is heard the note of Pascal, torn between the logic of reason and the irrepressible demands of faith. The visionary passion of a mind which refuses to accept the denial of spiritual hopes and is yet conscious of the sovereignty of the reasoning faculties finds dramatic expression in his book. Unamuno confesses an impotence of feeling when confronted by the unanswerable arguments of reason. The desire for immortality can find no rational confirmation, but reason leaves us no object in life and gives it no finality. Thought and feeling thus meet in a common despair. "The tragic history of human thought," says the author, "is simply that of a struggle between reason and life; the former trying to rationalize the latter, and to impose upon it resignation to the inevitable, to death; and the latter obstinately trying to vitalize reason by making it support its aspirations. That is the whole history of philosophy, which is inseparable from the history of religion."

In its own defense life finds the weak point in reason, which is scepticism, and from the despair engendered by scepticism is born "the holy, sweet, redeeming uncertainty, our supreme consolation." There are, then, three solutions to the problem of existence—either there is no after-life, which means despair in resignation and the eternal struggle, which is the theme of Unamuno. He is obviously a thorough and typical Spaniard. "I feel," he writes, "that I have within me a mediæval soul, and I believe that the soul of my country is mediæval, that it has perforce passed through the Renaissance, the Reformation, and the Revolution—learning from them, yes, but without allowing them to touch the soul, preserving the spiritual inheritance which has come down from what are the dark ages." Unamuno describes as Quixotism the struggle between the Middle Ages and the Renaissance, and he himself is the Don Quixote of modern philosophy. His book will be read by us rather for its poignant drama of the human soul than for its doctrine, which rests too easily upon assumptions which have long since ceased to be taken for granted outside Spain. Don Miguel de Unamuno is a rebel in his own country, but we are more likely to be surprised by his orthodoxy.

Although Unamuno's attitude toward political and social problems is the natural expression of his fundamental philosophy, it is not to the latter that his persecution through a long life is due. It is rather to his current articles and his personal influence, as exercised at Salamanca and at the Ateneo in Madrid, that famous institution which is so intimately associated with the intellectual life of Spain for the last hundred years. The Ateneo not only was a centre for reading, lectures, and debates, where every notable Spaniard contributed to its prestige, it was also a sort of collective entity whose opinion was eagerly awaited in every social or political crisis and which yielded a peculiar authority. General Primo de Rivera, known to the irreverent as the Royal Goose, closed up the Ateneo, his intention being obviously to terrorize the crowd and to intimidate the critical into silence. Only a few years ago Unamuno was condemned to sixteen years' imprisonment for *lèse-majesté*, but the King thought it wiser not to inflict the mediæval sentence. The verdict— for two articles!—was revoked by a royal decree. This time his underling was not so lenient.

In order to realize the position in which this great teacher and thinker found himself when the Royal Goose came into power, contrast the tone of Unamuno's writings with that of a letter which was inadvertently published in the Argentine review *Nosotros* in December, 1923.

I thought that this Royal Goose, who signed the impudent manifesto of September 12, a note of ignominy for Spain, was just an imbecile, with the brains of a grasshopper, a tragicomic barnstormer, but I see that he is a mass of abject, crawling passions. It is a disgrace to be a Spaniard, and that there should be people who imagine they can remain honest while

collaborating with these rascals, consumed by bullies' grudges
. . . the poisonous wells of what Menéndez Pelayo called
clerical democracy are reopened, the inquisitorial sense of
demagogy, and now the terrible cancer of Spain is visible—
envy, envy, hatred of intelligence. I am stifling, stifling,
stifling in this sink, and Spain makes my heart ache! And I
have to listen to them talking about mysticism and a new conception of liberty. Magnificent! . . . And lies, lies, lies!
Claiming, not in error, but by mendacity, that public opinion
is almost unanimous! Lying every time a new problem is
approached. . . . Liberalism to-day means waiting with a
gag in one's mouth until the saliva accumulates with which to
spit out the truth at this Bœotian rabble, for liberalism and
monarchy are incompatible in Spain.

In his *Life of Don Quixote and Sancho*, Unamuno
declares that "only men of passion achieve works
that are fruitful and lasting. Whenever you hear
anybody described as faultless, whatever be the
sense of that stupid term, avoid him, especially if
he is an artist. . . . The most unpoetic, antipoetic
artist is the impeccable artist." In the world of the
intellect there can be no peace, for "intellectual
peace simply means somnolence and lies." The author
of these words, however, is not in the least an anarchist, nor even what would be called a radical thinker
elsewhere in Western Europe or in America.

The doctrines of Unamuno will never stir the typical
Western mind, but, as Salvador de Madariaga points
out in *The Genius of Spain*, Unamuno's country,
like Russia, is "a border country," in which "East
and West mix their spiritual waters," and he incarnates the spirit of modern Spain "astride two enemy
ideals." Hence his importance, and the tributes
which have been paid to his genius by men as dissimilar as Havelock Ellis and Papini. The Spanish
critic I have mentioned, in his introduction to Craw-
ford Flitch's fine translation of *The Tragic Sentiment
of Life*, sums up the position of Don Miguel de

Unamuno in a passage which, while it explains the esteem and affection in which he is held, throws into relief the gravity of General Primo de Rivera's offense against the world of humane letters:

Miguel de Unamuno is to-day the greatest literary figure in Spain. Baroja may surpass him in variety of external experience, Azorín in delicate art, Ortega y Gasset in philosophical subtlety, Ayala in intellectual elegance, Valle Inclán in rhythmical grace. . . . Unamuno is head and shoulders above them all in the highness of his purpose and in the earnestness and loyalty with which, Quixote-like, he has served all through his life his unattainable Dulcinea. . . . Thus Unamuno, whose literary qualities and defects make him a genuine representative of the more masculine variety of the Spanish genius, becomes in his spiritual life the true living symbol of his country and his time. And that he is great enough to bear this incarnation is a sufficient measure of his greatness.

PÍO BAROJA

DON PÍO BAROJA Y NESSI, master baker, Nietzschean and novelist, is regarded by common consent as the most original writer of Spanish fiction since Galdós. Among the younger men there are distinguished artists like Ramón Pérez de Ayala and Ramón Gómez de la Serna, but in the famous generation of 1898, Pío Baroja is a typical and remarkable figure. When one remembers the roll-call of that generation, Unamuno, Azorín, Ortega y Gasset, it is evident that the stature of Baroja is not due to any flatness in the literary landscape. Out of the disaster of the Spanish-American War came a new intellectual era in Spain which has enriched that country with a modern literature, among whose chief ornaments must be counted the work of Pío Baroja.

The scope of that work is enormous and varied—over thirty volumes, ranging from provincial studies of Basque life to cosmopolitan pictures of London and Rome, and including an intellectual confession of faith, several volumes of essays, and a series of semi-historical novels. Of all these, six have been published in English: first *La Feria de los Discretos*, *César o Nada*, and *Juventud, Egolatría*; and then *La Busca*, *Mala Hierba*, and *Aurora Roja*, a trilogy, known as *La Lucha por la Vida*, which is held by most critics to be the author's greatest achievement. It can hardly be said that those earlier translations did more than make Baroja known to the discriminating. To the general reader Blasco Ibáñez still sums up the whole of contemporary Spanish literature.

72

Like Pérez de Ayala, whose charming fantasy, *Prometeo*, has been completely ignored in translation, Baroja must be regarded as the victim, to some extent, of the Blasco Ibáñez boom, which has done more harm to Spanish literature than mere neglect could do. It has provided publishers and readers with a set of false values, and a false standard, which the uncritical apply to every book that comes out of Spain. There will not be another Blasco Ibáñez, for, in spite of his age, he belongs to a period in Spanish literature, prior to 1898, which shows no signs of returning in the work of any of the original and significant writers of the present time. Pío Baroja, then, must be accepted as representative by those who desire to know something of contemporary Spanish letters. No better introduction to the man himself could be found than *Youth and Egolatry*, with which H. L. Mencken very appropriately inaugurated his "Free Lance Books" a few years ago. All his whims, his iconoclasm, his sardonic humor are concentrated in these notes on life and letters, which Baroja deliberately compiled in the midst of the war, in order to shut that event out of his mind, and to demonstrate his incuriousness about what seemed to him incomprehensible.

The English-speaking world rather prides itself upon its stock of eccentrics, and nothing delights us more than a real "character." Baroja answers that demand to a degree which ought to endear him to us. He is the antithesis of the professional intellectual, proud to have had his business as a master baker as a refuge from the disillusions of literary life. In *Cæsar or Nothing* he says: "Art is a good thing for people who have not the strength to live in reality. It is an excellent sport for old maids and deceived husbands, who need consolation as hysterical patients require morphine." He has written brief but very illuminating and amusing notes on all his own books, showing a detachment in relation to his writings which is, to say the least, unusual. Of *Mala Hierba*, the second volume of his trilogy, he says: "Like almost all my novels, *Mala Hierba* appears to be the rough draft of a book that has never been finally polished. That is what Blasco Ibáñez once said to me, and then he proceeded to write *La Horda* based on my material." Baroja regards *The Quest* as the most widely read of his books, adding: "When it was published I got the impression that I was now acceptable to the literary cliques, and that they were inviting me in. As I did not enter, having still got something, whether good or bad, to say, the door that had opened was again shut against me."

In his way Baroja resembles Shaw, except for this vital difference: he has no mission, no gospel to preach. He has Shaw's delight in mystification and paradox; his humor rarely lacks a touch of irony. He exalts the individual at the expense of society, whereas Shaw is an individualist who believes in the subordination of the one to the many. "We," he writes, "who have a world of unsatisfied desires and instincts, ought to join together and bury alive the weaklings who prevent us from realizing our craving for power. . . . When we have buried them, we shall then have leisure to devour each other." This anarchical strain in his character manifests itself in his work, in which there is a marked predilection for rebels and adventurers and outcasts, for those who live on the margin of society. The whole series of *Memorias de un Hombre de Acción* turns upon the adventures of Eugenio de Aviraneta, a swashbuckler who played many parts in the civil wars and conspiracies of the early nineteenth century, the Greek and Carlist wars, the July Revolution in Paris. Baroja avows that his sole interest is in this

adventurer relative of his, this "man of action," and
that he has no ambition to follow in the footsteps of
Galdós, with whose great historical series, *Episodios
Nacionales*, these books have been compared.

The Struggle for Life is typical of Baroja's interest
in the nether world of outcasts and strange characters. It is a work in the great picaresque tradition,
but the *pícaro* of Cervantes, Mateo Aleman, and
Quevedo is replaced by the *golfo* of to-day, the vagabond or loafer of urban industrial life. Manuel, the
central character of *The Quest* and the two subsequent novels, moves through the story in the traditional manner of such heroes; he is the servant in a
boarding-house, a shoemaker's apprentice, a rag-
picker's assistant, and the associate of thieves, passing through the strangest scenes and constant
fluctuations of good fortune. But the career of a
vagabond nowadays has little of the light-hearted
freedom of olden times; his revolt is sombre and
tinged with a philosophy undreamed of by Gil Blas
and his companions. And the writer's attitude is
modified accordingly. Baroja paints the scenes in
vivid colors but with absolute detachment, offering
no comment and drawing no moral. His power re-
sides in this impassive clarity, this reflection of life
in cold sharp strokes like the lines of an etcher bitten
with acid—the acid of an ironical and pessimistic
humor. The logical end of the lawless world surveyed by Baroja is anarchy, and that is the theme
of *Red Dawn*, the final volume of this trilogy.

Compared with *The Quest* neither of the two novels
which had previously represented Baroja in English
gives an adequate impression of his genius. *The City
of the Discreet* presents an interesting and characteristic type in Quintín, the climber, who returns to
Spain with an Eton education and British habits,
but with none of his fundamental ideas changed.

But the book is weakened by a piling up of incident and adventure which brings it too close to the feuilleton, and suggests all the defects of the picaresque manner usually adopted and adapted by the author to such advantage. *Cæsar or Nothing* is a better and more characteristic work, in which Baroja portrays more effectively the same type in César Moncada, a pseudo-Nietzschean, whose aim is to arrive at all costs, but whose Cæsarism has no higher ambition than petty political success. Even in this, however, he is defeated through his marriage, and the disproportion between his aspirations and his accomplishment is emphasized by his final acquiescence in the possession of a rich wife as a substitute for the worlds he set out to conquer. An amusing and almost Shavian interlude is the section of the book in which Moncada's impressions of Rome are recorded in terms of utter contempt for the grandeur of the classic heritage. Baroja tells us that he went to Rome to write a novel about Cæsar Borgia, but at the outset he renounced that plan because he could not be bothered obtaining all the details concerning the period, "which might turn out to be exceedingly tiresome."

In 1913 *El Aprendiz de Conspirador* inaugurated the series of semi-historical narratives, *Memorias de un Hombre de Acción*, in which the author has done for the period of the Carlist and republican intrigues, after the death of Alfonso XII, what Pérez Galdós did for the earlier history of Spain in his voluminous *Episodios Nacionales*. Thirteen volumes have been published and they may be extended indefinitely, but few, I fancy, of Baroja's foreign readers have had the patience and curiosity to follow these rambling tales, which are centred about the life and adventures of a relative of his, Eugenio de Avarineta. Avarineta was a stormy petrel in the swirl of mid-nineteenth-century revolutions and uprisings in different parts of Europe. The mere titles of some of those volumes, *El Amor, el Dandysmo y la Intriga*, or *El Sabor de la Venganza*, for instance, to cite two of the later publications, will indicate their vague historical import. The one is a curious collection of fragments, chapters of half a page sometimes, containing remarks on dandyism, on love, on women, or vignettes of old Madrid, the note-books of a loiterer amongst family and city archives, the other a story of judicial vengeance, telling the prison experiences of a survivor of that revolutionary time.

How naturally the picaresque novel is adapted to the genius of Spanish story-telling is shown here, where the author allows his pen to ramble on with the histories of the various personages whose names crop up in the course of the narrative. Baroja has succeeded by this method in giving an intensely living picture of a bewildering period in the history of modern Spain. More akin to his other fiction is *La Sensualidad Pervertida*, whose title is typical of his genius for finding the most attractive superscription to his discursive and chaotic narratives. It is also sufficient, I fancy, to arouse the ardor of Mr. Sumner and his moral cohorts. But they will be disappointed if it is ever issued in English with the same title. The author has thoughtfully provided, by way of a preface, a review of his book written in 1954, in which posterity is found declaring that it is a pity the book has no proper ending. If the form of this and other works of Baroja is vague, the content is packed with those delightful memories, that sharp psychology, and those disillusioned views of men and of life which give their peculiar savor to the writings of this novelist.

He is probably the most extensively translated and least known of all the important European writers who have been introduced to America during recent years. His case is unusual. Others are as little read: C. F. Ramuz, for example, the Swiss novelist, whose *Reign of the Evil One* was published in the European Library a couple of years ago, or Giovanni Verga, in D. H. Lawrence's excellent version of *Mastro Don Gesualdo*, or Pérez de Ayala, who had the good fortune to see his *Prometheus, the Fall of the House of Limón* and *Sunday Sunlight* beautifully translated. But these are all writers of whom a single volume is available, whereas six of Baroja's best and most characteristic works have been published here, yet he is as far as ever from success in this country. *The City of the Discreet, Cæsar or Nothing, Youth and Egolatry, The Quest, Weeds,* and *Red Dawn* have produced no response apart from the unanimous praise of all the critics who are interested in Spanish literature. They have reached only the converted.

Whenever I meditate upon the inscrutable ways of Providence, the case of Baroja overwhelms me with a sense of man's finite judgment, and with all the other platitudes which are invariably the result of such meditations. What is the cause of his failure? Not, surely, the character of his work, for it seems peculiarly designed to interest foreign readers. Not any obscurity in the manner of publication, for *Youth and Egolatry* is one of Mencken's "Free Lance Books," bearing his imprimatur and benediction, yet it has not benefited to any appreciable extent by the learned editor's far-flung moral influence in saving human souls. No one translator can be held responsible, for there have been several, of whom even the worst has proved himself competent. Moreover, I have yet to hear of a bad translation that has ever seriously hampered the success of a book which the public really wanted to read. Where specific transla-

tions of Baroja have been attacked, the terms of the
criticism have been vague, and have aroused the
suspicion in me that the translator was being blamed
for the author's defects, for the slipshod style of Baroja is notorious; it is as uneven and ungrammatical
at times as Dreiser's.

Pío Baroja himself has more than once expressed
his acquiescence in what appears to be the judgment
of the fates against him, for he is a thoroughly
cynical and dispassionate man of letters, entirely
devoid of the usual vanities and morbid fears of the
literati. He continues to write just as he pleases,
knowing that he can always count upon the appreciation of an intelligent minority, and indulging,
whenever possible, in a peculiar humor at his own
expense as an author. In his *El Laberinto de las
Sirenas,* for example, there is a prologue entitled
"Preliminary Conversation," which is typical of Baroja's manner. He is seated in the dining-car of a train
travelling out of Italy. Opposite to him is an Italian
lady who inspires him with the utmost distaste and
he is inclined to congratulate himself upon the fact
that he need not talk to her. She stares at him icily
and proceeds to eat her macaroni, a spectacle which
arouses in Baroja the following dissertation:

D'Annunzio, in collaboration with Mussolini, should issue a
decree to "the faithful on the way to eat macaroni, for it is
certain that people do not know how to do so with any degree
of elegance and decorum. When you cut it with a fork or a
knife it is very difficult to pick up the pieces. If you do not
cut it, but launch an enveloping movement with fork and
spoon, a manœuvre much favored by the Diazes and Cadornas
of macaroni, the strategic move is not sufficient, and you find
yourself half eating and half drinking, with the macaroni
hanging from your mouth like white tapeworms, a sight unworthy of Ruskin, d'Annunzio, and Mussolini."

The lady swallows her macaroni undisturbed by
these æsthetic considerations, and to Baroja's great

relief the lamp gradually moves from the side to the centre of the table, owing to the jolting of the train, and makes a barrier between them. However, his joy is short-lived, because the lady puts the lamp back in its place. It slips forward several times and is finally the means of starting a conversation, for Baroja tries to help her to fix it securely, but the lamp is too much for them. "What obstinacy!" he says; "this must be a pedagogical lamp. Only in pedagogues have I observed such perseverance in trying to spread light amongst the people," and soon the pair of them are talking about imagination and literature. Baroja reveals, under cross-examination, that he is an author, and listens to an appeal for a novel "with a nice love-story" which will enable us "to forget the ugly things in ordinary life." He declares his inability to write such a book, but she gives him her card and makes him promise to send her his novel. The card is that of a Duchess, so Baroja decides he will try to please her. "I was flattered at being able to have a reader like that, so insolent and solemn. Even now I should like to believe that she remembers me and I am going to send her a copy, with an old-fashioned inscription, full of epigrammatic, sonorous, and well-turned phrases."

Whether the Duchess was pleased or not is doubtful, for *The Labyrinth of the Sirens* contains little that will please those who have not already discovered in Baroja a highly diverting exponent of the honorable Spanish tradition of the picaresque novel. The wandering hero this time is Juan Galardi, a Basque sailor, and the book is the second in a group relating to the sea, of which the first was *Las Inquietudes de Shanti Andía*, it being Baroja's practice to classify his novels in groups according to their general subject, although the only actual trilogy is *The Struggle for Life*. Galardi and a friend land from their ship at

Marseilles and, as is the custom, fall in with two girls, one of whom, a Jewess named Raquel, appeals to Galardi so thoroughly that he remains in Marseilles with this first siren until all his money is gone and she leaves him. Then he goes off to Naples, where the second siren seduces him, a Stendhalian creature named the Marquesa de Roccanera, who is separated from her legitimate spouse, Robert O'Neill, who afterward becomes a great friend of Galardi's, though O'Neill knows that the sailor is one of his wife's lovers. As a lover, however, he finds the Marquesa almost as difficult as if she were his wife, so they agree not to see too much of each other. Galardi becomes a steward on the Roccanera estates, and there he meets a Nausicaa amongst the sirens, in the person of Santa, a simple maid with domestic virtues, whom he marries. But the sirens still sing seductively, and in due course Santa's cousin, an Amazon of imperious disposition named Otilia, conquers Galardi, but he is rescued by O'Neill, and in the end, when his wife dies, he enters a monastery.

Although of more ample texture than most of Baroja's recent novels, *The Labyrinth of the Sirens* is episodic and fragmentary; connected plot is alien to the author's temperament, and there is no story to outline. The strength and charm of the book lie in its restless, rapid movement, in Baroja's endless delight in strange, nomadic people, in the crowded life of tumultuous cities. The descriptions of Naples and Marseilles are finely executed, full of color and animation, and may be set beside the author's evocations of London in *La Ciudad de Niebla* and of Rome in *Cæsar or Nothing*.

His notation of country life, his landscapes, Roccanera, and the labyrinth of reefs which gives its title to the book—these are all pretexts for that descriptive writing at which Baroja excels. Follow-

ing the "Preliminary Conversation" there is a
lengthy prologue in which the adventures of the
author and a friend are described when they set out
for Naples to get the material for this book. Neither
of them liked antiquities and they thought Vesuvius
was an exceedingly disappointing volcano. It was
not a perfect cone, as they had always imagined from
pictures of it, and the smoke emerged from the
crater "not in solemn and majestic manner . . . in
a straight and decorative column," but in vulgar
puffs like smoke from a factory chimney. The whole
prologue is excellent fooling, full of that harsh dry
humor which Baroja displays when he sets out to reveal his own prejudices and limitations in conflict
with the prejudices and limitations of others.

Pío Baroja has been variously classified as a
naturalist of the Zola school, as a disciple of Dickens.
His own literary preferences are for *Le Rouge et le
Noir*, *Pickwick Papers*, and Dostoevsky's *House of
the Dead*, and these three apparently so disparate
figures, somehow, sum up the main qualities one
feels in Baroja's work. His clear, incisive, cold style,
in violent contrast with the flamboyant romantics
who preceded him, suggests the Stendhal who conned
the pages of the Code Civil in order to get away from
the prevailing cult of the sonorous phrase. There is
a touch of Dickens, grown sardonic, in the humor of
such scenes as the boarding-house in the opening
chapter of *The Quest*. With Dostoevsky, Baroja
shares a predilection for the underworld and its
strange heroes. But such comparisons have little
value in estimating the position of an isolated and
original figure like Baroja, whose genius lies precisely
in the fusion through his own personality of elements
common to the great masters of modern fiction.

The Shavian element in Baroja to which I have
referred is nowhere more clearly evident than in

Divagaciones Apasionadas. There is an address, delivered by Pío Baroja in Barcelona, reprinted in this
book, which is almost identical in its challenge to
Catalan nationalist sentimentality with Shaw's dis-
courses to his compatriots on the tender subject of
Cathleen ni Houlihan. There are some brief dramatic
criticisms, a record of the exceedingly brief period
when Baroja was sent to the theatre by an editor who
wanted to see the effect of an absolutely honest and
independent critic upon the theatrical world of Madrid. That effect was very similar to the effect produced by Shaw in London when he reviewed plays
for *The Saturday Review.* His first article on a classical play begins: "I am certainly no use as a dramatic
critic. I have left the theatre and I am damned if
anything occurs to me that is in the least worth saying.
It is the second or third time that I have seen one of
our classical comedies performed, and this time, as
on previous occasions, I ask myself: 'Am I such an
idiot that I cannot understand the beauty of this
work?' I look at the public and I see them listening
attentively. No doubt it pleases and interests them."
    In Barcelona, in the Ateneo, the very fount and
sanctuary of Catalan nationalism and culture, Baroja
proceeded to express his mind with characteristic
freedom on the subjects so dear to the hearts of his
auditors and his literary friends. "I do not hate the
Catalan intellectuals," he says, "but I believe I
should hate them if I were a Catalan. How can one
take seriously the weighty pedantries of my friend
Corominas, this great man whose thoughts seem to
be swimming in grease, or regard as definite the
brilliant flatulency of Gabriel Alomar, or attach any
importance to the snobbism, without ease or grace,
of Xenius in *La Veu de Catalunya?* As I say, I do
not dislike them, but they seem to me insignificant,
even more insignificant than the rest of us in Spain,

for there at least the people do not listen or pay any attention to us." Having thus described his attitude toward three of the most distinguished writers of Catalonia, Baroja then concluded with a prolonged and hostile criticism of the linguistic, racial, and political claims of the Catalans to independence. A typical performance, for in his discourse there is hardly a word which the ordinary type of official imbecile (such as the Dictator Primo de Rivera, who is now harrying the Catalans in every department of their national activities) could approve or exploit.

The most valuable part of this book of *Divagations*, however, is the section called "Divagations about Myself," which is an address delivered to the students of Spanish at the Sorbonne. Not even excluding *Youth and Egolatry*, it is the most important statement of Pío Baroja's attitude toward life and literature. He begins by describing the age of transition and uncertainty into which he was born, the last quarter of the nineteenth century, an era which culminated in the disaster of 1898. "I lived as a boy in Pamplona, a walled town, whose drawbridges were raised at nightfall, a town with the habits of an ancient fortress. I have seen a man passing before my house on his way to be executed, dressed in a yellow sack with red stripes, with a fool's cap on his head. I have seen him going to the gallows in a cart, supported by priests, between two long lines of Disciplinants, with yellow candles in their hands, singing the responses, while the hangman walked on foot behind the cart, and all the churches of the town tolled their bells for the dead."

On the subject of his youth in Madrid, under the Regency, Baroja has nothing good to say—"a period of indifference, laziness, and immorality," when Spain resembled "a feverish old woman who has painted her face and makes an effort to be happy." Of the third, contemporary, period of his life nothing good either. "The world is like a heap of cinders, while the sinister flame of the Russian revolution burns, a flame without heat, which does not leave in history a bloody and human drama like the French Revolution, but . . . the doctrinaire disputes of Marxian pedants, a cold, Oriental cruelty." Of his literary gods, Zola, France, Ibsen, Nietzsche, Tolstoy, and Dostoevsky, only the latter survives, "like an admirable monstrosity." "The number of imbecilities which our epoch is cheerfully swallowing is incalculable. There is no fake which it will not accept— spiritism and theosophy, dadaism or cubism, magic and Freudian psychoanalysis. Our age is an ostrich which swallows everything that is thrown to it. It cannot digest, because stones may be swallowed, but not digested."

"As students of Spanish literature," says Baroja, "some of you doubtless have read that there is a generation of writers in Spain, the generation of 1898, and that I belong to it. . . . I do not believe that there is or ever has been a generation of 1898. If there is, I do not belong to it. In 1898 I had published almost nothing; I was not known, and had not the slightest reputation. My first book, *Vidas Sombrías*, appeared in 1900. It never seemed to me a good idea of Azorín's, who baptized and almost invented this generation, to associate the names of a few writers with the date of a national disaster with which they had nothing whatever to do. Those of us who were beginners were men of all sorts of tendencies. The majority cultivated what was called and is still called, I believe, modernism, . . . but, as we had no common ideal, each went his own way. Benavente got his inspiration from Shakespeare, Musset, and the French dramatists of his time; Valle-Inclán got his from Barbey d'Aurevilly, d'Annunzio,

and Casanova; Unamuno from Carlyle and Kierke-
gaard; Maetzu from Nietzsche, and afterward from
the English sociologists; Azorín from Taine, Flaubert,
and then Francis Jammes. I divided my enthusiasm
between Dickens and Dostoevsky. As for Blasco
Ibáñez, also of our generation, who, I know not why,
is never included in the so-called generation of 1898,
he was a diligent imitator of Zola. . . . A generation
which has no points of view in common, nor the
same aspirations, nor intellectual solidarity, nor even
the bond of age, is not a generation. Therefore, the
alleged generation of 1898 is more imaginary than
real."

Baroja is an individualist. He began, he confesses,
by wanting to be universal, a citizen of the world.
Now he finds it excessive to be even a Spaniard, and
tends more and more to regard himself not even as
a Basque but as a citizen of the republic of Bidasoa,
whose motto is: "No flies, no priests, no cops." The
first means a clean community, the second a community with common sense, the third a state without
power—"all things that I think excellent."

RAMÓN DEL VALLE-INCLÁN

UNDER the title of *The Pleasant Memoirs of the Marquis of Bradomín*, the four famous sonatas of Don Ramón María del Valle-Inclán have been launched forth upon their career in English without any of the aids to immortality which have helped to make them and their author celebrated in Spain. Don Ramón is himself a legendary personage, and the fortunes of his books have always been closely involved in his picturesque existence and bound up with his romantic personality. If ever a work might have been helped by an introduction it was the English version of these sonatas, but there is no sketch of the author, no picture of that vivid figure strayed out of another century, no word as to the genesis of this book.

Yet it is a book which does not even exist in Spanish, for the four parts of the memoirs of the Marquis of Bradomín known as the *Sonatas* were never published as one work in Spain. The first to appear was the *Sonata of Autumn*, in 1902; in 1903 came *The Sonata of Summer*, followed in 1904 by the *Sonata of Spring*, and finally by the *Sonata of Winter*, in 1905. These are not, moreover, the only chapters from the life of the notorious Marquis which Valle-Inclán has imagined. Obviously the arrangement of these four volumes according to the order of the seasons in one English volume under the title selected, is something that might have been explained in an otherwise desirable introductory sketch of the author.

As the evolution of these stories has been boldly denied by an American authority on Spanish literature, it is of interest to establish the facts which, instead of being properly explained in an introduction, have been publicly obscured by a too zealous effort to justify the English version of the *Sonatas*. Valle-Inclán's first book, *Femeninas*, which appeared in 1894 or 1895—all points of Spanish bibliography are wrapped in an impenetrable obscurity—contained a story called *La Niña Chole*, which reappears in essentials as the *Sonata of Summer*. In the *Sonata of Autumn* will be found *Hierbas Olorosas* from *Jardín Novelesco*, a revised version of *Eulalia* from *Corte de Amor*, and part of *El Miedo*, from *Jardín Umbrío*. The *Sonata of Spring* contains *Fué Satanás*, which is also to be found in *Jardín Novelesco*. Thus only the *Sonata of Winter* can be regarded as a single and homogeneous conception. These transmutations of Valle-Inclán's stories are typical of his baffling bibliography, but become a simplification by reducing the works of importance to foreign readers, in prose, to the four *Sonatas* and the trilogy of *La Guerra Carlista*.

When the sonatas were beginning to make him known Don Ramón played a characteristic trick upon the public. Underneath a portrait of himself which was published he wrote: "The man whom you see here, of Spanish countenance and with an air of Quevedo, with his dark locks and long beard, is Don Ramón María del Valle-Inclán. My early life was full of risks and perils. I was a lay brother in a Carthusian monastery and a soldier in the lands of New Spain. My life was that of those second sons of the hidalgos who served in the armies of Italy in search of adventures of love, war, and fortune. . . . On board the *Delilah*—as I remember with pride—I murdered Sir Robert Yones. It was an act of vengeance worthy of Benvenuto Cellini. I will tell you how it happened, even though you be incapable of understanding its beauty. But, no. I had better not tell you; you might be horrified."

With this beginning he evolved an autobiography, which proved to be simply an adaptation of the *Pleasant Memoirs*. He has since rewritten his autobiography more than once, and the result is that an atmosphere of legend and mystery hangs around him, which his actual appearance does much to enhance, as his portrait by Juan Echevarría shows. He is a tall, Don Quixote-like figure, wearing a long beard, and with only one arm. His huge horn-rimmed spectacles are like those of his sixteenth-century forerunner Quevedo, and in his youth his long black hair, his enormous collars, and his threadbare garments, enveloped in a great cape, made him a spectacle which could not but stimulate the imagination of Madrid, the more so as nothing has ever been discovered about his life before he came to Madrid in 1895.

He arrived there armed with his first book, a volume of six stories, which had appeared the preceding year in Pontevedra, the town near which he was born in 1869. *Femeninas* contained "six tales of love" which, minus the style subsequently evolved, contained in germ the four *Sonatas*, and an ingenious critic, who has pursued the innumerable and elusive editions of Valle-Inclán's works through their various transmutations, argues that so frequently have those first stories been reworked and elaborated that one ordinary book of three hundred pages would actually contain all that is original in his writings, apart from some plays and his three novels dealing with the Carlist wars.

This first book had a certain resemblance to Barbey d'Aurevilly's *Les Diaboliques*, and the points in common between these two authors have since been stressed by many critics. The Marquis of Bradomín,

"ugly, Catholic, and sentimental," whose adventures
are a blend of religion and blasphemy, of sensuality
and mysticism, is a character that Barbey would
have loved. To the creation of this personage Valle-
Inclán has brought an imagination and a style which
are in perfect harmony. His imagination is mediæval
and decadent, his style is rhythmic, polished, and
languorous, full of the lovely cadences of his native
Galician poetry, with just the proper sense of archa-
ism.

This peculiar creation, with its appropriate style,
reaches its finest expression in the four *Sonatas*, and
is the work upon which Valle-Inclán's fame rests,
although in fact the novels of the Carlist wars are
better written, in the academic sense, and less deriva-
tive in general conception. Like Anatole France, the
Spanish novelist has a thoroughly classic indifference to charges of plagiarism, and thus is not disturbed by the fact that the *Sonata of Spring* contains
an incident taken almost textually from the fifth
volume of Casanova's memoirs, and the *Sonata of
Autumn* is in part an obvious adaptation of *The
Crimson Curtain* from Barbey d'Aurevilly's *Diaboliques*. His debt to d'Annunzio has been pointed
out, and one of his most effective stylistic usages, the
subtle linking and grouping of adjectives, comes
from the Portuguese Eça de Queiroz.

Such an author is naturally a problem for the
translator, and on the whole his American translators
have not betrayed him too badly. There are few
varieties of sexual experiences which the Marquis
of Bradomín does not illustrate in the course of his
adventures, and here the translators have been exceedingly cautious. Many passages are omitted
where the frank sensuality and literary perversity
of the Marquis reach a degree of intensity unsuitable
for chaste Anglo-Saxon consumption, and there is

a tendency to tone down unnecessarily the daring
but not obscene treatment of love. The cynical will
be amused by the fact that while the book has thus
been made suitable for Mr. Sumner's inspection there
are allusions whose implications are identical with
some of the suppressed paragraphs, so that one marvels at the tight-rope walking which such bowdlerization involves. Some of the Marquis's conquests are
allowed in English to disrobe, others merely let down
their hair, although in fact they loosened more than
that. The result is that the full-blooded, passionate,
religious, blasphemous reincarnation of Don Juan,
whose pleasant memoirs are related, appears before
his English-speaking audience in a state of relative
regeneration. He is still, however, an exotic figure
when he is set in the severe, undecorative frame of
Protestant English, where his Catholic blasphemies
lost much of their potency, and his pagan delight in
sin cannot find words at once adequate and acceptable to our censors.

The novels of Valle-Inclán fall into three groups,
of which the earliest is the series of *Sonatas*, written
under the influence and in the tradition of Barbey
d'Aurevilly and Villiers de l'Isle Adam. From these
a transition is effected by way of the studies of the
decadence of the nobles of Galicia, *Aguila de Blasón*
and *Romance de Lobos*, to the second group, the epic
stories of Galicia during the Carlist wars, *Los Cruzados de la Causa*, *El Resplandor de la Hoguera* and
Gerifaltes de Antaño, which constitute the trilogy of
La Guerra Carlista, published during the years 1908
and 1909. The third is his present and probably
last phase, as illustrated by *Divinas Palabras* and
Luces de Bohemia, in which the picaresque and the
diabolic combine in strange pictures of vagabonds
along the roads of his native Galicia, and dialogued
fiction which probes the lowest depths of social and

intellectual bohemianism. One is conscious of a certain rashness in trying to make such a classification, for the grouping of Valle-Inclán's work has tempted Spanish critics, with a decided diversity in the result. Julio Casares declared in 1915 that the division was, first, the simple manner, terminating with *Jardín Umbrío* about 1901; then the second, or florid manner, which reached its culminating point in 1903 in the *Sonata of Summer* and its decadence in the *Sonata of Winter*, in 1905. The third phase was *La Guerra Carlista*, a "return to the lyrical, melancholy, and mysterious spirit of Galicia." A much more authoritative critic—in fact, the only Spanish critic of modern literature who comes up to normal standards of clarity and skill—Eduardo Gómez de Baquero, who writes under the pseudonym of Andrenio—Don Eduardo asserts that the proper classification is, first the *Sonatas*, or the "Bradomín cycle," then the "Montenegro cycle" of *Aguila de Blasón* and *Romance de Lobos*, and finally *La Guerra Carlista*.

Both Andrenio's grouping and mine take account of the link between the Bradomín cycle and the Carlist War trilogy, for the Marquis of Bradomín is found again in *Los Cruzados de la Causa*, just as Don Juan Manuel de Montenegro recurs after having been introduced in *Aguila de Blasón* and *Romance de Lobos*. These two *hidalgos*, however, are no longer the central figures of the narratives, but are represented as types of the aristocratic society whose dissolution is the real theme of the trilogy. Valle-Inclán does not treat the Carlist wars as a national political event, and the series bears no relation to such undertakings as the vast *Episodios Nacionales* of Galdós. The Marquis of Bradomín, in the *Sonata of Winter*, gives us a clew to the author's attitude: "I have always found fallen majesty more beautiful than majesty enthroned, and I was a defender of

tradition for æsthetic reasons. For me Carlism has
the solemn charm of old cathedrals, and even during
the war I should have been satisfied if it had been
declared a national monument."

The lyrical, individualistic note of the *Sonatas*,
therefore, makes way in *La Guerra Carlista* for the
epic narrative of the rise of the people, the peasant
against a social order personified by the Marquis of
Bradomín and by Don Manuel de Montenegro,
whose son, Cara de Plata, represents the ultimate
fate and the final incarnation of the old race of warriors, great gentlemen, and lovers, who have no
place in the modern world. Ramón del Valle-Inclán
makes no effort to portray the actual Carlist war,
yet he has evoked the atmosphere of the time and
made the whole period live again in this series of
deft pictures of trifling incidents and obscure people,
for the most part, whose multiplication all over Spain
produced the upheaval which established the present
dynasty and the Spain of to-day. In *Los Cruzados
de la Causa* the Marquis of Bradomín returns to his
own territory to collect material for the war; he has
undertaken to get a supply of arms which are hidden
in a convent. The fact has been betrayed and marines
are searching the building, while the deep but latent
hostility of the people is felt in a thousand little
touches, but finds outward expression only in the
women. One of these discovers her son, a recruit,
whom chance has sent to this place, and who is
guarding one of the convent doors. Under his mother's abuse and supplications the boy's sense of discipline gives way and he deserts, is pursued, and shot.
When the marines leave the village, Cara de Plata
gets the arms down to the shore and they are despatched to the rebels.

There are just three capital scenes in the book—
the search, the death of the recruit, and the gun-

running; but into them Valle-Inclán has contrived
to inject the whole drama of the war, and to write
some of the finest pages in modern Spanish literature.
El Resplandor de la Hoguera is set, not in Galicia,
which was distant from the scene of action, but in
the very midst of insurrectionary events; but characteristically there is less of actual war in it than in
the preceding volume. It is a series of episodes
which show, as the title implies, "the glare of the
conflagration," the vast and far-reaching disturbance
of civil war in every class and type of the community,
the obscure conflicts, the disruption of Spain into
warring groups, "divided by ideas rather than by
interests," as Andrenio has said. The collectivity,
not the individual, is the hero of this novel, with the
simplest incidents as its theme, an affair of espionage
and one passage at arms between the followers of the
insurrectionist Miquelo Egozcué and a column of
government troops. Only in the last book of the
trilogy, *Gerifaltes de Antaño*, does Valle-Inclán handle
his subject in something like the traditional manner
of the historical novel. This time there is a central
character, Don Manuel Santa Cruz, the priest of
Hernialde, an actual personage in the history of
the Carlist wars. The cruelty and ferocity of this
man put him in the curious position of being pursued by both the Liberals and the Carlists, and the
author has made a wonderful study of the fanatical
soul of this bloodthirsty idealist, whom he compares
to "the vine-grower who lights fires against the pests
of the vine, watching the smoke rising from the
ground, as in a sacrifice, in the serene hope of gathering in the grapes one day under God's golden sunlight." When Santa Cruz is on the point of being
captured he is allowed to escape because his fierce
partisanship is worth too much to the enemies of the
Carlist cause which he, in his blind and ruthless
fanaticism, thinks he is helping.

Large as the Carlist wars loom in Spanish history and literature, for Galdós has treated them, and even Unamuno in his *Paz en la Guerra*, the subject has an inevitable remoteness for foreign readers, which must militate against the success of this trilogy outside Spain. Yet it is generally held that *La Guerra Carlista* is Ramón del Valle-Inclán's finest prose work, the most perfect in form and the most original. *The Pleasant Memoirs of the Marquis of Bradomín* has, of course, the fascination inseparable from all reincarnations of Don Juan, and, in the original, a harmony and beauty unsurpassed by any living writer, but as untranslatable as beautiful prose must always be. Having translated Eça de Queiroz, Valle-Inclán acquired a number of his mannerisms, as he borrowed quite freely from *Les Diaboliques*, but neither the Portuguese novelist nor Barbey d'Aurevilly ever brought such subtle harmonies into their perverse romances as Don Ramón María del Valle-Inclán. He is the pure artist and must, in consequence, count upon the reproaches of those who seek for morals in æsthetics. How antipathetic his outlook upon art and life must be to the Anglo-Saxon mind is beautifully demonstrated in *Semblanzas Literarias Contemporáneas*, by Don Salvador de Madariaga. This thoroughly anglicized Spanish critic, whose essays first appeared in English under the title of *The Genius of Spain*, reproaches Valle-Inclán with his "frivolity" and lack of "good form."

JACINTO BENAVENTE

THE English-reading public is now in possession of sixteen typical plays by Jacinto Benavente, who is regarded as the leading dramatist of contemporary Spain. The first volume of the series in English translation contained *The Bonds of Interest, His Widow's Husband, La Malquerida,* and *The Evil Doers of Good;* the second, *No Smoking, Princess Bébé, The Governor's Wife,* and *Autumnal Roses;* in the third are included *The Prince Who Learned Everything out of Books, Saturday Night, In the Clouds,* and *The Truth;* the fourth volume consists of *The School of Princesses, A Lady, The Magic of an Hour,* and *Field of Ermine.* It was a formidable task to make a choice that would be representative out of some hundred and fourteen plays, but Mr. Underhill has aquitted himself well. His versions are not too literal; they have the vivacity and color of dramatic speech, although, at times, they take liberties with the text. Patience, enthusiasm, and scholarship are necessary for such an undertaking.

It would be idle to pretend that Benavente's plays are widely known and appreciated outside Spain and South America, and it is certain that they cannot be translated in the casual, hit-and-miss manner which disfigures so many translations in recent years, particularly from the Spanish. The language, in spite of popular opinion to the contrary, is by no means easy, as those who are not contented with travellers' phrases and the elements of commercial correspondence are aware. The fame of the dramatist himself, although secure in popular Spanish esteem, is not such as to

encourage translators concerned only to exploit a
current vogue. When Benavente received the Nobel
Prize in 1922 he was scarcely more than a name to
most European readers unacquainted with Spanish.
The Swedes, who made the award, have only now
begun to translate his work, and the first venture
has not been welcomed with much enthusiasm. In
France, Benavente's pro-German sympathies during
the war have not facilitated the spread of his work,
and the bitterest and most abusive comment followed the announcement that he was the Nobel
Prize winner. In Italy, where a number of his plays
have been performed and published, opinion is
strongly divided on the subject of his merits.

In English, Benavente's reputation has hitherto
rested upon the success of the production by Miss
Nance O'Neill of *The Passion Flower*, that being
the rather cinematographic title chosen for *La Malquerida*. The Theatre Guild produced *The Bonds of
Interest*—which has also been played in London—
but without any of the success which attended *The
Passion Flower*, and the Washington Square Players
had previously performed a one-act farce, *His Widow's Husband*. Such is the record, so far as the general public is concerned, upon which opinion in this
country has based its judgment of Jacinto Benavente.
In the autumn of 1922 Miss O'Neill tried out another
play, *Field of Ermine*, which is in the fourth volume
of his plays in English. Its reception did not apparently justify its production in New York. It is evident that the Spanish dramatist has not yet secured
here the attention and consideration which he enjoys
in his own country.

What is Benavente's position in Spain? Is he, as
his fanatical admirers claim, the greatest Spanish
dramatist since Calderón? He is certainly the leading playwright of his country, and after some years

of unpopularity he is now a widely known and respected figure. But critical opinion is by no means unanimous as to his merits. Professor de Onís, of Columbia University, has recently pointed out that Benavente represents the culmination of a phase in the development of the Spanish theatre, and that a new generation has arrived which regards him as having accomplished his function. It is this generation, whose leaders are Pérez de Ayala, G. Rivas Cherif, and Luis Araquistain, which has systematically challenged the later work of Benavente. The older writers and the academic critics, as Mr. Underhill admits in his introduction to the third volume, are laudatory but vague. It is not easy to pin them down to more than a superficial comment, whereas the hostile critics have left no doubt as to what their objections are, and they have analyzed with frank, with brutal, precision the defects in his work. The spokesmen of clerical orthodoxy have also protested, not upon æsthetic but upon moral grounds, against what they regard as Benavente's materialism and indifference to spiritual values. In order to see the situation in perspective, a summary of Benavente's evolution is necessary.

Jacinto Benavente was born in Madrid in 1866, and belongs with Pío Baroja, Unamuno, and Azorín to the generation of '98; that is to say, the group of writers who, after the Spanish-American War, inaugurated a new era in Spanish literature. He began to write about 1892, and published a volume of Shakespearian fantasies, *Teatro Fantástico*, and a book of verse, before his first play, *El Nido Ajeno*, was produced in 1894. From that date his work was chiefly concerned with the theatre. He played an active part in the literary life of that exciting period, when the disaster of the war led to a transvaluation of values, and the intellectual life of Spain took a

new orientation. For ten years or so Benavente wrote
a series of brilliant social comedies, after the manner
of the French theatre of Capus and Lavedan. That
was when, as Mr. Underhill says, "Madrid dined
an hour earlier" whenever Benavente produced a new
play. Those were the years of *In Society*, *A Tale of
Love*, *The Husband's Train*, and *The Governor's Wife*
—to mention a few characteristic titles—and of
these early works only one, *The Governor's Wife*, has
been published in Mr. Underhill's edition. At that
time Benavente appeared as an acute satirist of the
society and manners of Madrid toward the close of
the nineteenth century. The plays had little action,
but were sharply etched pictures of *Well-Known
People*, to quote the comprehensive and descriptive
title of one of the best of these comedies.

The people satirized were themselves the audience
of the early Benavente, but gradually the scope of
the dramatist extended until it included themes of
more universal appeal. The ironical and sceptical
note is softened and a greater diversity of subject is
apparent. The first of these plays of the period of
Benavente's highest dramatic intensity is *La Noche
del Sábado*. Under the title of *Saturday Night* it
appears as the most important play in Mr. Underhill's third volume. In the second series he has already given us *Princess Bébé* and *Autumnal Roses*,
and in the first *The Evil Doers of Good*, all of which
belong to the second period of Benavente's evolution. It was this last-mentioned comedy, with its
indictment of professional moralists, and its plea
for human liberty, which secured for Benavente his
first real popular success in 1905. It had the good
fortune to offend some prominent lady philanthro-
pists, and enjoyed the adventitious fame which invariably accrues to any work that conflicts with the
conventions of the powers that be.

In such plays as these Benavente escapes from his preoccupation with a section of Madrid society. His satire, instead of playing with the surface manifestations of social life, takes on a wider and deeper significance. He uses the conventional forms of the theatre to express his opinions upon love and morality, politics and education, or human nature, in a word. He does not reproduce a milieu realistically, but frequently combines realism and symbolism. The background is perhaps the same as in the earlier plays, but now he introduces characters personifying ideas, or fundamental human characteristics. Benavente still looks at the world with the eyes of a satirist; he wears no rose-colored spectacles, and it is at bottom a disillusioned picture that he draws. But there is a note of melancholy, a vague hint of idealism, the beginning of a tendency to preach, to manipulate symbols which, some critics aver, he had from the first but which he concealed. J. Cejador y Frauca declares that Benavente's characters are chiefly abstractions, puppets, the unreal mouthpieces of the author. He roundly berates Fitzmaurice Kelly, the English historian of Spanish literature, who for many years completely ignored Benavente's existence, for repeating the statement that he is not a thesis writer. He quotes González Blanco, the dramatist's stanchest Spanish champion, only to say that the exact opposite of what he quotes is the truth.

Whatever may be said of this dispute, which is typical of the sharp disagreement amongst Spanish critics whenever Benavente is discussed, there is no doubt that the author of *The Bonds of Interest* and its sequel, as yet untranslated, *La Ciudad Alegr. y Confiada*, has abandoned his original objectivity. The lack of success which has attended *The Bonds of Interest* outside Spain must be attributed in part to its unhappy combination of sheer fantasy and thesis.

Society is symbolized by these puppets, and the didactic intention is even clearer in the sequel.

The first play shows us how vested interests establish themselves, and in the second we see the system at work. Harlequin, Polichinelle, and Crispin are masters, and are leading the public, their dupe, by the nose. A mysterious figure, known as the Outcast, symbolizes Truth, and tears the masks from the appearances of things and exposes the hypocrisy of the social order. There is an elaborate machinery set to work for the purpose of proving that politics are corrupt.

He has followed this play with such pieces of hollow symbolism as *The Necklace of Stars*, with the platitude of brotherly love as its point of departure, which are eagerly seized upon by his hostile critics as further proof of his decline. The truth is that the mantle of social prophet does not rest easily upon the shoulders of Benavente. He is involved, obscure, and turgid in the delivery of his messages to humanity, for that is not the rôle to which his undoubted talents assign him. Benavente is too profound a sceptic to succeed with a thesis play, even though it be disguised as a puppet-show. His adventures of late into this field, that dramatic No Man's Land once so tempting as the "theatre of ideas," cannot be called fortunate, though it is not unlikely that it was just this later appearance of solemnity which recommended the Spanish dramatist to the Nobel Prize Committee. Such moralizing Ibsenism as peeps through such recent works as *The Necklace of Stars* brings us back to Echegaray and completes the cycle of Benavente's evolution.

His initial success was based upon a definite break with the Echegaray tradition, and although it is hardly likely that the Sardoodledum of that dramatic platitudinarian can be restored, Benavente has resuscitated some of his peculiarities; notably, the use of a desolating and far-fetched philosophy expressed in hollow symbols, of which *The Necklace of Stars* is a typical specimen. The theme of this play is humanitarian; love of one's neighbor is its text, and the title refers to the stars in the heavens, to which the human family are likened.

Needless to say, these later plays have captured the general public, and the author need no longer complain that in all that has been written about the Spanish theatre there are "scarcely twenty expressions of opinion favorable to him." *La Ciudad Alegre y Confiada*, with its Scriptural title and undertones of Sodom and Gomorrah, was the occasion of a veritable triumph for the author, who, according to eye-witnesses, was hailed by the crowd as a genius. The Nobel Prize came as the final consecration of this conquest by Benavente of a public which, as he once said, "had to be made for his plays and not his plays for the public." A happy precept, which is true of almost every great work of genius, but hardly an accurate statement of the facts in Benavente's case. As one of the characters in *La Ciudad Alegre y Confiada* says: "Nothing is easier than to be a propagandist of ideas and to lead the mob. All that is necessary is to proclaim what one knows the public thinks." That is rather what Benavente has been doing of late, to the detriment of his talent.

He is not a writer with fundamental ideas, with a definite philosophy, like Shaw or Brieux, to name both a good and a mediocre dramatist, whose aim has been to create a public for the drama of ideas, the play with a criticism of social and economic conditions. Benavente's lack of equipment for such a rôle is evident in *The Bonds of Interest*, where he endeavors to satirize and expose the vested interests of the existing order in Spain without reference to the three basic factors of religion, capitalism, and monarchy. His real function is that of a genial and sceptical satirist of manners, who deftly and discreetly strips the gilt off the surface of society and reveals the eternal imbecilities and hypocrisies of the conventional world. His art is that of the miniaturist, and he often lacks the broad strokes which are effective across the footlights.

In his latest *Apologia pro Benavente suo*—the introduction to the fourth volume of translations—Mr. Underhill continues his demonstration of the transcendent merits of Jacinto Benavente over those of all other dramatists living or dead. Thus he asserts that the Spanish dramatist anticipated Schnitzler and Chehov, and all historians of the drama are admonished to take note of the fact, or be forever silent. The evidence in the case, however, is not very conclusive. It is obvious that both Schnitzler and Benavente were indebted to the French for the type of comedy in question. As for *The Cherry Orchard*, and its alleged predecessor, *La Comida de las Fieras*, if the Benavente play preceded the Russian by six years, Becque's *Les Corbeaux* preceded the Spanish by no less than sixteen years. It is true that the omission of Benavente's name from some of the standard histories of the contemporary drama is indefensible, but his name has no place there on such doubtful grounds as the claim that he anticipated the light social comedy of Schnitzler and the Russian realism of Chehov. In thus dissenting from the exaggerated esteem in which Benavente is held by some admirers, I am neither original nor unique. Compared with the heresies of Pérez de Ayala and others, my protests are mild indeed. This is what Ayala writes in *Las Máscaras*:

If one examines the complete dramatic works of Don Jacinto Benavente as a whole, like a panorama, it at once becomes apparent that this is a landscape whose flora and fauna correspond neither to the torrid nor the arctic zone, but to an epicene, transition zone, in which the climate changes arbitrarily from warm to cold and cold to warm, without ever touching any great extreme. It is not the land of palm-trees, or of firs; it is not the country of passion or of dreams. It is the territory of the white poplar with its silvery leaves like tambourine bells; the territory of the sentimental weeping willow. . . . The qualities of such a landscape are elegance and versatility. . . . The dramatic works of Señor Benavente are composed with that elegance which is partly artifice and partly nature, and as for his versatility it is simply prodigious. Señor Benavente has written all kinds of plays: monologues, comic sketches, dialogues, farces, middle-class comedy, aristocratic comedy, fantastic and children's plays, rustic comedy, hair-raising drama, detective drama, moralizing comedy, and, finally, a new kind which may be called patriotic comedy.

Among the kinds enumerated I have deliberately omitted to classify one into which Señor Benavente relapses with evident delight. I refer to those works whose characters are Emperors, Kings, Princes, Grand Dukes, and gentlemen, mixed up promiscuously with a mob of gamblers, criminals, thieves, prostitutes, acrobats, and others of that kind; the entire Almanach de Gotha, the real and criminal; in short, that crowd of people who make up the free and æsthetic world of comic opera . . . a world with no existence outside literature and the stage. To this order belong *Saturday Night*, *Princess Bébé*, *The School of Princesses*, and other works . . . which produce a disturbing effect . . . as if something were missing. What is missing is waltz music. They would make excellent libretti for operettas. . . . The souls of the characters are not interesting, only their costumes. Their souls are indistinct; the Princesses look like prostitutes and the prostitutes like Princesses. . . . The emotion they arouse comes from the suggestion of sex, an emotion that three-four time, waltz time, helps to intensify. That is why this kind of literature requires operetta music to achieve its maximum intensity.

Princess Bébé will be found in the first volume of Benavente's plays, *Saturday Night* in the third, and *The School of Princesses* in the fourth of Mr. Underhill's translation, where the curious may contrast their own impressions with those of the translator and those of Pérez de Ayala, who speaks for a group of most distinguished figures in the generation later than that of Benavente. Mr. Underhill thinks that *The School of Princesses,* "in range and imagination, in cunning mastery of all the tools commonly to be found in the dramatic workshop," is "wholly admirable." He says that "the wealth of its characterization, the glamour of its shimmering dialogue, and the prodigality of its ideas are blended in a sparkling sequence of mood and situation, with unflagging comic invention. The luxuriance and brilliance of Benavente's art have nowhere been seen to better advantage than in his royal comedies. . . . It is a type of drama that Benavente has made distinctively his own, in which the decorative elements, for all their opulence and arresting qualities, whether of dialogue or characterization, are yet all integral parts of the dramatic structure." Here is obviously an emphatic diversity of opinion.

The truth about Benavente, I need hardly say, lies somewhere between the pæans of Mr. Underhill and the inevitable revolt of such Spaniards as Pérez de Ayala, Luis Araquistain, and Rivas Cherif against the exaggerated reputation of a dramatist who has done good work. That work was the introduction into the Spanish theatre of good light comedy and social satire in the French manner. For foreign readers and playgoers, therefore, his interest is slight, and it is significant that over here, even after the Nobel Prize award, his *Field of Ermine* failed, as *The Bonds of Interest* had failed before it when produced by the Theatre Guild. It will be some time, I fancy, before the historians of the drama repair the omission with which Mr. Underhill reproaches them in his latest preface, by attributing to Jacinto Benavente an importance as an innovator and craftsman which he assuredly does not deserve, whatever his relative position may be in the history of the Spanish theatre.

AZORÍN

In spite of Pío Baroja's statement that there is no
such thing in Spanish literature as the "generation
of 1898," the term is generally accepted to describe
the writers who succeeded the Realistic school of
Pérez Galdós, Juan Valera, José María Pereda, and
Emilia Pardo Bazán, whose sole survivor to-day is
Armando Palacio Valdés. In the late 'eighties and
'nineties this group enjoyed a considerable vogue in
English, and more translations were made of their
works than of any Spanish author of the following
generation, with the exception of Blasco Ibáñez. As
Baroja reminds us, Blasco Ibáñez is never included
in the generation of 1898, but there remains one other
writer of that period, in addition to those whom I
have already discussed, whose name is usually linked
with those of Unamuno and Baroja as typifying the
new spirit of the times, José Martínez Ruiz, known
to letters as "Azorín." It is he whom Baroja credits
with having invented the generation of 1898 and
given it the name which literary usage has confirmed. In common with the others he has been
offered, without much success, to English-speaking
readers, who may observe one aspect of his peculiar
talent in an excellent translation of his *Don Juan*, by
Catherine Alison Phillips.

That tender and delicate narrative of the reincarnation of Don Juan, who is living humbly and happily
in a small town, having substituted for the luxuries
of his former high estate the contemplation of "the
faith of ingenuous souls and hope that never dies,"
and for the love of women "that higher love which is
pity for all"—this little book hardly gives the mea-

sure of the Azorín known to modern Spanish literature. Its series of charming vignettes of rural types
and landscapes is characteristic, but the caustic,
ironical, iconoclastic element is lacking, and it is
that element which has brought Azorín into the
front rank of Spanish essayists, beside Unamuno
and Ortega y Gasset. *Don Juan* is described as a
novel, but it has scarcely more title to that description than had its three more famous predecessors,
La Voluntad, Antonio Azorín, and *Las Confesiones
de un Pequeño Filósofo,* in which the author wrote the
autobiography of his own soul and generation, and
established his reputation.

He began to write in his early teens, contributing
"short and terrible articles of anarchist propaganda"
to *El Pueblo,* the paper which Blasco Ibáñez founded
and conducted during the nineties, when he was a
militant republican. Azorín has never denied those
articles, although he was subsequently to become a
Deputy of more or less conservative tendencies, but,
as Blasco destroyed the files of the paper for the
years of his editorship, nobody has been able to
confront this distinguished contributor with the sins
of his youth. Baroja compares the modification of
Azorín's attitude to "becoming a reactionary in one's
heart after being an anarchist in one's soul," and
Azorín himself states his position in terms which are
very similar to those employed by Anatole France
when describing his own tactics, except that France
began with the method which the Spanish writer
gradually acquired, as he admits when he writes:
"When an author has advanced in life, when he
knows something of the resources of literary technic, he realizes that he can now say substantially
everything he used to say, provided he changes the
form. And one realizes also that what we in Spain
call revolutionary is not the subtle and profoundly

new thought, but whatever is expressed in harsh, immoderate terms. How much more revolutionary are those writers who are masters of fine shades and gradual transitions than those who deafen our ears with strong words and violent expressions!"

Azorín did not achieve this wisdom early, as Anatole France did, and under the pseudonym of "Cándido" he published his first book, in 1893, an essay on Moratín, which was included the following year in a collection of satires and critical articles, entitled *Buscapiés*, and signed with his second pseudonym, "Ahrimán." After this he issued several volumes of a similar kind over his own name, José Martínez Ruiz, for which the signature Azorín was definitely substituted after the publication of *La Voluntad* in 1902. He declared of one of those early works, *La Evolución de la Crítica*, "if this book bears the title which it does, it is for phonetic reasons rather than for any appropriateness to the idea," which might well be applied to everything that he published before 1900. What chiefly interests us in his 'prentice work is the germ of that iconoclasm which was to set the orthodox by the ears when he finally combined maturity of manner with originality of matter.

Julio Cejador y Frauca, in his tortuous and strange *Historia de la Lengua y Literatura Castellana* succinctly states the grievance of the academic critics against Azorín when he says: "He has maltreated the most distinguished geniuses of Spain: Cervantes, Lope, Granada, Quevedo, Calderón, Bretón, Ramón de la Cruz, García Gutiérrez, Campoamor, Valera, el Duque de Rivas, Zorrilla, Pereda, Menéndez y Pelayo; and has extolled, on the other hand, mediocrities of the eighteenth and the beginning of the nineteenth centuries, because they were bad patriots and Encyclopædists." The Reverend Professor

cites some examples of Azorín's heresies. "Campoamor gives me the impression of an asthmatic gentleman reading a novel by Galdós and talking eloquently
about the September revolution." "Could there be
anything more hollow, verbose, incongruous, and
emotionless than the poetry of Zorrilla?" Calderón's
La Vida es Sueño is the "embryo of a masterpiece
. . . a sketch for a drama, a superb fragment, but a
fragment, none the less." One is reminded of Bernard
Shaw's dissertations upon Shakespeare and the Elizabethan dramatists by Azorín's continuous onslaughts
upon the classical theatre of Spain. "Nothing is
more brittle than our classic drama. If by any chance
a work is produced (after it has been pruned and
cooked up), we pretend to derive great æsthetic
pleasure from it. In reality, we feel nothing; if we
were sincere, we should say so openly . . . ; these
plays (with some exceptions) can mean nothing to
us who want drama to be based upon observation
and truth. Our old plays depend entirely upon chance
and improbability. . . . There is the same lack of
probability and logic in the picaresque novel. The
alleged realism of the picaresque novel is simply a
distortion of reality . . . a reflection which is an
exaggerated and distorted caricature."

The author of *Los Valores Literarios, Lecturas
Españolas*, and *Clásicos y Modernos*—to mention the
three volumes in which his literary essays are collected—has eliminated the Gallicisms and other
affectations of his nonage, but the irreverent "Cándido" and "Ahrimán" live on in the author who
could say of the unacademic things as harsh as any
levelled at Menéndez y Pelayo, as, for instance, this
exhortation to a youth desirous of entering journalism. "Well, my dear young man, since you are without dignity, shame, or sincerity, and know nothing
whatsoever about literature or art, why . . . be-

come a journalist!" Julio Casares, a Spanish critic whose pedantic incursions into the sources and the syntax of his contemporaries have made him the scourge of his literary world, takes a malicious pleasure in illustrating how Azorín emulated his own precepts in his callow youth, by making a character in *Antonio Azorín* play Beethoven's Ninth Symphony alone on the violoncello!

The same critic reproaches Azorín with his indifference to the writers who have followed the generation of 1898, and it is true that his essays on modern writers have been chiefly concerned with the Catalan, Xenius, with Juan R. Jiménez, and, above all, his close friend and kindred spirit, Pío Baroja. But here a question is raised which transcends the immediate object of the reproach, because that reproach applies generally to Spanish criticism. With the exception of Casares and E. Gómez de Baquero, whose later work, under the name "Andrenio," is alone first-class, Spanish critics of modern literature are so bad, so misleading, and so anxious to stuff up their books with irrelevant and undigested learning, that it is useless to turn to them for guidance. A. González Blanco and R. Cansinos-Assens write voluminously about their contemporaries, but the silence of Azorín is just as illuminating, and the pedantry of Julio Casares is more to the point. Andrenio is the only modern critic whose method, style, and critical attitude correspond to what we expect from the writer whose concern it is to interpret the living literature of his own time. Azorín's contribution to this field has been indirect, but his transvaluation of literary values cannot but have largely helped to clear the ground for the literature of contemporary Spain, which differs so markedly from that of the generation represented by Valdés.

While one may enjoy the iconoclasm of Azorín's

literary criticism, or resent it, there has been only
unanimous appreciation of his other works. Those
which he calls novels, *La Voluntad, Antonio Azorín*,
and *Las Confesiones de un Pequeño Filósofo*, scarcely
merit the term, for they are three volumes of contemporary Spanish history, even more loosely knit
than the four famous books which Anatole France
bracketed as *L'Histoire Contemporaine*. The love-
affair of Justina and Azorín in the first book is so
vague that the girl speaks only twice in the course
of it, and then she utters stereotyped platitudes, including "this life is a valley of tears." When she goes
into a convent and dies, we hear no more of her from
Azorín, who banishes her completely from his mind.
Instead of a story we get the reflections, ironical,
satirical, and serious, of Azorín upon all the trifling
and great problems of life, an exposition of the effort
of adjustment on the part of a man who is without
will, and who questions all things. It is an astonishing study of monotony, fatigue, and melancholy, in
a backwater of Spanish life, written in a suppressed
key appropriate to the tone of resignation that domi-
nates the book, and presenting a diagnosis of the
conditions out of which came the colonial disaster of
1898. *Antonio Azorín* continues the analysis, but
here the red lips and bright eyes of Pepita bring a
note of color into the calm of Azorín's existence and
lighten this picture of lonely and dreary Castilian
country life, this landscape through which only a few
figures move, preoccupied with death, indifferent to
life.

"Life," he wrote in *La Voluntad*, "is not a story
with a plot; it is varied, multiform, undulating, and
contradictory . . . anything but symmetrical, geometrical, and rigid, as it appears in novels," and he
cites with approval the brothers Edmond and Jules
de Goncourt who "do not give life, but fragments

and separate sensations." Azorín, however, has not the narrative skill which enabled the French writers to build up their mosaic out of those fragments until it overwhelmed one with its sense of tragic continuity. As Emilia Pardo Bazán noted, in terms peculiarly applicable to Azorín, although applied to the whole group to which he belonged, "the initial vibration of their sensibility is greater than their strength," so that this conception of life as unsuitable to the exigencies of conventional fiction is nothing more than a clear realization by Azorín of his limitations. After the third of the autobiographical books, *Las Confesiones de un Pequeño Filósofo*, he abandoned even the pretense of a fictitious setting until 1922—an interval of eighteen years—when *Don Juan* appeared. Here the autobiography is not resumed, but in essence the book is another of those charming volumes of impressions of Spanish manners and customs, like *Los Pueblos* and *La Ruta de Don Quijote*, those "plastic interpretations of Spanish life," as Salvador de Madariaga calls them. The same critic says that "this kind of short, dramatic picture, blending the plastic and the dramatic elements in him, is the most typical work of Azorín. Such books . . . are admirable little albums of Spanish life in which the reader is taken away from the beaten track, away also from exceptional and picturesque sights and incidents, and made to see, hear, taste, and enjoy the real commonplace Spain as it lives every day and everywhere—the whole through the sensibility of an exquisite artist endowed with a rare gift for atmosphere and detail," who "saw little, but saw so well that wherever his eye fell, there was life."

Azorín's friend Baroja has left on record the best impression of him, in spite of the demurrers of later critics, in his preface to the only play that Azorín wrote, a tragicomedy entitled *La Fuerza del Amor,*

which is a sin of his nonage and interesting mainly
because of Baroja's portrait. "He has not the great
imagination that creates types, nor has he tenderness. . . . He is an essentially Spanish mind, dry,
bitter, without that breath of pantheistic poetry
which disturbs Northern souls. . . . Do not seek the
cloud that makes you dream, tenderness for little
things, a mysterious vibration that comes from nowhere; no, in his works everything is clear, well
defined, and net." A smiling scepticism has replaced
the old truculence of the time when Baroja wrote
those words, but Azorín is still an impenitent doubter
who laughs at "the God of Sinai appearing in theatrical clouds and frightening a lot of miserable worms
with stage lightning"; there is not a trace of mysticism in him, as befits a child of the South, but, at the
same time, to the discomfiture of the Spanish theorists
of the contrast between the introspective North and
the spontaneous South, he has none of the athletic
vigor and simplicity of his neighbor from Valencia,
Blasco Ibáñez. He is as reflective and intellectual
as the Northern Unamuno, but he was born into an
age without faith, whose doubts he incarnated, and
he turned away from the quest for Truth, resting his
eyes upon the surface of life. His works are those of
one who sees rather than creates. In his own words,
they are "vivid and unconnected notes, like reality
itself."

GREGORIO MARTÍNEZ SIERRA

An already forgotten novel by Gregorio Martínez Sierra, *Tu éres la paz*, which appeared in English in 1921 under the title of *Ana Maria*, was the first serious attempt to exploit in English the alleged vogue of this voluminous writer. Since then we have been presented with two volumes of his plays, some of which were previously issued in separate form. Martínez Sierra shares with Benavente and the brothers Joaquín and Serafín Alvarez Quintero the honors of the Spanish theatre of to-day, and his plays may not be subjected to the same fate as his stories. Like the Quintero brothers and Benavente, Martínez Sierra is a prolific writer and the task of selection was not easy. Out of some hundred and seven plays by Benavente sixteen have been chosen so far to make up the American edition. The Quinteros have published over one hundred and twenty plays, and the list of Sierra's dramatic works totals about forty, although he is a much younger man; and in addition to his plays he has written fourteen volumes of verse and books of essays and travel sketches. He has translated five volumes of Maeterlinck's plays and made Spanish versions of *Hamlet* and *Romeo and Juliet*. From this mass of material we have in English nine plays, five translated by John Garrett Underhill and four by Helen and Granville Barker.

In his foreword Mr. Underhill refers briefly to Doña María Martínez Sierra, who has helped her husband through a series of collaborations, "whose precise nature," he declares, "the most patient criticism could not hope to disclose." The facts of this collaboration have been emphasized much more by

Spanish commentators, and Don Julio Cejador y Frauca, whose enormous and chaotic history of Spanish literature is the standard work of its kind, states that Martínez Sierra and his wife worked together from the very beginning of his career. They were married in 1899, in which year she published the only book which bears her signature, *Cuentos breves*, a volume of short stories. In 1898 appeared *El Poema del Trabajo*, a series of prose poems, which is Martínez Sierra's first work, but was written with his collaborator, who has always insisted that their joint productions shall bear the signature G. Martínez Sierra. This combination of masculine and feminine qualities is regarded by Spanish critics as the essential characteristic of the work of Martínez Sierra. The historian to whom I have referred dwells at length upon this point.

The literary personality of Martínez Sierra is an admirable and rare blending of the masculine and feminine elements which complete art that is really human. It is the work of two people, a man and a woman, in which perhaps the feminine note predominates in the manner, the effects, and, consequently, in the form, which puts its seal on a work of art. But it has a deep profundity of thought more characteristic of the masculine mind. . . . The literary personality known as Martínez Sierra is unique in our literature. Those who were accustomed to masculine literature found the work of Martínez Sierra rather feminine, as it is, relatively speaking, when compared with the traditional literature produced by men alone. But compare this work with that of the purely feminine Fernán Caballero. The temperament which seemed so feminine now appears to be much more masculine. The sentiment and delicacy, which are the notes of Fernán Caballero and Martínez Sierra, are not of the same quality. Neither of them ever dwells on those scenes of cruelty and barbarism which we find in the works of Doña Emilia Pardo Bazán, who seems at times to delight in the inhuman. That is because she tried to write like a man, and nothing is less human than for a man to imitate a woman or a woman a man. . . . The human way is for women to feel and write as women and men as men, and the most perfectly human is what is written both by a man and a woman, each contributing elements that are complementary. Such collaborations and agreements between the two sexes are rare in literature, but when they occur, as in the work of Martínez Sierra, the result cannot fail to be something essentially human and worthy of the fullest consideration. . . . The feminine is patently visible in Fernán Caballero. The exclusively masculine is as certainly absent from the work of Martínez Sierra as the exclusively feminine. But that does not mean that it is effeminate . . . it is simply human, belonging to both sexes equally. The truth is, that it brings a new note into our literature, a greater delicacy of sentiment than that to which purely masculine authors have accustomed us, but it is more masculine than is usual in our women authors.

While the qualities which Spanish criticism attributes to the dual personality implied by the signature of Martínez Sierra are evident in the author's verse and in the essays on femininism, they cannot fail to strike the readers of these plays. Sentimentality is their common feature and their outstanding virtue, or defect, as one prefers. He began by writing symbolical and mystical playlets in the manner of Maeterlinck, as the title of an early volume, *Theatre of Dream*, sufficiently indicates. He soon, however, found the vein of sentimental comedy which has produced the greater number of his characteristic works.

After a few experiences in collaboration with the Catalan dramatist, Santiago Rusiñol, Martínez Sierra made his first success in 1909 with a play entitled *The Father's Shadow*, which has not been translated. This edition in English, however, includes work of that period, for *Love Magic* dates back to 1908, and the other plays in the first volume, *The Cradle Song*, *The Lover*, *Poor John*, and *Madame Pepita*, were produced in 1911 and 1912. All five have been translated by John Garrett Underhill. The second volume, for which Helen and Harley Granville Barker are responsible, contains *The Two Shepherds*, *The King-*

dom of God, The Wife to a Famous Man, and *The Romantic Young Lady.* With the exception of the first, which was played in 1913, these four plays belong to the years of the war, but are as remote from the harsh realities of that time as though they had been written during the eighteen-nineties.

The Cradle Song was produced at the Times Square Theatre, New York, two years ago with moderate success. It is a typical Martínez Sierra play, with its slender story of a foundling child, who arouses the maternal instincts of the nuns in the convent where she has been left, is brought up by them, provided with a husband, and sent out happy into the world from which her mother intended to save her. Granville Barker, viewing it with the eye of an actor-manager, even rejoices in the fact that there are only two acts, "because his theme needs two, and no convention-satisfying third," so that we are asked to assume that the supreme excellence of the play is compensation for this violation of one of the practical rules of our own theatre. Equally slender is *The Lover*, a one-act comedy about a man whose admiration and affections are entirely absorbed in the Queen, for whose sake he allows his margarine business to go to ruin so that he may follow his idol everywhere. When at last he can claim a reward from her Majesty, all he demands is a railway pass, which will enable him to continue his Quixotic pilgrimage in her wake.

Madame Pepita, the only three-act play in the first volume, is also built up of the flimsiest materials. A fashionable dressmaker who is no better than she should be, an excessively innocent daughter, with a streak of real originality and character, and a world of crooked swindlers and decayed aristocrats. Into this group come two individuals of genuine distinction, the milliner's assistant Alberto, who is an artist of genius, and the fatherly academician Don

Guillermo, who befriends the girl, educates her, and finally marries her impossible mother in order to maintain a legal right to watch over her interests. With Don Guillermo's help the youth wins the Prix de Rome, the girl is saved from an adventurer, and the villains are driven away in disgrace. The curtain falls upon the incredible awakening of love in Don Guillermo's heart for Madame Pepita, his nominal wife. In brief, a thoroughly conventional piece of stage mechanism which, in its innumerable indigenous forms, is sure to run for at least a year, and has then long life before it "on the road."

In Mr. Granville Barker's selection the plays present very much the same characteristics. Here, too, is one play which has been presented to an English-speaking audience, *The Romantic Young Lady*, which was produced at the Royalty Theatre, London, in 1920. It tells of a young woman with vaguely feminist tendencies who revolts at the freedom enjoyed by her brothers and at their assumption that her destiny is either to find a husband or to be supported by them when they have got on in their careers and can afford to look after her. Why should she not do something for herself? Why should she not prove her individuality? She proceeds to do so by becoming involved in a romantic adventure with a man who climbs through the window. She thinks he is a burglar, but he is a gentleman in search of his hat, which was blown into the room through the open window, where the girl was sitting in the dark. Her hair gets entangled in his shirt-studs, as they stumble against each other in the dark. There is some mild love-making. The girl adores a certain popular novelist. The gentleman can get her a job as the novelist's secretary. In the next act she is applying for the secretaryship. Of course the strange man turns out to be the novelist. Circumstances conspire to destroy

her illusions and she runs off. In the third act the
tangle is straightened out and the novelist and the
romantic young lady live happy ever after.

The Wife to a Famous Man is a Spanish variation
upon the theme of What Every Woman Knows, with
the good-for-nothing husband who becomes a famous
aviator, tries to deceive his wife, who triumphs over
her fashionable rival, and then comes forward and
makes a speech about the trials of women, what a
handful men are, and so forth. Whereupon the curtain falls. In The Kingdom of God, which is probably
Martínez Sierra's best play, we are again in a convent,
but the heroine is a woman who has not taken vows.
She is seeking the kingdom of God, first in an asylum
for old men, then in a lying-in hospital for fallen
women, and in her old age as the head of an orphan
asylum. Here there is good character-drawing, if no
great depth or novelty of treatment.

The translators have successfully accomplished
an elaborate undertaking, which adds one more to
the roll of achievements in the field of foreign literature for which American publishers can claim credit.
The versions of Helen and Harley Granville Barker
are very much freer than those of John Garrett
Underhill, who has had the assistance of May Hey-
wood Broun in Madame Pepita. The English translators omit passages at their own discretion, apparently
because they had definite productions in mind and
prepared their manuscript for the theatre rather
than the book. Mr. Underhill, on the other hand,
has taken no liberties with the text, but his versions
read fluently and present no difficulties for the actor.
Most English-speaking readers of these plays will
be reminded of J. M. Barrie, and the comparison
very fairly represents the status of G. Martínez
Sierra in contemporary Spanish.

RAMÓN PÉREZ DE AYALA

DON RAMÓN PÉREZ DE AYALA is the most distinguished figure of the younger generation of Spanish writers, who followed that famous "generation of '98," Azorín, Unamuno, Baroja, Benavente, and the rest, whose work is the starting-point of every survey of modern Spanish literature. Since 1903, when his first book appeared, shortly after he had come of age, Ayala has published eleven volumes of fiction, three of verse, a book of impressions of the war on the Italian front, and three collections of political and literary essays. This total is sufficient to indicate that the author is not guilty of the besetting sin of overproduction; he has not aimed at seeing his name each season among the publishers' announcements, and it is this obvious care for his art as a man of letters, this conscientious craftsmanship, which have earned for him the high standing and esteem which he enjoys wherever Spanish letters are truly appreciated and understood. In 1920 he was introduced to this country through one of his most charming works, the three "poetic novels"—perhaps an unfortunate subtitle—translated as *Prometheus: The Fall of the House of Limon: Sunday Sunlight*; and an excellent novel, entitled *The Fox's Paw*, followed in 1924.

Although three small volumes contain all his verse, it is as a poet that students of Spanish literature will find him discussed in the studies which have been written upon him in his own country. His first book was a collection of poems, *La paz del Sendero*, which had its continuation thirteen years later in *El Sendero Innumerable*, and its sequel, *El Sendero*

Andante, in 1921. The similarity of these titles must
not be taken to imply any definite identity of theme,
but rather a common mood implied by the repetition
of the word "path," and its connotations of the progress of the soul through experience. The influence of
Francis Jammes, the French poet of rustic life, was
noticeable in that first volume of Ayala, but there
ran through his verses something more profound
than the ingenuous charm of Jammes. He had all
the latter's sensitiveness to natural beauty, his delight in the simple, eternal elements of country life,
but with an added vein of philosophic seriousness,
which became more marked in the later poems.
Here, with a rich and graceful vocabulary, a subtle
skill in the evocation of a landscape, is combined a
deep quality of intellectual emotion. A quotation
from Poe, which precedes *La paz del Sendero*, well
describes the intention of all Ayala's poetry: "The
struggle to apprehend the supernal loveliness." In
the course of that struggle he has given us some
of the loveliest poems in contemporary literature,
poems which, for all the difference of race and language, will inevitably remind the English reader of
Shelley. These lines from *El Sendero Andante*
typically illustrate the quality of his verse:

> "He salido a la ventura
> por el campo. Es primavera.
> Van mis pies a la ventura.
> Mis pupilas se apacientan
> de hermosura, a la ventura.
> Mi alma vuela
> a la ventura, indecisa.
> La brisa
> me sigue como un ferro y juguetea
> a la ventura. La dura
> piedra del corazón—muela
> que muele pan de esperanza
> con simiente de experiencia—,

la dura piedra se ha vuelto loca.
A la ventura, gira y voltea.
Se ha enternecido, volatilizado,
como nube, que del pecho sombrio sale fuera,
y por el cielo, a la ventura,
va resbalando, efímera . . . y eterna."

During the long interval which elapsed between the publication of his first and second book of poems Ayala gave his measure as a prose-writer in four volumes, which may be regarded as all part of a disguised autobiography: *Tinieblas en las Cumbres, A. M. D. G., La Pata de la Raposa,* and *Troteras y Danzaderas.* The first is a curious and chaotic study of what Shaw described as *Mrs. Warren's Profession,* and surpasses in irony and observation, though not in artistic excellence, Maupassant's famous variation upon the same theme in *La Maison Tellier. A. M. D. G.,* as those sardonic initials suggest, is a formidable indictment of education and school life in a Jesuit college, and quite impossible to reconcile with Anglo-Saxon standards of literary decorum. The same is true of *Troteras y Danzaderas,* although it is an amazingly interesting work belonging to an ancient and honorable tradition in the literature of Spain. This interest in strange types, in outlaws and rebels against the social order, is one of the fundamental characteristics of Spanish literature, which has endowed the world with the picaresque romance of roguery and adventure. In a form less startling to our own conventions, Pío Baroja has followed the impulse to explore the underworld, and his trilogy, *The Quest, Weeds,* and *Red Dawn,* belongs as surely as those early works of Ayala to the picaresque tradition. *La Pata de la Raposa* is rather different, being an interesting study of a type of psychological paralysis, the destruction of the will by the imagination.

The selection of the volume containing *Prometheus:*

The Fall of the House of Limon: Sunday Sunlight to bring Pérez de Ayala into English was well advised, for this is the first prose work in which he reveals the plenitude of his power as a novelist. His touch is surer, his craftsmanship vastly superior, and his style has the authentic ring of great prose. There is a suave irony in this semi-mythological narrative of modern Spain which is comparable to that of Anatole France, and which makes *Prometheus* one of the finest pieces of prose-writing in modern Spanish literature. The two remaining stories are excellent studies of provincial manners, with special reference to the political system which has created the sinister figure of the "cacique," who is to rural Spain what the "boss" is to American cities. The book deserves more attention than it has yet received in English. It has shared the neglect which seems to be the fate of so much that Spain has given us of real distinction in recent years.

Ayala's next novel appeared in 1921, *Belarmino y Apolonio*, a mature work of great originality, but one that defies translation, unless some translator of creative genius be persuaded to undertake it. It is hardly a novel in the proper sense of the word, but a fantasia upon the theme of the final poem, "Philosophy," in *El Sendero Andante*. Belarmino and Apolonio are two cobblers who incarnate in their grotesque persons two opposite human types. Belarmino is the philosopher in search of a word that will sum up all knowledge. Apolonio is a poet and a dramatist, whose dream is of glory and heroic action. The one represents the desire for knowledge, the other for expression. At the same time they are not mere abstractions, but fascinating human types, diverting eccentrics. The romantic element is supplied by the love of Apolonio's son for the adopted daughter of Belarmino. The pair are the rivals of Flaubert's

Bouvard and Pécuchet. Belarmino sees the universe in terms of the dictionary, his rival visualizes life in terms of the theatre. Ayala kindly supplies some pages from Belarmino's peculiar dictionary, for by a strange association of ideas words take on a meaning peculiar to himself and give a special savor to his numerous dissertations. For example, "to kiss" means "to envy, from the kiss of Judas"; "illiterate" means "impartial, without intellectual prejudices."

Although the novel which Ayala published in 1923 appears in two volumes under separate titles, *Luna de Miel, Luna de Hiel*, and *Los Trabajos de Urbano y Simona*, it is one story in two parts. He has taken a classical theme, a theme which served Longus for the pastoral poem of *Daphnis and Chloe*, and Molière for the comedy of *L'Ecole des Femmes*. Urbano is a youth as completely dominated by his mother and sheltered from the world in a monstrous "innocence" as ever Agnes was by Molière's Arnolphe. He is married by her to Simona, whose ignorance of the facts of life and nature is as perfect as his own. The brief honeymoon shows the young man that he is not prepared for his new estate. He runs away, is persuaded to return to Simona, and the young couple are on the point of learning to love each other when the mother again thwarts nature by separating them because a double bankruptcy has deprived them of the means upon which the marriage was based.

The second volume resumes the story at this point and develops the author's philosophy of nature versus convention. The "labors of Urbano and Simona" are directed toward overcoming the handicaps imposed upon them by a perverted and artificial education, and in the end they are brought together by natural instinct far more effectively than by the means employed by the formidable Doña Micaela, whose end is a terrible retribution for her denial of

the instincts and impulses of life. The secondary
figures in this curious tragicomedy are all types of
repression, of stunted psychological development:
Don Pablo, the complete specimen of Doña Micaela's
ideal, a mature man with a boy's mind; Don Castulo,
who is saved from an identical fate only by the
healthy normality of Conchona, the country servant,
who diverts Don Castulo's literary romanticizations
of love and life into the channel of marriage.

The entire narrative is informed by a great skill
of writing, an easy style, with just the right note
of irony, and a pleasant vein of genuine comedy
with a dash of what is usually called Gallic salt. The
scene in which the learned theologian, Don Hermo-
genes Palomo, is consulted on the question of divorce
is as amusing as Molière's treatment of the same
problem, though stated in different terms, when
Arnolphe tries to find out if Agnes has really out-
witted him. Ramón Pérez de Ayala has given once
more a work of classical distinction. His critical
writings, especially the two volumes of *Las Máscaras*,
are of interest to us, not only because of his discussion of such writers as Bernard Shaw and Oscar
Wilde, but also because they embody the views of
the school of younger Spanish writers who revolted
against the domination of Benavente in the theatre,
as I have shown in discussing the Spanish dramatist.

Discussing Oscar Wilde, the author enunciates an
ingenious theory which may be recommended to
those who do battle with Comstockery. There are,
he says, three categories of art: popular art for every-
body and subject to moral laws; artistic art, which
consists in a kind of skill only to be appreciated by
those who possess it themselves to some extent—
that is, by artists and dilettanti—art which, if it is
independent of morality, is not on that account
opposed to it; and exquisite or æsthetic art, still

more difficult to appreciate than artistic art—art
for a few superior individuals and not only indifferent
to morality but hostile to it.

Popular art does not express life as a whole, but
takes only what is pleasant, ethical, and agreeable
to general conventions. Artistic art professes to re-
flect all life, material and spiritual, but without selection on ethical grounds. Its main preoccupation
is the technical problem of exact and effective reproduction. Æsthetic art has no concern with life or
ethics, but with the creation of beauty, and when
that end is achieved no other question can arise.
Ramón Pérez de Ayala's choice is for "artistic art,"
since neither the moral excellence of inartistic workmanship nor the artistic perfection of vice can prove
the existence of a genuine work of art.

In the process of issuing a definitive collected edition of Pérez de Ayala's works, the Spanish publishers
have included a volume entitled *Bajo el Signo de
Artemisia*, where, "under the sign of Artemis," goddess of youth, the author shows us specimens of his
earliest work. The first tale is a *conte drôlatique*
called *El otro Padre Francisco*, which was written
when he was twenty-two, two years before his first
book, *La paz del Sendero*, appeared. It is a protest
against asceticism, with Rabelais as its central figure.
Cruzado de Amor is a romantic story of the trouba-
dours. *Artemisia* is a dramatic modern story absolutely in the manner of Maupassant. The value of
these juvenilia lies chiefly in their promise and in the
opportunity they at last afford us of studying the development of an author who actually published no
prose work over his own name until he was thirty,
when he established his fame with *A. M. D. G.* Prior
to that *Tinieblas en las Cumbres* had appeared, but it
was signed "Plotino Cuevas" and purported to be a
"posthumous novel" by that mythical personage,
which a reverend Jesuit had received from him on

his death-bed, as a preface explains. The book remained out of print for many years, but it is now part of the definitive Spanish edition, duly credited to Pérez de Ayala.

There is, however, one story in *Bajo el Signo de Artemisia* which has more maturity than the others, *Padre e Hijo*, a tragicomedy which contains a hint of the idea which is now developed in Ayala's most recent work, *El Ombligo del Mundo* (1924), a loosely connected cycle of five novelettes, dealing with the affairs of the inhabitants of the valley of Congosto. This obscure and scattered rural community is "the umbilicus of the world," as the author with irony implies, for here he allows us to observe on a small scale the natural imbecility, pettiness, and swinishness which make up the life of man. These ants scurry about in their ant-hill when Ayala pokes his stick in here and there, showing us the miracle of human nature. The stories themselves hardly bear summarizing; they are simply a series of incidents which enable the obscure protagonists to feel their own importance, and which involve them in all the usual pastimes of the great world: swindling, grafting, and profiteering; in quarrelling, in love, in marriage, in ruin. The charm of the book is its sardonic humor, its harsh irony, worthy of Flaubert's *Bouvard et Pécuchet*, in which effects are secured not by any emphasis or exaggeration, but by the continuous, meticulous notation of the actions, conversations, and reflections of these absurd bipeds who wear clothes. Far removed as the authors are in style, philosophy, and temperament, Pérez de Ayala presents in this book certain analogies with Ring Lardner's method in *Some Like Them Cold* and *The Golden Honeymoon*—the satire of absolutely faithful realism. The passion of *A. M. D. G.* and the wild, bawdy gusto of *Troteras y Danzaderas* has made way for this restrained, mellow, ironical detachment.

CONCHA ESPINA

THE Spanish attitude of gallantry toward Doña Concha Espina, the distinguished successor of Emilia Pardo Bazán as the foremost woman novelist of Spain, expresses itself more emotionally than is usual —at least in public—in this stern Puritan civilization of ours, where charming authoresses are concerned. One critic, writing of her most recent novel, *El Cáliz Rojo*, declares that she "is a beautiful woman, of a soft, dark, dramatic loveliness, which is very like that of Soledad Fontenebro, the unusual heroine of *El Cáliz Rojo*. What a mysterious, dark flame burns in the eyes of this distinguished writer, who combines intellectual brilliance with a marvellously graceful body! . . . Her eyes have the profound fascination of the Cantabrian sea. . . . Mountain and sea have moulded this extraordinary, feminine soul. . . . She is a master of style, this woman with her unique eyes and face full of tenderness, as though her spirit shone through the beauty of her golden amber skin."

This appreciation is not confined to words, for Concha Espina has been awarded no less than three prizes by the Royal Spanish Academy, first for her novel *La Esfinge Maragata*, in 1914; then, in 1919, for her only play, *El Jayón*; and last year for *Tierras del Aquilón*, a volume of sketches and impressions from Germany, which met the conditions of prize created by Baron Catillo de Chirel for "articles dealing in a literary manner with the situation in any of the countries of Central Europe since the war." Nor is this appreciation confined to prizes, for in August, 1924, her native town of Santander handed her a solemn parchment conferring upon her the title of "Favorite Daughter," and the Queen of Spain decorated her with the order of Maria Luisa. At the same time the first stone was laid of the Concha Espina Fountain, situated in what is to be known as Concha Espina Park. Beneath this stone is a brass box containing all the works of the author, and two envelopes. In one of these is Concha Espina's autograph; on the other is an inscription saying that "on no pretext whatever" shall it be opened "until a century has elapsed." Doña Concha is evidently a woman who believes that some people, at least, can keep a secret.

Just at the time when these impressive ceremonies were taking place, her first two books in English appeared, *La Esfinge Maragata*, under the title of *Mariflor*, and *Dulce Nombre*, under the title of *The Red Beacon*, both translated by Frances Douglas, to whose initiative American readers owe the first attempt to make Blasco Ibáñez known in this country, at a time when, as usual, it did not pay to pioneer in foreign literature. Their reception—also as usual —did not indicate that Concha Espina was about to displace the author of *The Four Horsemen of the Apocalypse* in the affections of the plain people, but the reviewers showed a quality of appreciation which should be reassuring to those whom a justifiable scepticism might incline to regard with suspicion an author so beloved of academic committees and City Councils. Concha Espina's fame depends neither upon her golden amber skin nor her capacity for evoking the enthusiasm of academicians and politicians. One has only to turn to the substantial body of her work—fifteen volumes between 1909 and 1924—in order to realize that these acts of official homage are the reflection of the well-earned esteem in which Spanish criticism holds her, and of a slowly growing success that is confirmed by the appearance of her works in French, German, Italian, Czech, and Rumanian, as well as in English.

Her achievement may be best measured in eight novels, which contain all the qualities found in her minor works, the sketches and prose poems of *Pastorelas*, *Simientes*, *Cuentos*, and *Tierras del Aquilón*, or even in her more ambitious volume of short stories, *Ruecas de Marfil*. The three-act play *El Jayón* is an elaboration of one of the stories in that volume, and does not throw any new light upon the character of her fiction, although it does show that Concha Espina, who is essentially a novelist, can produce a workmanlike drama. Like so many of her contemporaries, she has contributed her mite to the literature of Don Quixote. Her place as a Cervantista is not with the learned exegetists, like Menéndez y Pelayo and Menéndez Pidal, but with the Azorín of *La Ruta de Don Quijote*, with the Ortega y Gasset of the *Meditaciones del Quijote*, or, better still, with *La Vida de Don Quijote y Sancho* of Unamuno. Her book *Al Amor de las Estrellas* is a gallery of the feminine figures in *Don Quijote*, in which the women of Cervantes live and move again in the imagination of a Spanish woman of to-day. As Concha Espina recreates and interprets them they seem to be the ancestors of her own characters, for, above everything else, she is the interpreter of Spanish womanhood.

The novels are proof of this. In chronological order they are: *La Niña Luzmela*, *Despertar para Morir*, *Agua de Nieve*, *La Esfinge Maragata*, *La Rosa de los Vientos*, *El Metal de los Muertos*, *Dulce Nombre*, and *El Cáliz Rojo*; and, with the exception of *El Metal de los Muertos* and *El Cáliz Rojo*, they have but one theme, the pursuit of happiness through love, and its frustration, with marriage as a substitute—usually a mediocre substitute—for the dream of happiness. Only in the first of these novels does the author allow her autobiographical heroine Carmen to realize her dream by marrying Salvador, who is the Prince Charming of a perfect Cinderella story. Owing to her practice of carrying on the characters and their descendants from one novel to another, this unusual concession on the part of Concha Espina has had an unusual sequel. In *Dulce Nombre*, twelve years later, the morbid temperament of Nicolas de Hornedo is traceable to the fact that Salvador and Carmen had the same father, although originally the incest was excluded by Salvador's learning that, contrary to rumor and his own belief, Hornedo was not his father. Whether the author had forgotten in the interval that Salvador was supposed to be loved as though he were a son, but was not supposed to be Carmen's brother, when she reverted to that story for her later novel, it is impossible to say. She establishes a close parallel between the conduct of the Hornedo in *Dulce Nombre* and that of his forebear in *La Niña Luzmela*, and he clearly takes a sort of pride in his incestuous ancestry—all of which is a curious commentary upon the one romantic marriage in Concha Espina's novels!

As a rule, Concha Espina's heroines are thwarted of love in marriage. In *Despertar para Morir* she studies the two fundamentally opposed feminine types, María, who embodies the virtues of her sacred prototype, and Eva, who is the Eternal Feminine of the Garden of Eden. These ladies have each the husband whom the other should have: Eva is married to the dreamy poet Diego, and María to Gracián, a materialist who is fond of women, especially those least like María. Naturally, the inevitable interchange of interests and desires takes place; the practical Eva decides to grant her favors to Gracián, but awakens from her folly in order to die by suicide. María, on the other hand, returns Diego's love, tells him so, but suggests that he had better leave the country, so that they may both avoid temptation. Diego departs, María is henceforth his muse and inspiration, and she goes back to her husband. But she effects a reversal of Nora's famous door-slamming operation by slamming her bedroom door in Gracián's face. After her fashion she, too, has awakened, as the title suggests, only to die.

In *Agua de Nieve* Concha Espina introduces us to Regina de Alcántara, a type of Spanish emancipated woman, whose most interesting incarnation is to be found in Soledad Fontenebro, the heroine of *La Rosa de los Vientos* and of *El Cáliz Rojo*, whom, as I have noted, some Spanish critics regard as a definite piece of self-portraiture. The dark-eyed and red-haired Regina is quite familiar with Hobbes, Schopenhauer, and Nietzsche, while still in her teens, and one reverend commentator has traced to this pernicious taste her rejection of Carlos Ramírez, the man she really loves, in favor of Adolfo Velasco, a landed gentleman of importance, whom she takes away from the sister of Carlos, with truly Nietzschean deviltry. Whereupon she discovers that love is not, after all, "the contact of two epidermises," that one cannot be a free and independent female by that method, but that surrender is the basis of the emotion she sought. Fortunately, she further discovers that she is about to have a child, bursts into tears, and the symbol of the title is explained by this melting of the snows of her being, the cool stream of redemption.

Although Mariflor also renounces the man she loves, *La Esfinge Maragata* is something more than another variation upon Concha Espina's favorite theme. It is a powerful and fascinating study of one of the most remote and primitive communities in Spain, the Maragatan region, bordered by Galicia,

Asturias, and the Cantabrian Mountains. The men-
folk almost all migrate from their own countryside
during the winter months, which they spend in
Southern Spain, returning in spring to their homes,
when the warm winds and the melting snows sym-
bolize what has been rather quaintly termed the end
of "the nuptial armistice." But as one of Concha
Espina's characters indicates, there is a poor welcome
for the man who comes back to his *Weiberdorf*—to
quote Clara Viebig's title for her novel of similar
theme—with empty hands. The harsh poverty of the
Maragatan country imposes the migration, as it
imposes the demand for the hire rather than the
laborer, when he returns. Its vivid evocation of manners and customs, of folk-lore and folk-speech, and
its meticulous notation of elemental human types
and passions make *Mariflor*—to give the book its
English title—the most complete and original of the
author's novels, for these elements serve only as more
real and striking background against which to set
her woman's tragedy.

Concha Espina herself declares her preference for
her first novel and for *La Rosa de los Vientos* over all
the others, and it is impossible to escape the feeling
that in these this most subjective of writers has put
most of herself. In the later of the two novels one
encounters Soledad Fontenebro, who incarnates to a
supreme degree all the characteristics of Carmen,
Mariflor, and Regina. Here, however, she is more
conscious of her dilemma and more articulate. Soledad, like Regina, displays an interest in literature
which pious Spanish critics have dismissed as incredible in any nice young woman and unworthy of
the glorious traditions of Spain—the more so, as the
doctor and the priest who try to advise her in her
reading are mocked for their ignorance. She also
has sarcastic comments to make upon fashionable re-

ligion in Madrid, and her conclusions, in an equally fashionable hotel, as to the success of ladies who know how to uncover their bodies and to reveal their appreciation of carnal delight, likewise indicate an unbecoming perspicacity. But Spanish mothers doubtless reflected that Soledad is an orphan, on her father's side, whose mother neglects her after her second marriage.

Her mother also neglects her husband, with the result that the stepfather concentrates his affections upon Soledad, who feels for him, but cannot overcome a repugnance to his fatherly caresses. There is a curious uncertainty about the relations of these two which, in accordance with the best psychoanalytical procedure, would point to a repression of a love that is more than filial. Add to this Soledad's affection for her foster-brother, a humble sailor boy, which is as undefined as her repulsion from her stepfather. It is not until he has killed himself that something warmer than sisterly love awakens in her, and then— to the joy, I fancy, of all Freudians—Soledad flies to the arms of her stepfather; his eyes stir "the depths of my heart," and "for a long time, gazing into each other's eyes, we allowed our souls to quench their insatiable thirst." Finally an amiable and vague youth comes along to enact the part of her *fiancé*. The Spanish critic Cansinos-Assens, having interpreted Concha Espina as a "Northerly" writer and, therefore, unaddicted to the expansiveness of the Southern temperament, charitably concedes that the ambiguities of Soledad's relationship need not be probed too far, for in Northern countries "certain gestures which would seem lascivious in the South" are practised with impunity, "such as the English King instituting the Order of the Garter"! In Spain, evidently, they can still reckon without our Freudian hosts.

Whatever may be said of this naïveté, which is typical of many of the same kind in the essay of Cansinos-Assens on *Northern Literature*, his view of Concha Espina's work does explain the attraction exercised upon the Southern European mind by the reticences, the reserve, and the stoicism of a novelist whose world is the mountain region of Northern Spain, the hinterland of Santander. Her disconsolate philosophy which identifies love with pain and suffering seems to require that cold, harsh background in order to become intelligible to the easy-going children of the sun. For English-speaking readers there is perhaps more appeal in the two novels of Concha Espina which deal with social rather than with the peculiar personal problems of her other works. Of these, the most noteworthy is *El Metal de los Muertos*, a unique work in the canon of her writings and, I think, the best book which she has written. Like Zola's *Germinal* it is a novel of mining life—in the Ríotinto, and is linked up with the mountain stories in the person of Charol, whom Soledad was training to be a sailor in *La Rosa de los Vientos*. Charol, having abandoned the sea, and plied many trades, is now a mine-worker, known as Gabriel Suárez, who is the leader of the revolt of the miners against the conditions imposed by foreign capital. The author preaches no thesis, nor does she dwell upon such atrocities as Zola recalled, but her picture of the mining community, of the strike, and of the issue between capital and labor is more finely executed than anything which Blasco Ibáñez has done in the same field. Both in its superb realism and in its impressive symbolism this epic of "the metal of death," which is also the metal of modern industrial life, stands amongst the great novels of contemporary European literature.

El Cáliz Rojo also faces a social problem, that of

the Jew in his relation to country. The book is the product of a visit to Germany, of which Concha Espina's impressions are gathered in *Tierras del Aquilón*. In the novel we learn, without much astonishment, that Soledad Fontenebro's marriage was not a success, and she is travelling abroad in search of forgetfulness. Meeting a Jew from Salonica, she is drawn to this "Spaniard without a country," the descendant of Spanish exiles, and while the racial question is analyzed, the inevitable situation develops, in which the hopeless love of Ismael Dávalos is renounced by Soledad, in obedience to the precedents set by the author in all cases. This "symphony of grief," as it has been called, harmonizes with the poignant setting of Germany in dissolution, but still the Germany of the Romanticists, with all that the land of Werther and Obermann connotates to the Latin mind, for, after all, is not Concha Espina essentially a Romantic novelist of the school of Madame de Staël and George Sand? One social novel does not make a Realist.

RAMÓN GÓMEZ DE LA SERNA

THOSE who have been following the fortunes of Spanish literature outside Spain will have noticed here and there in the more esoteric reviews the name of Ramón Gómez de la Serna. A few years ago, when I first observed these references, with an occasional translation of some trifle by the author, I became convinced that in due course there would be a little "boom" in Don Ramón, as soon as London and New York had taken their cue from Paris. Ramón Gómez de la Serna is obviously destined to become a coterie idol, the centre of one of those cults which are the æsthetic mice produced by the labors of the mountain alleged to be pregnant with a new art. In due course, his works have reached London and New York via Paris. *Broom*, I think, can claim the credit of having first printed him in English, and when T. S. Eliot's *Criterion* appeared for the second time it was adorned by the name of Gómez de la Serna. Since then Valery Larbaud has published a volume of selections from his more typical writings, under the title of *Echantillons*, his novel, *La Viuda blanca y negra*, has been translated under Larbaud's ægis, *Senos* has appeared in French, and the French reviews generally have become aware of his existence, helped in the process, no doubt, by the fact that he has been the subject of a lecture by Valery Larbaud at the Vieux Colombier, and the recipient of a banquet given in his honor by the Cercle Littéraire International, which is affiliated with the P. E. N. Club.

It is no reflection upon the undoubted talents of Gómez de la Serna to call him a coterie author, for

in all such cases it is the coterie, the hierophants of
the cult who are absurd, not the often innocent object of their devotions.   Charlie Chaplin is not dead
because the heavy tombstone of *The Seven Lively
Arts* has been prematurely laid upon his reputation
by Mr. Seldes.   Guillaume Apollinaire, for instance,
was one of the most diverting people in Paris, and
an almost complete set of his vastly entertaining
and ingenious writings has accumulated on my
shelves ever since I read *L'Hérésiarque et Cie.*, nearly
sixteen years ago.   But when the æsthetes assert
with fanatical emphasis that Racine was a poetaster,
whereas Guillaume Apollinaire was *a very great poet*
—the *italics* representing a solemn rolling of the
eyes to heaven and a tone of awestruck reverence—
all one can do is to wish that Apollinaire were present
to share one's laughter.   It is just such a humorless
cult that may descend upon Gómez de la Serna,
especially as Spain is becoming increasingly the
prey of æsthetes in search of new idols.

He possesses two qualities which are usually found
in the coterie author, a whimsical, eccentric personality and extreme accessibility.   He is as easily identified and as obvious a sight for the tourist in Madrid
as the Prado and the Puerta del Sol, for he sits in
session at the Pombo Café, about which he has written
two comprehensive tomes, the second of which, *La
Sagrada Cripta de Pombo*, has recently been issued,
and contains a vast amount of information concerning the author and the many hundreds of literati
who have frequented the establishment. *The Sacred
Pombo Crypt* is a species of autobiography, with a
large section devoted to a general disquisition on
literary cafés in general, and on those patronized by
this incorrigible café-goer in particular.   There has
always been a certain mystery about Gómez de la
Serna's life, and here some facts are available which

have hitherto been unknown. The date of his birth, for example, has been sought in vain by all previous commentators and historians, not excluding the voracious and voluminous Cejador. He was born in 1891, and has more than sixty published works to his credit, which indicates, at least, that his devotion to cafés has not led him into slothful ways. It is true, many of these are mere pamphlets, but at least eighteen of them are books, and they represent a career which began at the precocious age of fifteen or sixteen, for his first book is dated 1904. His earliest work of importance, however, was published in 1915, *El Rastro*, followed by *Pombo*, *Senos*, *El Circo*, and *Greguerías*, in 1917. Then came *Muestrario*, *El Libro Nuevo*, *Variaciones*, *El Prado*, two volumes of plays, *Toda la Historia de la Puerta del Sol*, and several full-length novels, of which the most notable are *El Doctor Inverosímil* and *El Novelista*.

Perhaps the easiest way to suggest something of manner and mood of Ramón Gómez de la Serna is to say that his favorite form is that of the brief whimsical sketch, or aphorism, in the style, roughly speaking, of Logan Pearsall Smith's *Trivia*. It is these brief notations from life, these humorous meditations and little stories, which have made their author famous. Characteristic works of this kind are *El Rastro*, *Senos*, and *Muestrario*, from which the French edition has been selected. *Variaciones* belongs to the same order. Typical of all these books is the title *Greguerías*, which is hard to translate, but might be rendered by *Shouts and Murmurs*, for it means a confused noise, a hubbub, the chatter of birds. Under many variants of this idea the author contributes indefatigably these sketches to newspapers and magazines, illustrating them, in many cases, with his freakish drawings. The shouts and murmurs

which he hears are the confused cries of the subconscious, which suggest curious observations, un-
expected parallels, and incongruous metaphors. This
may sound rather more alarming than the facts
warrant, but as I have said, Don Ramón is the ideal
author for clique enthusiasm, and his impression of
his work is couched in appropriately profound terms.
Let me cite some characteristic specimens from his
Greguerías and *Muestrario:*

"The mooing of a cow is a labored imitation of a lion's roar,
to frighten children."

"Weathercocks are the birds' merry-go-rounds. The birds
know this, and take a special pleasure in perching upon them."

"*Lies:* 'My humble person'; 'It is forbidden to speak to the
driver'; 'Purveyors to H. M. the King'; 'Literal translation';
'Free list suspended'; 'An independent newspaper'; 'Irrev-
ocable resignation'; 'List of authors consulted'; 'This work
bears a certain resemblance to that of Maeterlinck'; 'We are
sure that the Government will not allow this work of art to leave
the country.'"

"The most terrible noise in the world is that made by a tall
silk hat when it falls."

"The streets are longer at night than in the daytime."

"The compass is an incredible creature, guided by God Himself. Its great, lucid mind has always amazed me. It is like
a miraculous relic, a holy relic enclosed in a glass case. One
must not trifle with a compass, or maltreat it. To do so would
be to maltreat a starfish of extraordinary sensitiveness. The
compass is full of sorcery. If it were handled differently, if it
were given letters of wider scope than N. S. E. W., it would have
many things to tell."

These shorter pieces illustrate the whimsical character of Gómez de la Serna's writings. The longer
sketches do not lend themselves to quotation, and
it is, therefore, not possible to given an adequate
idea of his more poetical moods, nor of the vein of
sensual poetry in the series *Senos*, nor the macaber
humor of such a book as *El Doctor Inverosímil*, with
its hideous pictures of disease and malformation.

As in all writers whose manner is more important than the matter, the interest in Don Ramón hardly survives the delicate task of translation, but, if I may judge by precedents, that is precisely why he tempts and will tempt the coteries, for the latter have a suspicious predilection for poetry in foreign tongues, as if that were not the final and most subtle test of one's sense of language. We shall certainly hear more of Ramón Gómez de la Serna from those who have had nothing to say about any of the older generation, nor even of his contemporary, Pérez de Ayala, whose work is vastly more substantial and universally interesting. But then the latter is not the leader of a school, known as the "Ultraists," who, like their equivalents nearer home, go through the solemn business of "discovering" Rimbaud, Laforgue, and Lautréamont—in brief, who live upon a belated enthusiasm for the obscurer novelties announced by Remy de Gourmont in his *Livre des Masques* nearly thirty years ago.

In his history of the Pombo there are innumerable reproductions of sacred and peculiar relics of Gómez de la Serna's personal life which are unique. One may contemplate a corner in his apartment in which stands a street lamp with his name where the street name should be. This valuable piece of interior decoration was acquired after prolonged and difficult negotiations with the Madrid equivalent of the Consolidated Gas Company, this body being somewhat alarmed at launching a street lamp on so unusual a career. Illuminated by this lamp is a scene in which the author may be discovered reading to a beautiful lady seated beside him on a sofa. She is fingering her necklace and gazing at Ramón with an air of concentrated rapture. In an earlier picture she is clad in those few garments which made the success of the strip-poker scene in *The Demi-Virgin* of hal-

lowed memory. When his friends call and find him
in polite seclusion with this fair creature they naturally tiptoe out and apologize for the intrusion. But
their discretion is as superfluous as the alarm of the
moral reader of this book, for the lady is a wax man-
ikin—the woman, as he says, of all men's dreams,
an unfading and ever-admiring beauty. Dolls of
all sorts fill his rooms, and he even has a full-size
skeleton to remind him of the eternal transience of
all things; likewise, and to the same end, a picture
on a corrugated surface, showing a young woman
when looked at from one direction and an old one
when looked at from another. He has a charming
cat's head which, by the pulling of a string, assumes
an expression of: "Is it possible? Can I believe my
eyes?" to quote its proud owner.

On his bookshelf there is a notice: "Do not touch!
Dangerous!" with a skull and cross-bones, which is
carefully reproduced here, together with a charming
collection of ornaments, such as a gibbet from which
is hanging the King of Bulgaria; a portrait of four
life-sized persons, purchased for five pesetas, as to
the merits of which Ramón's family is, he says,
equally divided; two sections of the ceiling showing
stars, comets, the sun, and a symbol of the Holy
Ghost; and one of those photographs in which the
sitter is seen in several positions simultaneously—
there are five Ramóns because it was used for publicity when five of his books appeared at the same
time. He is the owner of a monocle, which he strongly
recommends because it has no crystal and can be
changed without inconvenience from one eye to the
other and, as a diagram shows, may be hung comfortably on the forefinger; it never breaks and has
considerably influenced the author's view of life.

The editorial chambers of *The Smart Set*, under
Messrs. Mencken and Nathan, were adorned in a

manner somewhat comparable to that affected by
Ramón Gómez de la Serna, but the diversity and
elaborate absurdity of his tastes are a proof that he
is a more substantial morsel for the æsthetic novelty-
mongers, who will, if Apollinaire be a test, come along
some day and pronounce with the utmost solemnity
that Calderón and Galdós and Unamuno and Baroja
were just cheap hacks, but great, indeed, was the
genius of Ramón Gómez de la Serna. That he was a
great art critic will be established by the fact that he
discovered in Vasari that the armor on the statue
of Carlos V in the Prado Museum could be removed
and that a marvellous nude figure was concealed
underneath. In 1921 Spaniards had an opportunity
of beholding this unsuspected nude.

As to what the actual achievement of Gómez de
la Serna is, I submit, with becoming humility, that
he is simply a comedian. He actually does what
Logan Pearsall Smith has tried to do in those two
dreary volumes of *Trivia;* he plays effectively with
whimsical, sometimes poetic fancies. His capacity
for such work is extraordinary, and of course the
material is often very thin, for volumes multiply at
such speed that it is impossible to make a list of them
that will be complete.

His novels are of least importance, but it is not
excessive, I suppose, to claim that the sort of thing
quoted is as readable, if not more so, than Logan
Pearsall Smith's efforts to be funny when the bath
mat, turned upside down, confronts him cabalistically
as TAM HTAB, which I remember to have produced
an ecstacy in certain circles where this delicious
whimsicality is appreciated.

ITALY

GABRIELE D'ANNUNZIO

THERE are few more striking instances of the ephemeral popularity of foreign authors in English than that of Gabriele d'Annunzio, who, after all these years, still remains indubitably the greatest living master of Italian prose, and one of the enduring names in modern European literature. His great trilogy, *Il Piacere*, *L'Innocente*, and *Il Trionfo della Morte*, had their hour of fame in English twenty-five years ago. *Il Fuoco* and *Le Vergini delle Rocce* were also translated about the same time, but no major prose work of his has appeared in English since then, not even *Forse che si Forse che no*, which was published in 1910, nor *La Leda senza Cigno*, a pre-war novel, although not issued in book form until 1916, when it was adorned by an appendix relating to the war, which did not, of course, form part of the work as it ran serially in the *Corriere della Sera* during the summer of 1913. Whatever public there was for the first books in English might be presumed to have an equal interest in these later novels, but they were never put into English, although translated into French. The war and the consequent absorption of d'Annunzio in military and political adventures explain, to some extent, why his writings of the last decade have not awakened any response from foreign readers, but the facts show that he had fallen into disfavor long before 1914. Now that he has, at last, begun to write again out of his own life, and has ceased to find his inspiration in themes and events of Italian national and nationalistic importance, it is legitimate to hope that his audience may be extended until it includes once more those who once listened to the enchantments of his style and his imagination.

Under the general title of *Le Faville del Maglio* Gabriele d'Annunzio has begun to publish what promises to be another *Reveries over Childhood and Youth* and another *Memoirs of My Dead Life*. The first volume, entitled *Il Venturiere senza Ventura*, is offered to Aglaia, first of the Graces, and Thalia and Euphrosyne will be invoked for the second and third. The dedication is interesting: "To Eleonora Duse, last born of Saint Mark, melodious apparition of creative suffering and sovereign kindness." In a preface the author makes a challenging declaration of the scope and character of the work which he has undertaken, his first purely literary work since 1916, when *La Leda senza Cigno* concluded with a dissertation dictated by the poet after the loss of his right eye at the bombardment of Trieste. This dissertation on the war, coming as an appendix to a piece of fiction dating from 1913, was a symptom of the preoccupations which have ever since then diminished the pleasure of his foreign readers in the writings of d'Annunzio. His book on the Fiume epic, *Contro e Contro Tutti*, could have but little interest outside Italy, and although *Notturno* has many lovely pages of Italian prose in it, this document of his blindness is also too much involved in the events and passions to which he owed that mishap.

I have collected [he writes] in three very thick volumes the most beautiful, the most varied, and the most daring prose, boldly drawn from my book of memory. I know that I am breaking an ancient vow of mine, and I will not deny to Frate Jacopo that pride is the cause and principle of this transgression, as of all others. The false modesty of Petrarch is insufferable to me, when, having begun to write his colloquy entitled *The Secret* he apologized, as I perhaps might have once apologized, by saying: "Not that I wish this to be counted with my other works, or that I seek glory from it (better things stir my mind), but that the pleasure I once took in it may be renewed whenever I like to reread it." . . . I wanted to add to my *Laus Vitæ* a *Laus Mei* no less admirable in its rhythmic richness and power of evocation; . . . here I succeed in achieving a perfect correspondence between my will to expression and the subject I discuss, between thought and language. . . . My solitude preserves me from triumph. May it preserve me from triumph until my death! May it insure that until death my true soul be known only to dawn and storm, to garden and forest, to the lark and the eagle. The old world is dying out in a sort of putrid madness; coprophagous, it turns the prophetic cry into senile babbling. No less abject, its old art is being corrupted and extinguished, the dying paranymph of a Peace wedded to Opprobrium.

It will be seen from these quotations that the Prince of Monte Nevoso counts himself as one of the company of great poets who were also great heroes and patriots, whose egoism usually becomes the delight of posterity, but is often trying to their contemporary friends. D'Annunzio's Byronism reached its supreme consecration during the war, and a real sense of dramatic values underlies this well-advertised but none the less genuine withdrawal from the world. He may be sure that the sparks which now fly upward from his strokes upon the anvil will be greeted with something of that rapturous and long-drawn-out "a-h!" with which crowds invariably greet firework displays. His purely literary fame during the decade before the war had undergone a species of eclipse. Croce had devoted to him a celebrated article which set the tone for a generation of critics, who rang the changes upon Croce's epithet, "a dilettante of sensations," while the younger generation of Papini and his contemporaries professed the utmost scorn for the florid classicism of d'Annunzio's style. To English and French readers, who have never, I may remark in passing, read his most famous novels in other than bowdlerized translations, d'An-

nunzio was a sort of superman of the 1890's. His
Fiume adventures did nothing to endear him to the
English-speaking world, which had begun to forget
him as a writer. On the death of Eleonora Duse he
was again remembered unfavorably, and the most
dramatic stories of their relations were exhumed
indignantly, an operation to which the dedication
of *Le Faville del Maglio* makes a curious retort.

The tone of the preface to this book is a significant
indication of the position in which d'Annunzio now
finds himself in Italy. His war record was the final
confutation of his critics, who declared that he was
a dilettante, that his art was insincere, that he played
with the idea of war and glory as he had played with
love. Now he is greeted as a Renaissance figure,
the man in whom the spirit of the Rinascimento and
the Risorgimento meet; the great artist of the Cinque-
cento and the patriot of a united Italy, these are
the two phases into which Italian criticism now divides the work of Gabriele d'Annunzio. The period
of artistic isolation, of anarchy, closes with *Il Fuoco*
in the last year of the nineteenth century. Up to
that moment art is elevated to the level of a religion
and life itself is an art, for no other theme or aim
seems worthy. Then comes the period of the patriotic and historical writings, the *Odi Navali*, the
Canzone di Garibaldi, and *L'Armata d'Italia*, at a
time when no such glories illumine the Italian horizon,
when a socialistic and bourgeois materialism domi-
nates. Naturally Croce is moved to accuse d'Annunzio of idealizing war and slaughter; the ethics of
heroism have replaced the old æstheticism, but
d'Annunzio's compatriots know that this is just the
talk of an irresponsible literary man, that perpetual
peace is more or less certain, and that men of sense
have realized that life is simply an economic problem,
a simplification *à la* H. G. Wells.

Now Italy has seen the poems of d'Annunzio translated into action, and very largely, moreover, through the action of the poet himself. The "insincere" æsthete, the cruel tormentor of Duse, the dreadful Don Juan of the novels and early poems, lives on earth, on the sea, and in the sky, the raptures which inspired some of his most beautiful verse invoking those elements; the poet turns warrior, and a victorious warrior. He can now afford to retire to his mountain seclusion and send forth this magnificent chronicle of his life. The charm of these pages lies in the beauty of the prose, for d'Annunzio's style is a prolonged and exquisite enchantment, and the fragments from his life follow one another in a lovely rhythm, which tempts one to translate, and then defies one with the mockery of the result: a moment on the road to Vincigliata at eventide, the close of a burning day; the cicadas are singing in the dark cypresses; the bushes that line the road are silent, but in the underbrush the singing goes on, as if to prolong the sunset. Finally only one shrill insect is heard—its cry diminishes; there is silence. The poet waits anxiously. He is afraid that the cicada will begin again and that the shadows will burn once more. A vivid picture of the railway-station at Ancona, the flickering lights in the station, the nuns in the waiting-room; high up on the hillside the sound of guitars and mandolins; the tapping of the telegraph-machine; the melancholy lowing of cattle confined in a waiting goods train.

From these brief vignettes the author leads us back through his memories to longer chapters from his past, culminating in the lengthy piece entitled *The Second Lover of Lucrezia Buti*, which runs to two hundred pages and is packed with autobiographical details from d'Annunzio's childhood; his infatuation for Suor Lucrezia Buti, whom Fra Filippo Lippi loved; the prank he played when he decided he would serve mass in the Greek of St. John Chrysostomos; his delight in scandalizing his teachers by declaiming with great fervor Virgil's second Eclogue, and reading Xenophon of Ephesus—so very different from the more familiar perpetrator of the *Anabasis*—to his schoolmates. After the vulgarity of Papini's *Storia di Cristo* it is an agreeable surprise to find here the parables of the prodigal son, of Lazarus and the rich man, and of the wise and foolish virgins developed into stories with a peculiar d'Annunzioesque savor and beauty. One of the most perfect chapters deals with an American artist and may be recounted in more detail.

In 1896, d'Annunzio relates, he was in Venice, and a friend had given him a plaster cast of a torso which he tried to tone down in color by washing it in strong tea, hoping to give it the tone of "wild honey which the torso of Subiaco has acquired in the obscurity of centuries." In the midst of these labors his companion enters and asks if he knows Miss Macy. He confesses he never heard of the lady. Whereupon he is taken to see her, for she knows the secret of changing plaster into "old stone, old stucco, old wood, and old ivory, into everything out of which are made living objects of art which crack, crumble, and blacken." Miss Macy is

an American, sent by the barbarians from overseas to Venice to copy in miniature the important buildings. For six years she has been working to reproduce in plaster the Ducal Palace. With infinite patience she has modelled every arch, every column, every capital, every balustrade, every fresco, every little detail. Her work is like a huge instructive toy for a childish people.

She meets me at her threshold with a smile. Her smile is multiple, like a ray of sunlight on a ruffled stream. I experience at once and strongly the sensation of being in the presence of a living person, of that exceedingly rare phenomenon, a person who is really alive. She is dressed in a long blouse of a bluish tinge. She is blond, with her hair thrown back from her forehead and streaked here and there with gray. Her eyes are blue, splendid, pure, childish, and emotion passes through them continuously like running water. She has the rough, strong hands of a worker.

Having described the garret in which she lives, looking out on to the Giudecca Canal, d'Annunzio gives us a glimpse of her peculiar art:

She disappeared into a dark corner and returned with an object in her hands. She showed me a little ivory Byzantine triptych, of the Macedonian epoch, yellow and consumed with age, in a case of old green velvet.

"*Xè, gesso* [it is plaster]," she said with an indescribable Anglo-Italian-Venetian accent.

She goes off and returns many times, showing him on each occasion some object of art, looking like old enamel, like marble, like copper, and her laughing comment in each case is, "*Xè gesso*"—for all these things are plaster, colored according to her secret method. She shows d'Annunzio her workshop and the kitchen where she eats with her assistants, for she lives in simplicity and poverty. "Here poverty seemed to me to have the bareness of strength, the simplest and noblest statue of life."

"I also work," said I to her, when I saw her looking at my hands that were too white, my nails that were too glossy.

I told her of my discipline, of my nights of study, of my patient researches, of my power of staying fifteen or twenty hours bent over my table, of the amount of oil I used in my lamp, of the heaps of paper and pens, of my well-worn inkstand, of all the instruments of my trade. Then I showed her the palpable sign: my middle finger deformed by constant use of the pen, a smooth furrow, and a hard welt.

Suddenly she was moved. Her whole expression was one of maternal tenderness. She took my finger, looked at the mark, and then, all at once, with a graceful gesture which I shall never forget, she brushed it with her pure lips.

"God bless you!"
The running water flowed out between her eyelashes, shone,
trembled, ever fresh.
"God keep you forever!"

Such is the strange variety of the incidents in this
unique book, which promises to be one of the most
interesting of modern autobiographical works. Of
all the famous and notorious adventures of Gabriele
d'Annunzio with women none has prepared us for
such a story as this meeting with Miss Macy, so
typical both of her own race and the poet's imagination. *Sparks from the Hammer* is infinitely varied
and surprising and always surpassingly lovely in its
orchestration of a beautiful language. It is a book to
console d'Annunzio's admirers for the volumes of
politics which he has given us now for eight years.

GIOVANNI VERGA

WHEN Giovanni Verga died in 1922, aged eighty-two years, he was the most famous and least read novelist in Italy. Indeed, it is probable that he had more admirers and fewer readers than any famous writer of his time. His career was unique, for in the first ten years, from 1866 to 1876, he was a successful and popular author of novels in the manner of Octave Feuillet, which, to this day, far exceed in sales the later and important works on which his permanent fame must rest. Then he published the volume of short stories containing *Cavalleria Rusticana*, and had the sardonic pleasure of seeing that work become known all over the world as the more or less anonymous libretto of Mascagni's opera. The following year his masterpiece appeared, *I Malavoglia*, and seven years later, in 1888, came *Mastro-Don Gesualdo*. These were announced as the first two volumes of a pentalogy with the general title of *The Defeated*, but the third was never finished, and the fourth and fifth volumes, so far as is known, were never written. Verga's literary life may be said to have ceased thirty-four years before his death. During that time his youthful novels were in every bookstore and railway newsstand, but the two greatest works of fiction in Italian literature since Manzoni lay neglected, except for the praise of the critics, beginning with Croce, who recognized what their predecessors in the eighties had been too blind to see.

Verga's fame abroad has followed very much the same course. In spite of the efforts of Edouard Rod, who translated *I Malavoglia*, the book had no success in France. In America the novel appeared in

1890, under the title of *The House by the Medlar Tree*, with an introduction by Howells. This English version is far from satisfactory, but according to Verga it sold well enough to induce an English publisher to make an agreement for *Mastro-Don Gesualdo*, which duly appeared in London in 1893. This edition so completely lapsed into oblivion that thirty years later D. H. Lawrence came forward with a translation which was greeted as the first appearance of this book in English! Yet, in those mid-Victorian (metaphorically speaking) American eighteen-nineties, *I Malavoglia* was available in English nine years after its appearance in Italy. Some day, when we have recovered from our delight in our own progressiveness, some one will point out all that was done in that benighted era to bring the literature of Continental Europe within the reach of the American public. Meanwhile it is interesting to note the parallel between the fate of Verga's work in his own country and in this. One thing, however, must be said at the outset: this translation of *Mastro-Don Gesualdo* is far superior to that of Mr. Lawrence's predecessor. Verga is an exceedingly difficult author to "get" in another language. His use of Sicilian dialect is discreet and effective, but he adapted Italian to the rhythms of Sicilian, its turns of speech, very much in the way Synge gave English the flavor and tang of Irish. Nothing of this was in *The House by the Medlar Tree*, which was also prettified and bowdlerized, nor in the same translator's "Master Don Gesualdo"; there is a great deal of it in the new version of *Mastro-Don Gesualdo*, which is one of the best translations I have seen for some time. We have too many translations by translators and not enough by men of letters.

The second volume of *The Defeated*, like the first, is a vast picture of Sicilian life, but now it is not the

ruin of a peasant family, as in *I Malavoglia*, but
the disintegration of the middle class that Verga
has studied, destroyed, when it emerges as wealthy
peasantry, by contact with the ruined nobility.
Gesualdo Motta is a self-made man who has accumulated his fortune slowly and painfully, with all the
pertinacity of those who are close to the soil and who
struggle with the forces of nature. The time has
come for him to move definitely out of the sphere
which has been his for generations, so he marries the
daughter of a penniless family of nobles, who thus
acquire his wealth and get rid of the problem presented by a girl who has given herself to a man of her
own class but cannot marry him because she has no
dowry. The marriage, naturally, is a failure, and
the child that is born to this ill-matched couple does
not redeem it. Gesualdo concentrates upon Isabella
his frustrated hopes, but the more he gives her the
less she is his, for he provides the education, the
luxuries, the ease, which are the essence of her aristocratic being. She is her mother's child, not his. She
marries into her own class, moves off to the city, and
lives in ducal splendor remote from this rugged old
man. Her mother dies, and Gesualdo is left alone to
witness the crumbling away of his own fortune, and
the disruption of the whole social order which has
seemed as immutable and eternal as the land and
the succession of the seasons.

His own life is bound up with that of the period,
which is the middle of the nineteenth century, and
the political movements of the time, the revolutions
of 1820 and 1848, have their strange repercussions in
that remote Sicilian village where the scene is laid.
The peasants are in revolt against him; he is old
and sick and has no bond of affection with a living
soul except Diodata, once his servant and the mother
of his children, whom he had to dismiss in order to

make his way in the world. Like a wounded animal he bears his sufferings, suspecting those who would help him, filled with atavistic superstitions concerning the wiles of doctors and the peasant's distrust of medicines because of the money they cost. Finally he sets off for Palermo to live with his child. The magnificence of the palace overwhelms him; the extravagance and luxury break his heart, as he thinks of the good land that is being squandered; the insolence and number of the servants terrify him. He takes refuge in an isolated apartment in that great house, watches from his window the frittering away of all that his labors built up, reads in his daughter's eyes a misery comparable to his own, and knows that her marriage and life have been defeats as surely as his.

The final pages, in which the death of Mastro-Don Gesualdo is described, are among the most powerful in modern literature. Balzac never surpassed them in *Père Goriot*, and it is arguable that, on the whole, Gesualdo is a finer, a more complete, conception of the type than Balzac's. Verga succeeds in conveying the tragedy of this central character with marvellous poignancy, but, at the same time, he never loses sight of the vast social drama of which he is an infinitesimal part. Mastro-Don Gesualdo is the peasant in relation to property, and within these two limits Verga shows us the whole gamut of human experience. Verga was born in the same year as Daudet and Zola, his best work was contemporary with that of Maupassant, and with all three he has been compared by the historians of Naturalism. He is not dwarfed by the comparison, for his short stories hold their own even with *Boule de Suif*, and neither *L'Assommoir* nor *Le Nabab* equal their Italian counterparts, *I Malavoglia* and *Mastro-Don Gesualdo*.

LUIGI PIRANDELLO

WHAT Shavianism was to the English theatre in the high and far-off days of British repertory theatres and "the drama of ideas," Pirandellism now is to the Italian theatre, since Luigi Pirandello has become the most famous dramatist in Italy. His art is so peculiarly his own; it stands out in such sharp contrast against that of his contemporaries that Italian critics can now recognize a "Pirandellian" situation when they see one, just as Messrs. William Archer and A. B. Walkley gradually discovered that plays by Bernard Shaw were peopled by "Shavian" women, and dramatists endeavored to secure effects in the "Shavian" manner, when the bloom had worn off the novelties of Ibsen, and the "well-made" play had been abandoned by the intellectuals. The fact that Pirandello has supplied a noun and an adjective to the dramatic vocabulary of his country must be regarded, I suppose, as evidence of the seriousness of his success, for Pirandellian and Pirandellism are not terms of reproach, like Pineroesque or Robertsonian; their lineage is that of Ibsenite and Shavian. In fine, the implication is that the author of *Six Characters in Search of an Author* has introduced into the theatre something as new and as revolutionary as Shaw and Ibsen were in their day.

If great changes must be effected slowly, then Pirandello is great indeed. He has been writing since 1889, but it was not until 1921 that his *Six Characters* achieved the success which makes for international renown. Luigi Pirandello belongs, with Giovanni Verga and Luigi Capuana, to that group of Sicilian writers whose work is so considerable a part of contemporary Italian literature. He began by publishing several books of verse, in which it is impossible to discover even the germ of the author, who was subsequently to become famous as a humorist. He has translated Goethe's *Roman Elegies*, made a version in Sicilian dialect of *The Cyclops* of Euripides, and published several volumes of verse and criticism, including a learned German treatise on *Laute und Lautentwicklung der Mundart von Girgenti*, which is a dissertation upon the speech of his native Sicily. In 1894 he published his first collection of short stories, *Amori senz'amore*, and from that date until shortly before the war he was known exclusively as a story-teller. His novels *Il Turno*, *L'Esclusa*, and *Il fu Mattia Pascal*, to mention the more important, were not so successful, with the exception of *The Late Mattia Pascal*, which has been translated into French, German, and finally into English. Luigi Pirandello was definitely classed and accepted as a writer of short stories, a humorist like Panzini, but with a more cynical and sardonic touch. His humor consists in his capacity for seeing the amusing side of sad and mournful situations. There is little gaiety in the works of this humorist of disillusionment. When the author does indulge in pure fun, it descends, as a rule, to the level of the slap-stick and the custard pie of the vaudeville and movie.

All of these activities did not suffice to make Pirandello known to a wide circle, and it was not until he began to write plays that Fame relaxed from her coyness and rapidly surrendered with a truly feminine decision to make up for lost time. So far as I know, his first play to be produced was *Sicilian Limes*, which was published here before the rise of interest which now attaches to all his work. It was played a couple of years previous to the war without exciting much comment, and nothing is more amusing than to read the brief and perfunctory references to Pirandello, the playwright, in all books on the Italian theatre, even after he had written such plays as *Pensaci, Giacomino*, and *Il Piacere dell'onestà*. Nowadays, as Prezzolini has said, "when the theatre is mentioned in Italy, only one name comes up: Pirandello."

The first production in New York of a play by Luigi Pirandello, *Six Characters in Search of an Author*, coincided with the issue in Italy of a definitive edition of this author's works. Under the collective title of *Novelle per un Anno* the first six volumes of his short stories have appeared, *Scialle Nere, La Vita Nuda, La Rallegrata, L'Uomo Solo, La Mosca*, and *In Silenzio*. In a foreword Pirandello explains that his original intention was to bring together all the stories hitherto scattered and to make one monumental tome containing three hundred and sixty-five stories, one for each day of the year. Hence the title *Novelle per un Anno*, a sort of super-Decameron, in which the story-teller undertakes to keep his listeners amused, not for a thousand and one nights, like Scheherazade, but for a year. The edition will consist, however, not of one, but of twenty-four volumes, each containing some fifteen stories.

Pirandello is at his best in the creation of ironical situations, and in his sketches, skilful and malicious, of strange and eccentric characters. The moral and spiritual absurdities of human nature are the material from which he secures his best effects. He is happily innocent of any didactic intention, but he has in common with Bernard Shaw the faculty of seeing both the external comedy and the internal tragedy which arise out of the contrast between the appearance and the reality. As he himself once said:

Let a man see himself in the act of living, a prey to his passions; hold up a mirror before him. He will either start with

astonishment at his appearance, or he will turn away his face
to hide the spectacle, or he will spit at his own reflection out of
sheer rage, or he will angrily thrust forward his fist to smash it.
If he was weeping, he will no longer be able to do so. If he was
laughing, he will be unable to do that. . . . In short, there will
of necessity be some manifestation of pain.

It is with that pain of humanity confronted with its
own absurdities that the art of Pirandello is concerned. He likes to describe the profound transformation which takes place in a person to whom is suddenly revealed a situation in which the individual
has lived for years unconsciously, when that individual appears to himself as he has always appeared
to other people. Obviously, the stage, rather than
the short story, inevitably became the medium for
the expression of a genius so constituted.

Thus it came about that Luigi Pirandello, after
publishing novels and stories for the greater part of
his life, graduated late as a dramatist and finds himself famous, the most celebrated playwright in Italy
to-day, especially since the production of *Six Characters in Search of an Author*. In his plays one finds
carried to their highest point of expression all those
qualities which informed the best of his work in
narrative fiction. His humor consists essentially
in the dissociation of ideas, in a violent confrontation between the ideal and the real. This aspect of
his own method is actually exteriorized in *Six Characters*, where we are shown the futile effort of the
real characters to see themselves in the representa-
tions of the actors. The artistic creation is eternal
and immovable, but life is changeable and ever-
flowing, and so these living beings cannot recognize
their own image in the stereotyped gestures of the
players. One more instance of the clash between
reality and illusion. The idea here developed into a
play is first met in *La Trappola*, a book which he

published during the war. In the preface he explained that he is "at home" every Sunday morning to his characters, who visit him and urge their claim to be projected into life via literature. Even characters from other novels than his own come to see him and beg him to confer upon them an adequate existence when they have been the victims of unskilled creators. But, he tells us, he never accedes to such prayers. It is a characteristic fancy of Pirandello, who loves to play with his characters, to trifle with them until they apparently convince him that they are real enough to be allowed to take control of their own literary destiny. Then they enter that form of artistic being which is, in the author's philosophy, death, for it congeals living human beings in eternal attitudes, and separates them from the ceaseless flux of life.

This sudden and belated fame as a dramatist came to Pirandello in the space of the last six years, when he made himself known as the author of *Henry IV*, *Right You Are (If You Think So)*, *Each in His Own Way*, *The Pleasure of Honesty*, and *Naked*, to mention only those works which are now published in English. Ordinarily one might be justified in thinking that a writer who thus finds his true vein so late in his career must have been deceived during the best years of his life as to the real nature of his talent. But the truth is Pirandello in his plays has simply carried to their most effective point of expression ideas which visibly preoccupied him as a story-teller. When he came to the theatre, he did not submit to the exigencies of the existing dramatic conventions, but imposed his own form and his own technic. His plays have revitalized the Italian theatre just as the theatre called forth a fresh flowering of his own creative imagination. He has written comedies that are new, but whose novelty does not lie in scenic effects or even in the quality of their structural innovations. Their novelty is in the workmanship and thought behind them. He gives us the theatre of ideas—with a difference. Hence his plays are difficult, but they have the decided advantage of pleasing the crowd, which can be amused by externals, and of stimulating the initiated who read into them a philosophy of life which some term Pirandellism.

By this time the subject has been so often discussed that I need not launch into any very elaborate exposition of this alleged philosophy, the essence of which is that reality and illusion are meaningless terms, that a hair's breadth divides the noumenal from the phenomenal—to use the jargon of the metaphysicians. We are what we think we are, largely as a result of the pressure of the opinion of others upon us. Apart from their conception of us, what are we? Have we any objective existence? To recapitulate these pleasant conundrums, which are suggested by the plays, is to thrust oneself back into the (for me, at least) dim period when Schopenhauer's *Welt als Wille und Vorstellung* was something that made life brighter and better. Pirandello's dramatic exposition of such enigmas is possibly softer pabulum. For greater simplification of his method he has provided two plays in which the process is exteriorized by the device of having the living characters in a drama witness an attempt to give artistic expression to that drama on the stage—*Six Characters* and *Each in His Own Way*. Yet, in Pirandello's view, a life of fiction may be the only genuine life, and in *Henry IV* the madman who thought himself a king, when he returns to sanity, reproaches his attendants with their inability to live the actual dream which his madness created. He prefers to simulate madness in order to escape from the unreality of the world, which he sees with eyes strangely clairvoyant, but life drags him out of his dream world in the end.

The defect of such plays is their artificiality. If Shaw conceived of the theatre as a place in which to dramatize social propaganda, Pirandello uses it to dramatize metaphysical conceptions. If ever plays were "talking" plays, Pirandello's are, but his use of words is sparing, and there are none of those elaborate dissertations with which Shaw entertained or exasperated his public when the critics clamored for action. He has no message of hope, no indignations, no belief that some wrong or other has got to be righted and that he must write a play about it. Wherefore, I suppose, nothing has been said about the purely intellectual appeal of Pirandello, his lack of emotion, although the same case could be made out against him as against Shaw on this score. The success of *Six Characters* should not be taken as an indication of what may happen to his other plays. *Come Prima Meglio di Prima*, which was played here under the fantastic title of *Floriani's Wife*, is an equally typical Pirandello piece, but it failed to convince, not because the production was wretched, but because the situation is inherently weak and makes demands on one's credulity which are never satisfied.

That, in fact, is one of the complications in the case of Pirandello; he likes to postulate a situation, or a character, or both, which are incredible. They are often as preposterous as those in the cheapest melodrama. When that happens, and when at the same time all the emotional effects of melodrama are eliminated and ingenious variations upon the author's favorite philosophical theme are substituted, the result is a somewhat strange if often fascinating combination. *The Pleasure of Honesty* may be cited as an example, although there are others, not yet translated, which are even more alarming. Baldo-

vino marries Agata, when she is about to have a child
by Fabio, who is already married. He is a gentleman
of dubious reputation and he is glad of this opportunity to lead a respectable life. Agata and Fabio
may continue to be lovers, but they must be careful
of Baldovino's reputation, not for his own sake, but
for the sake of his position, which is that of the law-
ful husband of a respectable woman. Baldovino
acquires such a respect for his new office as a husband
and an honest man that he subordinates his real self
to this artificial conception of respectability. The
effect of this upon Agata is that she breaks off her
relations with Fabio, although it was precisely to
facilitate them that this marriage with a man of
straw was arranged. Fabio tries to involve Baldovino in a theft in order to disgrace and get rid of him.
Baldovino finds out the trap, and offers to go away,
provided Fabio becomes the thief, not he. Then he
changes his mind; he discovers that he loves Agata;
he is a man confronted with a woman, not a husband
in name with a wife in name. Each tears off the mask
of the artificial personalities they have presented to
each other, and love conquers all. . . . Italian audi-
ences riot over little things like this. In our less
demonstrative Anglo-Saxon way, we just seem to
become a little bored.

GIOVANNI PAPINI

In January, 1903, there appeared in Florence a luxurious and aristocratic-looking periodical, printed on hand-made paper and illustrated with woodcuts, in which, amongst other then obscure names, was that of a writer who signed himself "Gian Falco." This signature concealed the identity of the founder and editor, who was none other than the redoubtable Giovanni Papini, and this paper, *Leonardo*, which ran until 1907, represents his début in the world of Italian letters, of which he has since become a dominant figure. Probably his earliest appearance in America was the article in the Chicago *Monist* of July, 1903. Since then his work has been appearing more and more frequently in periodicals, and after *Four-and-Twenty Minds* had languished in semi-obscurity the colossal vogue of *La Storia di Cristo*, in Dorothy Canfield Fisher's adaptation, lent a little reflected glory to that work, as well as to *The Failure*, which was subsequently published as the English translation of *Un Uomo Finito*.

Giovanni Papini was born in Florence in 1881, so that he had just attained his majority when he began to make himself known as a new force in modern Italian literature. He wrote indefatigably for the reviews in those first years, challenging all the accepted idols in literature and philosophy and acquiring for himself that reputation as an "excoriator" which he finally accepted to the extent of calling a collection of these essays *Stroncature*, some of which are contained in the translated volume *Four-and-Twenty Minds*. This book is not a translation of the Italian volume of that name, but a selection from

168 STUDIES FROM TEN LITERATURES

the three volumes of his polemical essays, 24 *Cervelli*, *Stroncature*, and *Testimonianze*. His first book, *Il Crepuscolo dei Filosofi*, was published in 1906, and was followed in rapid succession by *Il Tragico Quotidiano*, *Il Pilota Cieco*, *Memoire d'Iddio*, *La Vita di Nessuno*, and *Un Uomo Finito*, to mention a few of his more important works prior to *La Storia di Cristo*.

Papini's friend, Giuseppe Prezzolini, has given a personal description of the man himself which is worth quoting, for his physical characteristics are symbolical of his literary personality. He is "like those pears which are coarse to the touch but sweet to the palate. At first sight he is not good-looking; his features are ugly. Speak with him, if you can get over the initial rudeness which marks his attitude almost always toward strangers, and you will see how in conversation his whole face lights up. You will become conscious of the spirit glowing within him; and he who might remain coarse and common to vulgar eyes takes on the noble aspect of a man whose soul is alive with genius—a man whose queer, misshapen exterior stands for a nature no less strange and exceptional."

Papini's *Life of Christ*, following his conversion to Catholicism, represents the culmination of a long series of intellectual and spiritual adventures which are better understood now that his autobiographical masterpiece, *The Failure*, has been made available for American readers. It is the logical expression of a state of mind which became more and more evident in his writings after the war, when he decided that only an act of faith could resolve the doubts and antagonisms engendered by the conflict. Nothing of the fire and passionate energy of the old unregenerate Papini is lost; the converted heretic approaches his task of spreading the gospel of Christ

in the same mood as inspired his onslaughts upon
Croce and the other literary idols of his earlier campaign. Nietzsche is now the chief butt of his in-
vective, and he reviles the unbelievers, even those
unfortunate pagans who had no choice in this particular matter, with the vigor and brilliance which
earned him a reputation comparable to that of H. L.
Mencken.

Papini approached his subject in a mood and in a
manner as unlike those of Strauss as of Renan.
There is no learned exegesis, no effort at scientific
criticism of texts, no ingenious attempt to interpret
Christ as a myth. He begins with an explanatory
foreword in the old manner, the unregenerate, unre-
pentant manner of those excoriations with which his
critical fame has been identified. He denounces the
sceptics as he once reviled Croce, and delivers himself of many vigorous diatribes which remind one of
nothing more than Mencken lampooning the Puri-
tans. Nietzsche is, naturally, the chief enemy, and
he makes contemptuous play with the circumstances
of "the last Antichrist," the product of "a German
presbytery and a Swiss professorship." He invites us
to contemplate the Dionysian cult, full of "that
grace which you might expect from a German born
of a Lutheran clergyman and lately released from
his chair of Helvetian learning." In fine, Papini's
controversial prologue is saved from the rougher
charms of the Billy Sunday technic only by his
superior literary power. Intellectually his attitude
is barely distinguishable from that worthy's abuse
of "four-flushers" and "dirty, stinking bunches of
moral assassins." His style is not so vernacular.

However, this *Story of Christ* does not purport to
be a controversial volume, although its Italian title
promises something more historically elaborate than
the word "story" would imply in English. Papini has

relied solely upon the Four Gospels, making sparing use of the apocryphals and a few traditions to fill out his narrative. He makes no effort whatever to distinguish between what reasonable criticism has now rejected, and accepts what even the theologians have ceased to argue. Where the gospel accounts are at variance he does not choose the one which is most probable, but confounds them all together, as if afraid to omit even the most incomprehensible incidents. Papini just tells the story in his own words, based upon the gospels, with personal observations and descriptive particulars, which, although invented, do not exceed the limits of what is convincing. His historical allusions are always useful and sometimes remarkable, as in the chapter devoted to a summary of the history of the Jews, which begins with an idyll in the Garden of Eden and ends in the tragedy of the Crucifixion.

> Never was a people so greatly loved by God and so terribly punished. It was chosen to be the first of all and it was the slave of the least; it wished to have its own country and to be victorious and it was exiled and enslaved in the countries of other peoples.

The chapter on Octavius, which describes the state of the world into which Christ was born, is another example of Papini's sense of historical drama. He begins: "When Christ appeared on the earth criminals reigned and the world obeyed them. He was born under two masters—one, more remote and stronger, at Rome; the other, nearer and more infamous, in Judea." Summing up the character of the Roman Emperor, he concludes: "This deformed weakling was the master of the Western World when Jesus was born and he never knew that one had been born who was destined, in the end, to destroy what he had built up. For him the facile philosophy of the little fat plagiarist, Horace, was sufficient: 'Let us enjoy to-day wine and love; death without hope awaits us; let us not lose a day.'" Equally fine is the historical synthesis in the chapter entitled "Achilles and Priam," in which he argues that the idea of love did not come into literature or into the hearts of men until Christ taught them to love their enemies. Ulysses, Socrates, and Seneca, like Achilles, are moved in certain circumstances to compassion, but Papini's analysis of their motives is designed to prove that "in the most lofty and heroic world of antiquity there is no room for the love that destroys hate"; that love was not known until proclaimed in the Sermon on the Mount.

So long as the author sticks to his last, telling his story and commenting with all the ingenuous ardor of the proselyte, he is, if not convincing to the sceptic, at least plausible and intensely interesting. He cannot, however, resist the temptation to indulge in textual hypotheses, and then he becomes frankly ridiculous. He refers, for example, to the scene by the Sea of Tiberias, when Christ asks Simon Peter, "Lovest thou me?" and the latter answers three times, "Thou knowest I love thee." According to Papini, it was not until the third time that the answer came in this form. Twice Simon Peter's answer was "I like thee," for he did not dare to say "love" after having denied Christ three times. This ingenious notion is based solely upon the form of the Italian version of the New Testament where "*ti voglio bene*" occurs twice and "*ti amo*" once. In English, French, and Latin the word love (*aimer-amare*) is used by Peter in all three replies. In the Latin text it is Christ who varies the word by employing "*diligere*" in the first two questions and "*amare*" in the third. Perhaps Papini is prepared to attach some special significance to this, since he has apparently no hesitation in theorizing about words which were not, in any case, actually employed either by Christ or Peter.

There have been instances in literature where popular success has had the effect of lowering the standard and quality of the author's work. Under pressure of circumstances, or perhaps half consciously, a writer proceeds to exploit his success by publishing work because he discovers it will be accepted whether good or mediocre, or because he discovers that a certain element in his writings is sure of a wide response, though it be a most inferior element. Giovanni Papini, however, presents a curious variation in the sense that his popularity and success have come to him precisely because he has deteriorated. Success has not spoiled him; he did not succeed until he had become spoiled. The result is that the boom in Papini produced in this country by his *Life of Christ* has coincided with his definite eclipse in Italy as an author of any rank other than that conferred by mere quantities of paper consumed and copies sold. He shares this distinction as a circulationist with Guido da Verona, whose stories of incest, and romantic adulteries in absolutely first-class hotels, with champagnes, perfumes, and translucent and transcendent underclothes, make his novels the delight of hundreds of thousands of Italian stenographers.

Papini has not enjoyed in England anything like the vogue which he has over here, nor in France, where they have recently discovered him. There is a curious irony in the fact that, just as William James was the first foreigner to recognize Papini at the outset of a career that seemed so brilliant, so, at the moment of his eclipse, it is the compatriots of James who take him seriously, or at least enthusi-

astically. The critical literature on Papini in Italian
is an interesting evidence of his fate. Ever since the
Storia di Cristo, that is to say, since 1920, there has
been a vast diminuendo of appreciation. The last
study of Papini which is comprehensive and favorable dates from 1914, Prezzolini's *Discorso su G.
Papini*, unless one except a volume issued two years
ago by Papini's publisher, a vague and wordy piece
of house publicity by R. Fondi, entitled *Un Costrut-
tore: Giovanni Papini*. The latest study of Papini
strikingly illustrates the disfavor into which he has
fallen with his more intelligent compatriots. The
book is a little volume in a new series which is frankly
popular in design and scope, and is not addressed to
any clique or any cenacle of superior persons. One
naturally turns with some curiosity to the volume
on Papini in such a series, for it affords an opportunity
to judge how he appears to the average cultivated
Italian reader.

The author of the Papini volume is Nicola Moscardelli, one of the most distinguished poets of the
younger generation. He was just twenty-one when he
went to the front, and was wounded in 1915, and his
first book was published in 1913. I mention these
facts to indicate that Moscardelli belongs absolutely
to that generation of the war which is supposed to
be in sympathy with the revolt against rationalism
and to be particularly well disposed toward the contemporary continental European enthusiasm for
Catholicism, Fascism, and the æstheticization of
sport—the generation, in brief, from which the American æsthetic borrows his half-baked ideas. Moscardelli's analysis of Papini's alleged conversion and
of *The Life of Christ* is not only excellent in itself,
but it also sums up exactly the feeling of intelligent
Italians toward this latest phase of Papini's career.
He shows the evolution of Papini from pragmatism

via futurism to Christ, and then demonstrates how
shallow, intellectual, unemotional, and irreligious,
in the true sense of the word, the Papini of *The Life
of Christ* is: how the book lacks every element of
genuine faith and spiritual emotion. "In it Papini
proves that he encountered the Gospel in a library.
He treats Christianity as he treated Pragmatism.
But Christ is not James." How does Papini talk
about Christ? Moscardelli asks. "By spreading over
more than six hundred pages what the Gospels tell
us in less than one hundred. The reader would never
notice that Christ is being discussed if it were not
mentioned in the title. It might just as well be about
Christopher Columbus or Garibaldi or Napoleon.
The lofty themes suggested to the human mind by
the Gospel are never developed by Papini, but are
worked out like a schoolboy's theme. . . . With the
same words Papini could prove the exact opposite
of what he is trying to prove if a 'no' were substituted
for each 'yes,' and 'good' for 'bad.'"

Moscardelli points out that the chapters of *The
Life of Christ* can be traced back to preceding works
of the author's pre-Christian phase, that they spring
from no change of heart, and are mere prolongations
in an incongruous field of the spirit animating *Four-
and-Twenty Minds* and other earlier untranslated
works. "Papini has written over six hundred pages
to tell us that he has known Christ, but there arises
the well-founded doubt: has he not written about
eternal truths rather than eternal truth? He has not
confronted us with his resurrection but told us about
it. Six hundred packed pages without a single
thought of three lines comparable to the splendor of
Pascal, to an image of Hello, or the illumination of
Dostoevsky. The moral problem, which is man's
capital problem, seems to have become just a publishing problem. Write a big book and it will appear

great; little thoughts which literate and illiterate alike leave unsaid." Anybody can expand the story of the gospel, but "not every one can write a hundred little pages in which Christ is never mentioned but from which it is evident that Christ is born."

The famous *Dictionary of a Savage*, Papini's most recent work, is rightly cited by Moscardelli as the final proof of the author's collapse. It will be remembered that this is the book which is full of the grossest insults to America, and the most impudently ignorant besmearing of reputations and ideas that do not coincide with the hooligan type of Catholic obscurantism which Papini now affects. It is the perfect expression of a crude anticlerical's return to clericalism, and, when American dollars for lectures were dangled before Papini, strenuous efforts were made to evade the evidence of this book and to dissociate Papini from it. It was written with a collaborator, who could be used as a convenient scapegoat. In Moscardelli's analysis the obvious relation of this dictionary to Papini's present state of mind is clearly established, with the further charge that this work alone is sufficient to dispose of the notion that Papini has found Christ, or understood even the rudiments of Christianity. Here again the author of this invaluable little book traces the ideas in the dictionary to their source in Papini's earlier writings, just as in the case of *The Life of Christ*. He accuses Papini of having emptied into these pages the insults, the blasphemies, and the filth which he could not use in the days of his polemics of a different character in *Lacerba*. "There is no personal vision nor Christian vision of life. It is not a buried world revivified by the light of Christ, nor splendid thought illuminated by the love of Christ— just the blasphemies of yesterday and always, reversed, that is to say, the same."

Such is the Papini whom the movie magnates are paying for the use of the New Testament! The filming of his *Life of Christ* is an appropriate culmination, for even Papini himself has never pretended that there is anything in the actual narrative itself which is not in the Gospels. Papini's contribution consists of opinions, ideas, comments, and arguments, which obviously cannot be screened. The film version of *The Life of Christ* will, therefore, resemble Papini's "conversion"; it will correspond to nothing that it purports to be. It will be a thing without sound or fury, signifying nothing but the fact that Giovanni Papini can "sell" the New Testament story of Christ to a Protestant country which professes to regard the English Bible as one of its priceless possessions and deathless literary heritages.

AN ITALIAN CRITIC: G. A. BORGESE

ALTHOUGH he is known in this country as the novelist who wrote *Rubè*, that remarkable study of Italian youth during and after the war, G. A. Borgese has for many years been familiar to readers of Italian literature as a distinguished and discriminating critic. He was one of the group of Croce's disciples and successors who have built up a body of critical work which is sharply differentiated from that of the schools preceding Croce—the schools of de Sanctis and of Carducci. The Croceans are numerous, for the reason that it was almost impossible for the generation reaching maturity at the beginning of this century to escape the charm and influence of Croce æsthetic philosophy, but the outstanding critics of the school are Renato Serra, Emilio Cecchi, and G. A. Borgese. They represent the last critical phase of the epoch which closed in July, 1914. Since then new names have come up, notably Adriano Tilgher, Silvio d'Amico, and Pietro Pancrazi, and the literature of another era has its own interpreters.

It is not that Borgese at once abandoned his functions as a critic, for since the war he has published *Tempo di Edificare*, which, with the three volumes of *La Vita e il Libro*, *Risurrezioni*, *Studi di Letterature Moderne*, and his *Storia della Critica Romantica in Italia*, present the main body of his work as an active critic. They offer, as he says, "a picture that is doubtless incomplete and imperfect, but sufficiently unprejudiced and comprehensive, of Italian literature from the noontide of Pascoli and d'Annunzio to the dawn of a new day." If the appearance of *Rubè*, followed by *I Vivi e i Morti*, was an indication that Borgese the critic was making way for Borgese the novelist, the matter is now clearly explained in the preface to his latest book. In *La Vita e il Libro* he salutes his successors in the field of criticism, "a new group of critics, different from us as the circumstances and conditions of their labors are different from those of 1913," and his hope is that they will be able to discover in his work "some decipherable sign of an epoch that felt itself to be intellectually a prodigy, but historically mediocre, and which was, in fact, the contrary." In giving its title to *Tempo di Edificare* he wished to emphasize the fact that a certain stage in his own development had been reached; it was now "the time to build," to turn from critical to creative writing:

"I was an artist in the process of evolution even when I was practising my profession as a critic; a large number of the writings here collected are coeval with *Rubè*. But it is morally and intellectually difficult to write novels, verses, and plays while retaining one's function of ceaselessly passing judgment on the writings of one's contemporaries and compatriots. For that reason I say that the time has long since come for me to build, to become fully what it is my duty to be . . . and to leave to the new critics the task of passing judgment in their turn."

As Borgese himself points out, the situation which confronted him and his contemporaries when they surveyed Italian literature was peculiar. The great artists Pascoli, Fogazzaro, and d'Annunzio had done their best work; they were accepted modern classics. Verga, though still alive, had so long been silent that he belonged to the past that was dead beyond recall. There was no promise in the literature then in being, and the duty devolved upon the critics of analyzing the causes of this sterility and of trying to preserve the public taste from destruction by the substitution of inferior values in the place of those that were gone. Gradually certain figures began to emerge, Federigo Tozzi, Marino Moretti, Giovanni Papini, but their obscurity during the decade prior to the war can best be measured by the scant space they occupy in the three volumes of *La Vita e il Libro*. Even Panzini and Pirandello did not come into their own until relatively late. There is only one reference to the latter in *La Vita e il Libro*, an article on the short stories entitled *La Vita Nuda*, whereas in *Tempo di Edificare* Pirandello is the subject of an interesting essay in which Borgese shows that the theme of the plays, the contrast between appearance and reality, is found in his earlier work, particularly in his novel *The Late Mattia Pascal*. The recent fame of Papini may also be measured by the fact that there are only two passing allusions to him in the whole of Borgese's work previous to 1914. The comment upon his conversion and his *Storia di Cristo*, and the Neo-Catholic resurgence in general, which forms a chapter in *Tempo di Edificare*, is well reasoned and welcome after all the nonsense which has been written about Papini's return to the fold of orthodoxy.

The contrast between this last book and its predecessors lies in the increasing concern with Italian literature pure and simple, where, before the war, English, French, and German authors were most frequently the subjects of Borgese's criticism. *Studi di Letterature Moderne*, for instance, one of his most stimulating works, devotes only a quarter of its space to Italian authors; the rest of the book consists of studies of Emile Olivier, Bergson, Mallarmé, Rimbaud, Claudel, Poe, Wilde, Kipling, Shaw, Heine, Hebbel, Hauptmann, Sudermann, Cervantes, Tolstoy, Dostoevsky, and Eça de Queiroz. *La Vita e il*

Libro is not quite so cosmopolitan in its range, and its chief interest and historic value must be sought in the general reflection it gives of a transitionary period in Italian literature, when criticism was the whole duty of man, and there seemed to be no "time to build." The war between the Croceans and the Carduccians raged furiously, and Borgese was involved in it, as the epilogue to the second volume of *La Vita e il Libro* records. In this, Borgese, with considerable vigor, disentangles himself from the implications of mere Croceanism, which he was more and more to disown as his own critical philosophy developed. Prezzolini has described the divergence of the older and the younger critic in a passage worth quoting:

His criticism is the true expression of his own spirit, which has always tended toward construction, even though useless; toward ornament, even though florid. Hence the contrast with Croce. In the early day in *Leonardo* he used the latter's ideas, and in his magnificent *Storia della Critica Romantica*, as all have done, for they all start from Croce. But his temperament was so far removed from the harsh and puritan temperament of Croce, his artistic aspirations were so contrary to the bourgeois tastes of the latter, that it is easy to understand that they should clash. Borgese is sincere when he asserts his belief in a classical æsthetic, in which the beautiful takes on an appearance of solidity, of deliberate plan, and his silence is comprehensible concerning the few sincere and authentic but poor poets of this generation.

Borgese now declares that the principle, "physician heal thyself," is applicable to the critic, who must produce something of his own that is worth being criticised, and so he has given us *Rubè*, *I Vivi e i Morti*, *L'Arciduca*, a tragedy based upon the Mayerling drama of Rudolph of Hapsburg. In so doing he cites the example of Sainte-Beuve, but the fortunes of *Volupté* are hardly a good omen, for the novel surely lives merely because of the critical achievement of its author. Admirers of his work as a critic will always be interested in anything he may care to write, and they will welcome this handsome edition of his essays during the constructive period which he curiously fails to regard as *Tempo di Edificare*. At the same time they hope that the volume so entitled will not be the last of his contributions to a literature which will otherwise be abandoned entirely to Croce. Among the newer critics whom he so kindly welcomes I see none, as yet, who is comparable to G. A. Borgese.

Since Borgese turned away in 1921 from critical writing to publish the novel exclusively known in America, political events in Italy have shaped themselves, under the ægis of Mussolini, in a manner to which this study of war neurosis furnishes a valuable clew. While violence has gradually been sanctified, and hysteria has taken the place of rational ideas, the story of Filippo Rubè has been translated by the indefatigable Doctor Goldberg for the edification of those who would like to know something of the stuff of which Fascismo is made. The English version is fair to middling.

I regret to say that, as so often happens with Doctor Goldberg's translations, I have more respect for his great industry than for his skill in the manipulation of English. And I am depressed, every now and then, by definite blunders which are so elementary as to be almost inexplicable. It is incredible, for example, that he should be unaware of the Italian for "Come in!" in answer to a knock at the door. Yet such was the first slip that caught my eye as I turned over the pages of text and translation for purposes of comparison. However, let nobody pretend that such errors are a valid excuse for neglecting an interesting novel.

Some of the English versions of Anatole France contain "howlers" that would disgrace a schoolboy, but the argument has not been made that this is due to the audacity of mere Americans in daring to undertake so delicate a task, for the French master has been translated exclusively in London, where they are so fond of condescending to American translations. Doctor Goldberg has done his task, on the whole, in a workmanlike manner. In view of the success of certain atrocious translations which are selling to the satisfaction of all concerned, I intend to be sceptical if any one attempts to saddle the translator with responsibility for the success or failure of the book!

When I read *Rubè* it was with something of the same interest and curiosity as must send many readers to Sainte-Beuve's *Volupté;* it was also the first novel of a distinguished critic, who had previously published a book of verse but no fiction. Naturally one asks: what sort of novel will such a man write? *Rubè*, it seems to me, is precisely what one would expect from a writer whose criticism is the antithesis of Sainte-Beuve's, cosmopolitan and objective, more concerned with ideas than with personalities. *Volupté* was equally as characteristic of that first "naturalist of souls," whose interest in the all-too-human weaknesses of literary human nature corresponded to a feminine element in himself, to which may be traced the jealousy that prompted him to prefer the second-rate figures of his own time to those of first-rate significance. Sainte-Beuve's novel, to this day, provokes naïve and belated protestations against its lack of traditional masculine discretion where a woman's reputation is concerned. But he had a feminine streak in his character, which was the defect of his other qualities as a critic.

To begin with, *Rubè* is as far removed as possible

from the conventional standard of Italian fiction, especially that which is most familiar in English translations. The harsh realism of Giovanni Verga, the flamboyant romanticism of d'Annunzio, the passionate emotion of Grazia Deledda and Matilde Serao are as conspicuously absent from the pages of *Rubè* as is the cloying sentimentality of de Amicis or the sublimated theatricalism of Fogazzaro. Borgese has written the story of "a child of the century," an analysis of the type which is representative of the transition in Europe.

Filippo Rubè is a young man from southern Italy who comes to Rome shortly before the war to make a career for himself as a lawyer. He is vain, egotistical, but clever, in a sense. He has the gift of the gab, and he fancies there is a great future for him at the bar and in politics. But he is not of the type that succeeds, because, while he is cynical and clever enough to perceive the profound buffoonery of life, he is a self-tormenting logician and introspective sentimentalist, eternally engaged in searching his heart for answers to enigmas which had better be left unsolved. Borgese shows with great subtlety how Rubè has actually failed, long before the war comes to disrupt his personality completely.

The war is the supreme dissolvent which hastens the process of disintegration. He goes into the army as a junior officer in the artillery, and for a long time he is stationed back of the line with Major Berti and his daughter Eugenia. He is not popular with his comrades, and he is torn constantly between his terror of death and his vanity. In a moment of hysteria he confesses his cowardice to Eugenia, then he makes her his mistress, feeling that this bond will close her mouth effectively so far as his confessions are concerned. He is sent to the front, receives a wound, is decorated, and returns to Rome to convalesce.

Now he is physically happy, brutal, and more egotistical than ever. Eugenia submits to their liaison, and when he sets off for Paris on a mission he promises to marry her when the war is over. His life in Paris is centred about the wife of a French general, Lambert, a charming, wholly immodest, but technically virtuous woman. Rubè's sole concern is to get on and have a good time. The war ends, and like thousands of his type he is reduced overnight to the ranks of the unemployed, in the fullest sense of that term. The comfort, interest, and certainty of his military career are gone. He becomes an entirely unimportant civilian once more.

Here begins the second and most original part of the novel. Rubè marries Eugenia, and in an aimless manner attempts to live in a quiet way in Milan, where he has secured an appointment. But the war has spoiled him for whatever kind of useful work he might once have performed. He is discharged. In a night's gambling he wins a large sum of money, and with this he sets out on a crazy pilgrimage. At Stresa he meets Mme. Lambert again, and this time she does not hesitate to give herself to him, for her husband is away on some patriotic mission in Roumania. The amorous couple are overtaken by a storm on a lake, the boat capsizes, and the woman is drowned. Rubè is accused of murder, but is acquitted. That experience is the last straw. He wanders from place to place, from the priest, to whom he frantically but uselessly confesses himself, to his friends, from his native village back to his wife. Nobody can help him. A neurotic wreck, mad with self-torture and insomnia, he goes out into the streets of Bologna and becomes involved in a riot. Holding, with symbolical gesture, both a red and a black flag in his hands, he is caught in a cavalry charge and is fatally injured. Thus ends the futile quest of this drifting and unstable soul in an ignominious accident, characteristic of the undecided and purposeless generation of Filippo Rubè.

As this summary outline will have shown, *Rubè* is not lacking in movement and action, although it is tightly packed with ideas, analyses, and conversations, which at times seem overemphasized. Borgese has drawn for us in *Rubè* a type corresponding in our own time to Turgenev's *Rudin*. This book has been compared to Stendhal's *Red and Black*, and even to Bourget's *The Disciple*. There is some analogy with the former in the relationship of Rubè to women, in the psychology of the sex element. But to find any parallel for such a dissection of the mind of an epoch, for so fine an analysis of a type that is a symbol, one must look not to the literature of any other Latin country, but to Russia and Germany. It is not unnatural that the intellectual element should dominate in the first novel of a man of the stamp of G. A. Borgese.

It is that element which renders the book vastly superior to the pseudo-Russian mysticism of *The World's Illusion*. The tiresome, cinematographic flicker of endless incident in Wasserman's novel bored me more than passages of too lengthy dissertation with which some critics have reproached the author of *Rubè*. In this book G. A. Borgese has done more than write a brilliant first novel: he has brought the keen insight of a fine and sensitive critic to a profound diagnosis of the malady of an era that is dying.

PORTUGAL

EÇA DE QUEIROZ

THERE is a curious absence of any principle in determining the selection of works translated into English from foreign literatures. The erratic response of the public to translations is equalled only by the freakishness of the choice in the first instance. Rarely is an author introduced by means of a first-rate and representative book. Of André Gide we had, for some time, only his *Prometheus Ill-bound. Colette Baudoche* alone represents the novels of Maurice Barrès; there is not one volume of the famous series of *Le Culte du moi;* long before Remy de Gourmont's philosophical essays were published in English, his *Night in the Luxemburg* stood alone. When Carl Spitteler was awarded the Nobel Prize, the English translators ignored *Conrad der Leutnant* and *Imago,* but presented us with *Two Little Misogynists,* which was relegated to the limbo of "juveniles"—a strange fate for the author who forestalled Nietzsche's *Also Sprach Zarathustra.*

However, I cheerfully grant that there is no more reason why intelligence should be displayed in this field than in any other, that the possession of knowledge is entirely unnecessary, and that in publishing translations, as in other things, fasting and prayer are liable to be more helpful than familiarity with the subject concerned. No translation is bad enough to spoil the success of a book, provided the book be sufficiently mediocre. There is no evidence that a first-rate representative book by a foreign writer succeeds better than a tenth-rate and unrepresentative work. Proofs to the contrary are abundant, but I am willing to admit that there is something to be

said for both kinds. Excellence may be a positive
hindrance. One should be thankful if it is not and
demand nothing more. *La Garçonne* is clearly not
precisely the author's masterpiece, but it has been
greeted with the encouragement of actual cash pay-
ments, whereas the charms of earlier translations of
the work of the Marguerittes are unhonored and un-
sung outside the pages of the college manuals. There
is one book by Blasco Ibáñez which self-respecting
Spaniards read, *La Barraca*. If I am not mistaken, it
is the least known of all his works in its English form
as *The Cabin*. In brief, not even for translation can
the reading leopard change his spots or the publishing Ethiopian his skin. Nevertheless, as a mere
matter of pedantry, based, not upon any faith in the
tastes of the plain people, but upon the assumption
that the purpose of translated literature is to enable
intelligent people to see what other intelligent peoples
read, the eccentricities of selection divert and fasci-
nate me.

The most astonishing case is that of Eça de
Queiroz. In some book-shops one may observe a
gaudy tome, with classic designs and Græco-Roman
decorations, entitled *Perfection*. It is the work of
the Portuguese novelist Eça de Queiroz, and is the
third book of his which I have seen in English. The
other two are *The Sweet Miracle* and *Our Lady of the
Pillar*, pious and precious volumes destined for the
fate which assuredly awaits *Perfection*. Nobody ob-
serving the succession of these little books would
guess that Eça de Queiroz is the outstanding figure
in contemporary Portuguese fiction, although he died
in 1900; that he is the author of a vast collection of
novels, short stories, essays, and travel sketches, of
which these three little fragments give an utterly
misleading idea. He has been translated into Spanish
by no less a person than Ramón del Valle-Inclán,

and some of his more important works are available in German and Italian. His chief novels are *A Reliquia*, *O Primo Bazilio*, *O Crime do Padre Amaro*, *Os Maias*, *O Mandarim*, and *A Illustre Casa de Ramires*. His career coincided with the rise of Naturalism in France, and the resemblance between *O Crime do Padre Amaro* and *La Faute de l'Abbé Mouret* is noticeable, as indeed the greater part of his work is strongly influenced by Zola and the French Realists.

A Reliquia is a curious work, and ought long ago to have appeared in English, for it is an excellent illustration of the strange hybrid character of Eça de Queiroz's imagination, of the defects and qualities of his style. It is the story of a ribald nephew's struggle to elude and delude his bigoted and inquisitorial aunt, ending in one of the most farcical tragicomedies imaginable. Teodorico Raposo's ideals are as much of the earth earthy as those of D. Patrocinio das Neves are of the most intolerant purity. She controls the fortune which this youth hopes to inherit, but his sinful ways are a constant source of irritation and suspicion to his aunt. Partly to escape her and partly in the belief that he can do something to secure her permanent approval, Teodorico sets out on a pilgrimage to the Holy Land, where he promises to find a relic which will cure the old lady's rheumatism and bring her spiritual consolation. At Alexandria he finds an English girl, who charms him to such an extent that, not for the first time, both of them succumb to the weaknesses of the flesh. He has a pleasant sojourn in the land of this Circe and on leaving her carries away, as a trophy and tender souvenir, a perfumed garment that had lain next to the skin of the fair creature; in a word, her chemise.

Comforted by this batiste relic he arrives in the Holy Land, where Eça de Queiroz, with characteristic versatility, reconstructs the sacred scenes of which it

is the background. After this interlude we again
behold the sinfulness of Teodorico, who procures for
himself a fake relic of the kind likely to appeal to his
aunt's piety and credulity. His own relic and hers
thus repose, carefully wrapped up, in his trunk, as
he turns his steps homeward, conscious of several
things accomplished and something done. As he
nears Lisbon, however, he decides that it would be
wiser to preserve only the more important and irre-
placeable memento of his pilgrimage, so he throws
one of the parcels away. On his arrival home he joyfully announces the success of his quest and mysteri-
ously invites his aunt to come into her private chapel
to inspect the holy treasure. Trembling with emotion
Maria Patrocinio das Neves assists at the impressive
ceremony, in the presence of her spiritual adviser and
several worthy old friends of her household. The
parcel is opened, and amidst the not too suave perfumes affected by the Alexandrian charmer the aston-
ished group contemplates the gauzy chemise ornamented with ribbons of tender blue, which he had
carried away for remembrance.

On this framework of burlesque humor Eça de
Queiroz constructs a story in which a classical severity
of style in the descriptive passages is allied to a savage
and brutal analysis of character. Aunt and nephew
are examined with impartial contempt, the stupid
bigot and the stupid libertine are reduced to a common denominator—their abject, fleshly egotism. The
old lady believes that she is serving God, when all
she is doing is indulging her fear of bodily pain and
death, trying to obviate the one and facilitate the
other by obedience to certain rites. Teodorico imag-
ines that he is free and progressive, that his rejection
of religion springs from a healthy paganism, but his
life is merely sordid and lazy. Both types are incapable of the real ardors they pursue. She is as in-

capable of saintliness as he of passion. Within the
limits of this sordid and blasphemous, this grotesque
and satirical, novel, Eça de Queiroz has drawn a picture of the Portugal of his day during the last quarter
of the nineteenth century, which is one of those
caricatures whose every stroke tells more than the
strictest realism could have done. It is not a great
novel, for the author had not the power of a Flaubert
or an Anatole France, but it is a remarkable one.
Eça de Queiroz was a Zola with a sense of burlesque
humor, a poet with something of Flaubert's imagination, but without the discipline of form and style.

Yet Eça de Queiroz was destined to have a considerable influence upon an author who is perhaps
the greatest stylist in contemporary Spanish literature, Ramón del Valle-Inclán. Curiously enough, he
was not very well known in Spain until after his
death. *A Reliquia* appeared in Spanish in 1901, and
in 1902 a second translation was made by Valle-
Inclán, from which interesting deductions have been
made as to the source of some of the Spanish novelist's most characteristic and effective turns of style.
In his *Crítica Profana*, Julio Casares, in addition to
his demonstration of the absurdity of the claim that
The Pleasant Memoirs of the Marquis of Bradomín is
a single, homogeneous work, makes a detailed analysis
of the similarities of form in the Spanish and the
Portuguese writers. He notes the trick of grouping
three adjectives at the end of a sentence, which Valle-
Inclán uses to such good purpose, and he finds that
the typical phrase "perfumed with love and violets,"
which recurs as the description of the profane "relic,"
occurs in the *Sonata of Autumn*, where it has been
admired as peculiar to Valle-Inclán. Violently contrasted adjectives, the abrupt juxtaposition of sacred
and profane, the combination of abstract and con-
crete in a single comparison prove, on analysis, to be

the essence of Ramón del Valle-Inclán's style, and they all come from Eça de Queiroz.

With Castello Branco, who belonged to an earlier generation, but died only ten years before Eça de Queiroz, the author of *A Reliquia* is the only modern Portuguese novelist whose reputation extends beyond the frontiers of that little country. Branco's *Amor de Perdição*, in its Spanish version, with a somewhat dithyrambic Prologue by Azorín, has been more widely read than perhaps the merits of this Portuguese Octave Feuillet warrant—or it may be, indeed, precisely because of the analogies between *O Romance de un Homem Rico* and *Le Roman d'un Jeune Homme Pauvre*. Compared with his younger contemporary, he lacks force and flavor, in spite of the excess of romantic incident and invention with which he burdened his stories. The choice of three minor tales by Eça de Queiroz for translation into English, rather than one of his major novels, has tended to obscure his immense superiority over Castello Branco. But the difficulties which he presents to the translator are considerable. *Os Maias* is an exceedingly long novel of Lisbon life, a picture of futile people and of ignorant provincialism, of existence drifting as aimlessly as in a play of Chehov's. *O Primo Bazilio*, which is highly esteemed by Portuguese critics as "a masterly, almost perfect book," is actually nothing more than an average specimen of the French Naturalistic school, and Cousin Bazilio might have been a creation of Maupassant's, in a Portuguese setting, a more restricted Bel Ami. But whereas Maupassant's sensual imagination does not really exceed the limits of Anglo-Saxon decorum, in this book Eça de Queiroz does not shrink from refinements of eroticism worthy of Zola, or rather of d'Annunzio, for he is not so crude in his perverse allusions.

Mr. Aubrey Bell, who is one of the very few

Englishmen who have tried to enlist attention for modern Portuguese literature, quotes Eça de Queiroz's description of *O Crime do Padre Amaro* as "an intrigue of priests and devout women, hatched and murmured in the shadow of an old Portuguese provincial cathedral," a phrase which explains, I think, why it has never enjoyed abroad even such success as attended *La Faute de l'Abbé Mouret*, which did not appear until after the Portuguese novel on a similar theme. There remains, therefore, *A Reliquia*, "an extraordinary book—vulgar, repulsive, blasphemous, fantastic, amusing, sordid, horrible," to quote Mr. Bell. From the second of these adjectives I dissent, but the others may well stand as summarizing the qualities which ought to bring foreign readers to Eça de Queiroz through this most entertaining and original novel.

SWITZERLAND

CARL SPITTELER

When Carl Spitteler appealed for the neutrality of German Switzerland against Germany, in the winter of 1914, he deliberately sacrificed his popularity in the only country outside his own which had known and appreciated him. Since then France has been stirred to notice him, and five of his prose works have been translated into French. In 1915, on the occasion of Spitteler's seventieth birthday, which was publicly celebrated by his countrymen, the French Academy sent him fraternal greetings, and in 1919 he was awarded the Nobel Prize for literature, but the only book of his to appear in English was a minor work which was published as a children's book under the title *Two Little Misogynists*.

Carl Spitteler was born at Liestal, near Basle, in 1845, and died at Lucerne, in 1925. He spent his youth in Switzerland, and studied at the universities of Basle and Heidelberg, prior to his departure for Russia as a tutor, at the close of the Franco-Prussian War. In 1879 he returned to Switzerland and earned a livelihood as a teacher and journalist. It was not until 1892 that he enjoyed any degree of leisure and independence. His earliest attempts at composition were, he tells us, submitted to the Swiss poet Gottfried Keller, who found them "lamentable as to form, but unusual in content," and so long did Spitteler strive to perfect his work that he was thirty-six years old before he ventured to publish his first book. The two volumes of *Prometheus und Epimetheus* appeared in 1880 and 1881 over the expressive pseudonym "Felix Tandem," and a quarter of a century was to elapse before a second edition was issued in the author's own name. Meanwhile, he had written a number of books, both verse and prose, which had failed to make him known beyond the borders of his own country. When the German musician Felix Weingartner wrote his enthusiastic pamphlet, *Carl Spitteler, ein Künstlerisches Erlebnis*, in 1904, his admiration had been aroused by the poet's last and finest work, *Olympischer Frühling*. Only then did German criticism begin to "discover" the remarkable writer of the intervening years between 1880 and 1900 when the first book of *Olympischer Frühling* appeared.

It is a coincidence that the World War should have brought Nietzsche into universal discussion and at the same time the writer whose whole career was thwarted by the publication of *Also Sprach Zarathustra*. That famous evangel followed by a few years the publication of Spitteler's *Prometheus und Epimetheus*, but in spite of a certain fundamental identity of spirit, and some analogies of form, the unknown poet was ignored and the philosopher gained the credit which priority should have given Spitteler. Indeed, so long did the latter suffer from this almost simultaneous expression of a similar doctrine that he was obliged to publish in 1908 a pamphlet entitled *My Relations with Nietzsche*. At the time *Prometheus und Epimetheus* appeared Spitteler had not read a line of Nietzsche's work, and, although subsequently the two writers corresponded, there could be no question of borrowing. In the case of the Swiss, whose book was conceived during his stay in Russia, and existed in draft during the long years of preparation that preceded its much-delayed appearance, his originality is beyond doubt. Moreover, we know that Nietzsche was one of the few who had read and appreciated *Prometheus und Epimetheus*, and all his life he expressed his esteem for Spitteler, whom he mentions with gratitude in *Ecce Homo*.

It is, perhaps, unfair to a work of extraordinary richness and beauty to attempt a summary of its contents, but in order that the points of contact between Nietzsche and Spitteler may be established, we must have an outline of the latter's conception before us. Prometheus is the superman of Spitteler's prose poem, who knows no law but that of his own soul, and will suffer every indignity rather than be false to himself. His fate is to see his brother, Epimetheus, rise to power and honor while he himself is rejected and insulted by men. Epimetheus does not possess wisdom, but a cleverness which enables him to barter his free soul in exchange for a comfortable and useful conscience. Thus equipped, he can live in accordance with the common laws of man, and he is chosen, instead of Prometheus, to be lord of the world. Prometheus wanders off into slavery and exile, followed by two animals, a lion and a dog, as Zarathustra was accompanied by an eagle and a serpent, and there he submits to humiliation and grief, rather than sacrifice his spiritual freedom.

Epimetheus reigns, meanwhile, wisely and successfully according to his lights. His conscience keeps him within the straight path, and mechanically operates to the disadvantage of any promptings of "master morality," as Nietzsche would have termed it. One day, however, peasants bring him the secret gift of Pandora, and Epimetheus is in doubt as to the value of this offering. Neither the priests nor the goldsmith can estimate Pandora's gift, and Epimetheus appeals in vain to his conscience for enlightenment. That acquired, an artificial sense of values is powerless to judge of Eternal Beauty. The disappointed peasants cast the treasure from them; it is found by a Jew, who hides it hastily beneath his dress and disappears forever with the unappreciated gift. Thus, Epimetheus learned the first of his limitations, but was powerless to profit by the experience. Consequently he is betrayed into even greater difficulties.

As King of Man his most sacred office was the care of the three children of deity, Mythos, Hiero, and Messias. When a grave sickness fell upon them, hope dawned upon the powers and darkness. King Behemoth is advised by his cunning servant, Leviathan, in the art of cheating Epimetheus, so that the three children may fall into his satanic power. Leviathan explains how easily the conscience of man may be circumvented by the virtuous professions of the wicked. It is only necessary to give a religious tone to one's actions, to disguise one's movements in a cloak of sanctity, in order to get the better of the common people. The scheme is put into practice, and works so successfully that humanity, including the "sharp and highly cultivated Athenians," is caught in the trap of the devil, who seizes the divine offspring, killing Hiero and Mythos. The same fate awaits Messias, whose death would mean the disappearance of divinity for all eternity, but fortunately the despised Prometheus is remembered by his brother. Epimetheus sees now that in driving Prometheus into banishment he has punished only himself, and, through the intermediary of the goddess Doxa, he recalls the wanderer. Prometheus defeats the forces of evil with their own weapons, not being bound by any conventional weaknesses. But he no longer covets his legitimate reward, the lordship of the world. He prefers rather to reveal his nobility and strength of soul by a supreme act of courage, when he embraces his brother, and lifts him up out of the depths where shame and despair had plunged him. Epimetheus, having strangled the conscience which played him false, is now fit to soar above the earth with his brother soul Prometheus.

Such, briefly summarized, is the action of Carl Spitteler's prose epic, which lay forgotten during the twenty-five years that saw the rise to fame of the author of *Zarathustra*. No *résumé* can give an adequate idea of the beauty and profundity of this work, in which the transvaluation of all values was preached to a generation as yet unfamiliar with the Nietzschean doctrine. From the beginning we find that extraordinary faculty which has enabled the poet to clothe the most abstract ideas in a garment of delicate imagery, and to breathe life into the teachings of an abstruse mysticism. Where Nietzsche is the poetic philosopher, Spitteler is the philosophic poet, in the best sense of the word. The former was the evangelist of a new gospel, the latter has aimed solely at the creation of beauty, without a thought for his didactic mission. Spitteler is content to please, while Nietzsche's purpose was to convince, and herein lies the fundamental difference between Zarathustra and Prometheus. The one announces a potential superman, the other represented man at his highest and best, when his actions accord with the dictates of a noble soul. Yet Spitteler's offering, like the gift of Pandora, was unrecognized by more than a discerning handful, which included Boecklin, Brahms, Conrad Ferdinand Meyer, and Gottfried Keller.

The approval and encouragement of the few, while it strengthened the poet's faith in himself, did not obtain for him a hearing in Germany, so Spitteler was compelled to earn his living, as "a schoolmaster in a small town, burdened with thirty hours of teaching in the week." In these circumstances, the greater part of his maturity was passed, until a measure of recognition for the work so produced brought release from such drudgery. A couple of years after

the publication of *Prometheus und Epimetheus* his
second book followed, under the title *Extramundana*.
The writing of the earlier book had developed in
Spitteler a sense of mythology which was not part
of his original epic genius: "Even as a twenty-two-
year-old student I was convinced that epic poetry
was to be my life-work," he said once, in reply to
those who had argued that the epical quality of
Prometheus und Epimetheus indicated it as the work
of mature age. But the thirteen years devoted to
its composition brought with them an expansion of
his talent which was expressed in his second volume.
Extramundana was nothing less than an attempt to
rewrite the story of the creation in verse. The author
has since dismissed the experiment with a contemptuous reference which does not altogether do justice
to its many fine pages. Nevertheless, his criticism
of a too elaborate allegory, "cold and rhetorical,"
refers to much that will drive away all but his more
enthusiastic admirers. There is a banality of thought,
and a carelessness of form, which partly confirm
Spitteler's description of the book as a piece of
"hasty botch work."

For six years, from 1883 to 1889, no publisher could
be found to accept the manuscripts of a poet who refused to write for the age of realism in which he lived.
Finally, however, Spitteler persuaded his original
publisher in Jena to issue *Schmetterlinge*, his first
essay in rhyming verse. The transition to this form
from the beautiful rhythmic prose of *Prometheus und
Epimetheus* was the blank verse of *Extramundana*.
So uncertain was Spitteler of his power of versifica-
tion that he struggled for a long time with a rhyming
dictionary, yet no trace of such labor will be found
in these graceful poems, whose actual subjects are
the butterflies of Switzerland. They have more,
however, than an appeal to the poetic entomologist,

for they give us the first of those memories of childhood and youth which Spitteler later developed in
his prose stories. As soon as the poet sought his
themes in his own country the Swiss element, as
distinct from the German, became noticeable in his
work, and *Schmetterlinge* served as a natural prelude
to the four volumes of prose which now followed.
The national characteristics are as unmistakable in
Carl Spitteler as in Gottfried Keller, whose *Zürcher
Novellen* and *Leute von Seldwyla* could not have been
written by a German.

In their order of publication these four works are,
Friedli der Kolderi, *Gustav*, *Konrad der Leutnant*, and
Die Mädchenfeinde. Although not published until
1907, the last-mentioned belongs to the same period
as its three predecessors, all having been written
between 1890 and 1900. Spitteler has modestly
termed them "experiments," made in pursuit of
his plan to leave no field of literature untouched, but
their success justifies what must seem to be a rather
doubtful form of literary ambition. The author
urges the example of the painters of the Renaissance
in support of his theory that the artist should learn
by experimentation. "Development comes through
essaying and mastering precisely those domains of
art which lie farthest from one's talent." As he thus
states it, the theory is open to obvious objections,
which are not answered by the undeniably fortunate
results of Spitteler's own efforts. If the prose form
of these stories was not akin to the mood of the epic
poet, their content responded to a natural impulse
toward self-expression. Their composition may have
imposed the discipline of an apprenticeship, but
their inspiration was wholly personal and national.

Friedli der Kolderi, his first work to be published
in Switzerland, consisted of seven of the most varied
examples of prose narrative, four "feuilletons," two

fairy tales, and the "study," which gives its title to
the book. This last is by far the most remarkable,
being an interpretation of Swiss character after the
manner of the modern Russians. As a sketch of
folk life it may rank with the best that Keller has
written. It is composed of the simplest elements,
yet, in its own way, it leaves an impression as lasting
as any of the Russian story-tellers.

The idyllic little tale, *Gustav*, and the children's
story, *Die Mädchenfeinde*, are both charming elabo-
rations of autobiographical material. The young student of medicine who has failed at his examinations,
to the great distress of his parents, returns to his home
cherishing the dream of becoming a great composer.
His philistine relations have little confidence in his
genius, but one of his compositions eventually reaches
a distinguished musician and all ends well, as befits
an "idyl"—another of Spitteler's experiments. If
the gods have been less prompt to intervene in the
reality of his own case than in the picture of *Gustav*,
the personal interest of the story is not thereby diminished. The precocious misogynists of *Die Mädchenfeinde* are the occasion of a delightful picture of the
child world, in which the problems of existence are
faced with the same, if smaller, weapons as afterward serve in the struggles of manhood. It was
characteristic of Spitteler that the *nouvelle* should
have suggested to him this exposition of the psychology of childhood. Experimenting with a new
genre, he succeeded in achieving the maximum of
external dissimilarity, while preserving the fundamental identity of method employed by its recognized exponents.

A volume of satirical verse, *Literarische Gleichnisse*,
preceded Spitteler's next and most important essay
in contemporary prose fiction, *Konrad der Leutnant*.
In this book the author undertook to meet his ene-

mies the Realists on their own ground. We have seen how he suffered from the possession of a talent utterly opposed to the literary fashion of his time. While all his Swiss stories approximate to the demands of realism, they nevertheless failed to satisfy the critics, owing to their inherently poetic and idealistic qualities. Finally, Spitteler decided to surprise his literary opponents by providing them with a new formula, which he illustrated in *Konrad der Leutnant.* "Before writing another epic I wanted to prove to myself that I could employ even the Naturalistic style, if I so desired. I chose the difficult form of the 'description' (*Darstellung*), in order to make my prose writing less easy." The subtitle of *Konrad der Leutnant* is *Eine Darstellung*, which term is defined by the author as follows: "By 'a description' I understand a special form of prose narrative, with a peculiar purpose, and a particular style which serves as a means to that end. The object is to obtain the highest possible intensity of action, the means are: unity of person, unity of perspective, consecutive unity of time." In other words, the principal character is introduced immediately the story opens, and remains throughout the central figure, only those events being related of which he is conscious, and as he becomes aware of them. The action develops uninterruptedly, hour by hour, no interval being passed over as unimportant or unessential. Naturally, such a narrative can cover only a comparatively short period of time.

The story of Lieutenant Conrad is told in the space of twelve hours, and relates how the young officer comes into conflict with the jealous authority of his father, the proprietor of the Peacock Inn at Herrlisdorf. From the beginning of the day until its close Conrad is engaged in a constant effort to assert himself against the domination of the old man, who will not recognize his son's right to control the affairs of the inn, in spite of his own manifest incapacity. With patient skill Spitteler unfolds the series of inconsequential thoughts and actions which bring out the clash of wills between these two, and as the incidents become increasingly violent a close atmosphere of suppressed passion envelops the scene as the presage of a storm. Every moment the tension grows, until at length the emotional pressure is relieved by the necessity of quelling two rioting factions who have met at the inn through the owner's obstinacy in not heeding Conrad's warning and advice. The fight, however, gives the latter the chance he has sought of imposing his authority, for he alone is young and vigorous enough to quell the disturbance. At last his moment of self-assertion comes and is reluctantly recognized by the father, but before he has fully realized this rehabilitation Conrad is murdered. One of the rioters thus revenges his forcible expulsion from the inn, in addition to paying off an earlier score incurred in a personal quarrel with the lieutenant.

In its bare outline *Konrad der Leutnant* offers no unusual interest, although the picture of rural manners is drawn with Spitteler's customary insight, and gives a value to the story which admirers of Keller will appreciate. Perfect is the characterization Kathri, who is the female counterpart of Conrad, and to whom a natural affinity draws him in the course of that tragic day. The whole household lives before us, as the members in turn cross the path of the central character, each contributing to the unfolding of his destiny. But the main interest of the book is, of course, technical. The mechanism of the *Darstellung* itself will suffice to hold the reader, apart from the intrinsic worth of the narrative. Spitteler has certainly given an ingenious demonstration of the logical development of literary Naturalism. The disadvantages of the method need hardly be emphasized, for we have long since seen the fallacy of the theory which gave birth to the school. Not every detail in *Konrad der Leutnant* is interesting, since no life can possibly be composed of uniformly valuable elements. The author, like all Realists, labors under the obligation of completeness, which imposes a vast fund of unprofitable material. Spitteler, however, is here frankly an experimentalist, and is entitled to some concessions to the success of his experiment. It is not improbable that he wished to effect a *reductio ad absurdum* of the Naturalistic doctrine, while incidentally proving his capacity as a Realist. The temptation to translate this book into French was obvious, its appeal being more popular than that of the other Swiss stories. Yet, while welcoming this effort to make Spitteler more widely known, one cannot but regret the choice of an interesting, but unrepresentative, volume.

The year 1898, which saw the publication of *Konrad der Leutnant*, was marked by the appearance of a work which came as near to finding immediate recognition as is possible for Spitteler. *Lachende Wahrheiten*, a collection of critical essays, was, strange to say, the occasion of this unusual experience. Most of these had appeared in the German *Kunstwart*, and in the *Berner Bund*, whose literary editor, the late J. V. Widmann, had been Spitteler's earliest friend and critic. All his life Widmann stood forward as a champion of Swiss culture, and he died with the reputation of being one of the foremost critics in the world of German letters, his fame having passed beyond the confines of his own country. His appreciation and encouragement of Spitteler must be remembered amongst his chief claims upon the gratitude of his countrymen. But he was not alone in his estimate of Spitteler's merits as an essayist. Nietzsche had pushed admiration to the point of inviting the Swiss writer to collaborate with him in *The Case of Wagner*. These "laughing truths" revealed Spitteler as a critic who knew how to combine a gentle freedom of manner with considerable æsthetic originality and a graceful style. The essays are *causeries*, rather than formal expositions of literary doctrine, although the remarkable discussion of the ballad leaves nothing to be desired from the point of view of exact knowledge. Stimulating as his theories appear, their translation into practice was more helpful, as when Spitteler's next book, *Balladen*, was published—after a long silence—in 1905.

The following year Spitteler made public a work which undoubtedly belongs to the same period as *Prometheus und Epimetheus*. In spite of the twenty-five years' interval, *Imago* stands in evident relationship to the author's first volume, with whose second edition its appearance coincided. The book is thinly disguised autobiography, and within the limits imposed by the fiction it may be regarded as a fairly reliable account of the events which attended the creation of *Prometheus und Epimetheus*. Victor, the young poet, returns home to a little provincial town where his former love, Theuda, has since settled down as the eminently respectable wife of a typical German professor. An intensely sensitive, imaginative temperament, Victor had renounced marriage for the sake of his muse, but he is filled with a desire to shame the woman who preferred the comforts of bourgeois domesticity to emulating his own act of self-immolation. Needless to say, "Frau Doktor Treugott Wyss" does not feel in the least perturbed when confronted by her idealistic admirer, and the effect of this disappointment upon the overwrought fantasy of the poet provides the leading motive of

the story. Victor loves Theuda all the more because
of his renunciation, but his imagination has made of
her an unreal image, quite unlike the Frau Doktor,
and increasingly identified with the poet's muse.
Spitteler describes how these two beings, the real
and the imaginary, alternately project themselves
into the visionary's inner consciousness, until finally
they are as one. Theuda, whom Victor had bitterly
nicknamed "Pseuda," is at last identified with
Imago, "the supernatural being of symbolic origin,"
who had come into the poet's imaginative world as a
personification of his first love and inspiration. He
finds, however, that his emotion toward Theuda is not
spiritual, as the transformation implied, and when
he at length reaches a compromise in this conflict of
sentiment, it is only to find that Theuda feels nothing
more than pity for him. He flees away to solitude,
and, as the fruit of this prolonged spiritual crisis, he
writes his masterpiece.

"An acute crisis of the soul" was the reason alleged
by Spitteler for his decision to publish *Prometheus
und Epimetheus* after thirteen years brooding over
it. The choice of "Felix Tandem" as a pseudonym
indicated the nature of his emotion at having emerged
from a spiritual conflict which had given him the
power to affirm his artistic personality. The points
of resemblance between that early work and *Imago*
extend beyond the identity of mood out of which
they were written. There is a similarity of rhythm
in the prose of both which is not found elsewhere in
Spitteler, and a like tendency to clothe emotional
impulses in a personal form. But the book has an
interest quite distinct from its relation to the poet's
entry into literature. As a novel of contemporary
manners in provincial Germany, *Imago* deserves to
be read by all who can share Spitteler's almost
savage delight in candid analysis. The long chapter

entitled, "In the Hell of Gemütlichkeit," is an exposure of essentially German conditions. Even that virtue of *Gemütlichkeit*, which Germany's worst enemies and best friends agree in conceding to her, does not soften the heart of Spitteler. He has many bitter things to say of the pseudo-culture of such typical institutions as the "Idealia *Verein*," and his comments upon the social distractions of the middle classes are as unfriendly as his reflections upon "the dogma of the mystery of German womanhood." At bottom Spitteler's strictures are directed against the provincial philistine as he universally exists, but the German setting of *Imago* lends a special piquancy to his satire at the present time. Once again the ideas of Nietzsche and Spitteler coincide, in this commentary on German society, which has inexplicably escaped the attention of translators.

Spitteler's masterpiece, the great epic, *Olympischer Frühling*, appeared in four volumes between 1900 and 1905, and, after ceaseless revision, received its final form in 1910. In what may be accepted as the definite version, the poem consists of five parts, divided into thirty-three cantos, in rhymed iambic couplets. From the wealth of epic material which had haunted Spitteler from his youth *Olympischer Frühling* alone achieved adequate expression. His first conception, *Johannes*, "a romantic epopee," has neither been published nor altogether abandoned by the author; unlike *Atlantis* and *Die Hochzeit des Theseus*, which were both adapted to ballad form and included in *Balladen*. It is a remarkable testimony to the intellectual quality of the man and the writer, that Spitteler should have devoted practically a lifetime to the creation of such a work. *Olympischer Frühling* is not a lifeless reconstruction of antiquity, but an original mythology, into which the poet has breathed the life of his own spirit. The classical nomenclature is preserved; we read of Zeus, Hera, Apollo, and Dionysos, but they are human gods and very close to our age. In fact, a dissociation of ideas is necessary before we can comprehend these figures who, in spite of their names, are moderns, living in a world familiar with the cinematograph, the steam-engine, and the airship! The classical student must rid himself of his preconceptions, if he would avoid mistaking for anachronisms these elements in Spitteler's mythology.

Kronos and his companions, the representatives of an obsolete religion, are cast into Hades by Ananke, who calls upon the new gods to succeed them in Olympus. Apollo, Zeus, Eros, Hermes, and Poseidon are those chosen to compete for the hand of Hera, and a series of trials must decide who is to wed her and reign over the world. Zeus, for his insolence, is at once excluded from the contest, and chance seems to favor Apollo, yet where Ananke rules, there is no place for the god of light and goodness. The judges are unanimous in their decision as to Apollo's superiority, but on the last day of the contest Zeus, by force and craft, seizes the throne and enforces recognition of his authority. Later he seeks Apollo in the mountains, and appeals to him to lighten the burden of the world governed by violence and crime. Zeus has the equipment of the true *Realpolitiker*, he is domineering and unscrupulous, yet he confesses his need of an alliance with Apollo:

"Er sprach. Mit diesem Schieden friedlich und versöhnt,
Er, der die Welt beherrscht und der, der sie verschönt."

While the first two books are thus concerned with the development of the main narrative, the voyage of the new gods from Hades to Olympus and the wooing of Hera, the third and fourth are rather in the nature of interludes. Moira, the fateful daughter of Ananke,

grants the world a season of springtime, which shall
last so long as there is peace between Zeus and Hera.
During this interval of peace the gods are free to
visit the earth and to mingle in the lives of mortal
men. Their experiences furnish Spitteler with a
number of episodes where the serious and the burlesque, the tragic and the pleasant, alternate to the
greater glory of the poet's exuberant fancy and brilliant imagination. *Apollo the Discoverer*, *Hermes the
Deliverer*, or *Dionysos the Seer*—it is hard to decide
which of the twelve cantos is the finest, but these
three are enough to vindicate the genius of the
author. The apotheosis of Apollo in the first-mentioned canto has been greatly admired, yet who could
resist the charm of the fourth book with its narrative
of Aphrodite's adventures? Excellent satire is this
account of Aphrodite's sojourn on earth, where she
becomes ever more involved in human activities,
and finally believes her power over mankind warrants
her leading a revolt against the domination of Zeus.
The humorous element is developed in such incidents
as the visit of the goddess and her naked nymphs to
the town hall, where the worthy councillors first admire the statuesque beauty of the group, until pious
horror is aroused by the discovery that the figures are
living. Characteristic is the plan of Aphrodite to
lead a procession of mankind, as the Pied Piper of
Hamelin led the children, for the amusement of the
deities in Olympus. This levity is too much for
Ananke, who paralyzes the activities of Aphrodite
by a stroke whose simplicity is that of genius. A
downpour of rain forces her to seek shelter in a hay
barn, where the most grotesque accident occurs, in
confirmation of the dictum, "None can be a god when
it rains!" Ananke then sows the seeds of a distrust
of Zeus in the mind of Hera, and "the fête of the
world's springtime" is at an end.

The fifth and last book of *Olympischer Frühling* opens with the awakening of Zeus to the duties of his kingship. Calling the gods together, he confronts them with an enigma, to which they may find, if they can, an answer. Several perfect theories are advanced to justify human existence, but, alas, none of them is true! Zeus descends among men in search of a solution, but in vain. The universal respect for the paraphernalia of his authority, rather than for himself, convinces him that Aphrodite was right in saying that she alone was a justification of life. In anger and disappointment he is about to destroy the world, but refrains at the intercession of Pallas and Gorgo. In a splendid vision Zeus sees the world redeemed by justice, and the whole animal kingdom rejoicing at the triumph of Man, become Lord of Creation. Zeus is still sceptical, but resolves to make a supreme test by sending Herakles down to earth as the forerunner of the Superman. Meanwhile Hera, the only mortal deity, is haunted by the fear of death and tries by every means to ward off her impending fate. Denied her hope, she resolves to commit some evil deed before she dies, and Herakles is her victim. Her gift to him, as he starts on his journey earthward, is a cynical revelation of the destiny which awaits him. "The enemy of falsehood and the opponent of mob cowardice and hypocrisy," Herakles counts upon the gratitude and love of the best among men. Hera disillusions him with the truth, that he will not only live lonely and misunderstood, but will be mocked and despised for his "soft-hearted foolishness." Herakles does not allow himself to be deterred. Upheld by the blessing of Zeus and his own proud courage, he enters upon his earthly mission.

No summary, however detailed, can do justice to this beautiful work, whose place is with, but above,

Wieland's *Oberon* and Klopstock's *Messias*. Carl Spitteler has effectively disposed of the theory that epic poetry is possible only to a young people. *Olympischer Frühling* is a demonstration of arguments advanced in *Lachende Wahrheiten*, when, in the essay *Das verbotene Epos*, the poet combated the judgment which excluded the epic from modern literature. With wonderful skill and imagination Spitteler has combined the elements of humor and thought, of action and song, so that, for all its length, the poem is as diversified and as interesting as the epopees of the classical age. A deep note of pessimism runs through this, as through all his works, but it is not the bitter despair of mere personal disillusion, and just suffices to give *Olympischer Frühling* the mark of contemporary philosophy. Moreover, in the second version, the key of resolution in the face of experience is made more perceptible by the rewriting of the last canto, which describes the lofty faith of Herakles in his task of regeneration. The despondent nihilism of the earlier edition has been abandoned.

Spitteler's style is absolutely his own, being an expression in the German language of the spirit most remote from that which we know as Teuton. His idiom is national in its affection for the strong accents of that older tongue which survives on the lips of German-speaking Swiss, for Spitteler is never afraid to draw upon the verbal treasure of his own country. Here, indeed, we have a clew to the fundamental difference between the author of *Olympischer Frühling* and his German contemporaries. Carl Spitteler is Swiss, and as such he shares the privilege of Switzerland to serve as the point of fusion between Germanic and Latin culture. The Swiss spirit has been moulded by these two dissimilar linguistic and intellectual traditions, and the literature of Switzerland has always expressed this compromise. Often the result has been to render somewhat colorless the writings of men who were neither wholly French nor wholly German, but in Spitteler this compromise has found its happiest illustration. Superficially the form of his work is German, but its content is essentially Latin, and this has reacted upon the manner of its expression, giving the latter a suppleness and plasticity not characteristic of the Teutonic genius. An adequate translation of Spitteler's epic in verse is hardly conceivable, so intimate is the relation between the style and language of *Olympischer Frühling*. The poet's masterpiece must, for many reasons other than linguistic, remain the possession of a few, but not so the epic prose of *Prometheus und Epimetheus*. This remarkable work only demands a sympathetic interpreter in order that a wider audience may learn to admire, in its earliest and most original manifestation, the great genius of Carl Spitteler.

A SWISS NOVELIST: C. F. RAMUZ

THE literature of French Switzerland, like Anglo-Irish literature, dates from about the eighteenth century, and in both cases the early writers have come to be wholly identified with the more powerful neighboring country whose language they used. Rousseau and Mme. de Staël have been annexed by France, just as Goldsmith and Swift have been claimed by England. The note of Swiss nationality was heard for the first time in Philippe Bridel's *Poésies Helvétiennes*, which appeared just a few years before the birth of Thomas Moore, who was the first of Ireland's national poets to write in English. Le doyen Bridel, as he is called, may be considered the father of French-Swiss literature, for it was he who first revealed the consciousness of a distinctive Helvetian tradition embracing the German and French elements in the composition of the nation. He aroused in his compatriots an intelligent interest in their country and its history and tried to give literary expression to their legends, folklore and stories. He resembles the Irishman, Samuel Ferguson, whose part in the Irish literary revival was somewhat similar. Both writers tried to serve the two masters of history and poetry, to the prejudice of their actual poetic achievement. Philippe Bridel's collection of *Les Étrennes Hélvetiques*, a veritable repository of national lore, verse and prose, history and biography, criticism and anecdote, is more important than his verse. By a coincidence, it was completed just when Moore's *Irish Melodies* came to remind Ireland of her own national treasures, which were in danger of being forgotten since the decline of Gaelic.

Romanticism came into French literature largely
under the impulse of Mme. de Staël, and Swiss literature is greatly indebted to the romantic movement.
A notable figure was Juste Olivier, who, though
resident in Paris, turned to the folk-songs and legends
of the Swiss countryside, and he succeeded even in
using the old poetic forms still preserved in *le pays
romand*. It is this traditional folk element in his
poetry which survives, while his formal, imitative
work is forgotten. His regionalism deprived Juste
Olivier of any permanent success in France, where he
was condemned to play the part of a mere provincial.
How humiliating that part was may be seen in his
correspondence with his great friend Sainte-Beuve.
His contemporary, Etienne Eggis, the last of the
Swiss romantics, and companion of Maxime du Camp
and Arsène Houssaye, was more fortunate. Eggis
enjoyed some fame both in France and Switzerland,
and Jules Janin described him as a "poète gallo-
allemand," a term which aptly sums up the characteristics of Swiss literature. Eggis was an interesting
combination of Musset and Heine, with the passionate melancholy of the other. Granted the German
origins of the Romantic movement, it is not surprising that Switzerland should more easily respond to it
than France, where its fundamental racial qualities
conflicted with the essentially Latin tradition of
French classicism.

While a definite national literature was slowly
developing, Switzerland continued, like Ireland, to
produce writers who were not particularly identified
with the land of their birth. Alexandre Vinet, the
Protestant Pascal, and Frédéric Amiel were the two
more important Swiss contributions to French literature in the middle of the nineteenth century. Amiel's
celebrated *Journal Intime* is a classic even in English,
and its profound note of Protestantism, which stamps

the author's nationality, doubtless explains its appeal in England and America. It is perhaps not so well known that Amiel was one of the first historians of Swiss letters, for in 1849 he published *Le Mouvement Litteraire dans la Suisse Romande*. The contemporary work of Cherbuliez, the novelist, had little trace of the author's origins except a truly Genevese spirit of cosmopolitanism. More significant is the poet and critic, Eugène Rambert, whose *Ecrivains Nationaux* appeared in 1874 and greatly stimulated the sense of literary independence which Switzerland needed. Rambert was so devoted to this task that he refused to join the staff of *La Revue des Deux Mondes* because that would involve the sacrifice of his ideals for Swiss literature. "Absolutely unintelligent hostility to everything not Paris" was, he found, a condition of being accepted by that review. "Obliged to choose between apparent success and what I consider essential to my originality, I prefer to be myself." Thus he admirably defines the struggle which at all times confronts the writer in a small country whose literature is written in the language of a powerful neighbor.

Edouard Rod is probably the best-known French-Swiss writer of modern times. Like Rambert, he refused to sacrifice his nationality to success in France. He would not become a naturalized French citizen in order to be elected a member of the Academy. Having demonstrated his capacity to challenge the French novelists on their own ground, as in *La Vie Privée de Michel Teissier*, he returned to Switzerland, where he wielded an influence on the contemporary literature of the country which was enhanced by the prestige of his work abroad. When he died in 1910, a flourishing literary movement had grown up under his inspiration and encouragement. It is to that movement that we owe C. F. Ramuz, one of the most arresting figures in contemporary French fiction.

Charles Ferdinand Ramuz, who was born in Lausanne in 1878, is one of the group of young French Swiss intellectuals who founded the *Voile Latine* movement at Geneva in the autumn of 1904. At that time Edouard Rod was the only Swiss author of more than local fame, and his reputation, like that of Cherbuliez before him, was essentially French, although in his later years he returned to Switzerland and associated himself more closely with the intellectual life of his own country. Ramuz and his friends, while agreeing with Rod's frank criticism of Swiss literature for its dulness, its provinciality, and its incurable moralizing, could not accept him as their leader, for he was precisely the type of Parisianized Swiss against which the *Voile Latine* group protested. Their avowed task was very similar to that of W. B. Yeats and his associates in Ireland thirty years ago. They wanted the art of Switzerland to be national, and they wished to set up æsthetic standards in place of the facile judgments of a public which accepted local celebrities for moral and patriotic reasons but always looked to Paris for serious work.

The first number of the *Voile Latine* appeared in October, 1904, shortly after Ramuz had published his first book, a sheaf of poems collected under the title of *Le Petit Village*. Amongst the other contributors who have since become well known were Gonzague de Reynold, the critic of the movement and recent biographer of Baudelaire, and Henry Spiess, a distinguished and delicate poet, whose work, with that of Ramuz, is the chief accomplishment of this renaissance of French-Swiss literature. Very soon the review attracted all the best talents, Louis Dumur, Madame Burnat-Provins, and Robert de Traz, who now edits *La Revue de Genève*. It ran until the end of 1910, and in 1914 its place was taken by *Les Cahiers Vaudois*, designed after the plan of Charles Péguy's *Cahiers de la Quinzaine*. This publication is now valuable and important, for in it Ramuz published all his work during several years: *Raison d'être*, essays half critical, half biographical; *Chansons*, a collection of poems; three major works of fiction, *La Guerre dans le haut Pays; Le Règne de l'Esprit Malin; La Guérison des Maladies*, and *Le grand Printemps*, reflections upon the war. Most of these works have not been issued in any other form. The purpose of the *Voile Latine* was to satisfy "the need of a renaissance which a few young writers of French Switzerland have felt, and to give complete freedom of self-expression to every individual." During the seven years of its existence *La Voile Latine* represented a definite movement in the direction of national tradition in art and literature, a tradition at once Helvetian and Latin, classical and modern, above all, Swiss. It turned the creative impulse toward the sources of nationality, and aimed at an art which, in all its branches, would be as truly of the soil as the mountains and chalets of Switzerland.

Although C. F. Ramuz began with the traditional little book of poems, to which he has since added *La Grande Guerre du Sondrebund* and *Chansons*, his fame rests entirely upon his work in prose fiction. His first novel, *Aline*, was published in 1905, and was followed by *Les Circonstances de la Vie* (1907), *Jean-Luc Persécuté* (1909), *Aimé Pache, Peintre Vaudois* (1911), and *La Vie de Samuel Belet* (1913). These represent a definite period in his development which seems to have terminated with the war, for since then his work has entered upon a new phase, of which *Le Règne de l'Esprit Malin*, which has been translated under the title of *The Reign of the Evil One*, is the most brilliant illustration. His first period was one of realism, in which it appeared as if a successor to Rod had been found whose genius was wholly Swiss. In an early number of the *Voile Latine*, when the eternal question was being debated as to whether there could really be a distinctively Swiss literature, Ramuz formulated the point of view from which his own position must be estimated. He reduced the rôle of French culture to one of pure æsthetics, looking to France not for ideas but for models in the art of writing French. His novels and stories are as indigenous as the strongest nationalist could wish. He is not just another French author who happened to be born in Lausanne instead of Paris. He is more intensely and exclusively Swiss than Rod; at the same time he is not a mere parochial celebrity of the chocolate and Swiss milk variety, several of whom, it so happens, have long ago been translated into English! M. Ramuz is a writer in the same category as J. M. Synge and James Joyce, an artist whose appeal is universal, though the form and content of his work bear the deepest imprint of purely local and immediate circumstance.

There is, indeed, a suggestion of Synge in the method of M. Ramuz, at least in the earlier novels of his realistic period from *Aline* to *La Vie de Samuel Belet*. They spring from the very soil of the country in which the scene is laid, and are the creations of a mind which has adapted itself with great skill to the simplicity of the folk manner. As he sits in the village inn of some Swiss hamlet, his ear notes the turns of phrase, the savory idioms of the country people. The slow rhythms of this speech possess him, and in this close contact with man and nature he gradually earns some half-forgotten legend, the fragment of an idyl or the vague tradition of a rustic tragedy. Then he has the theme of a novel, which he will proceed to elaborate in the deliberate, naïve style of the narrators, reconstructing the fable piece by piece, with scrupulous notation of every detail of time and place. The limitations of this method are obvious. There is a lack of spaciousness, of perspective, in these pictures filled with scarcely articulate figures, and where every detail is recorded with the same minute care. The art of M. Ramuz is essentially narrative and plastic, and his canvases have the charm of the Primitives. *Aline* is a little peasant romance with a tragic denouement; *Jean-Luc Persécuté* tells the story of drama of infidelity in a mountain village. In themselves they are trifles, but the author has recaptured the movement of life in them.

While those two books, together with *Nouvelles et Morceaux*, are peasant studies pure and simple, revealing in their brevity the author's method, it is in his three long novels, *Les Circonstances de la Vie* (1906), *Aimé Pache, Peintre Vaudois* (1911), and *La Vie de Samuel Belet*, that M. Ramuz has shown his greatest power. Here the technic is the same, but it is applied to the richer material of provincial manners, in a country where the small town is nearer to the village than to the city, and where the absence of large cities makes it possible to contain the whole panorama of a people's life in this framework. *Les Circonstances de la Vie* may be called the history of a Swiss Charles Bovary, the ignominious defeat of a mediocre individual by the force of circumstances as ignoble as they are implacable. Emile Magnenat, the good, respectable, commonplace notary, is the central figure. With meticulous care M. Ramuz sets this character upon the stage, describes his social background, his wedding, his family, the family clergyman, and the rest. The German Swiss servant Frieda Henneberg is the instrument of the catharsis which destroys all the second-hand morality and smug security of the family, when she establishes her domination over the man and finally ruins him. In *Aimé Pache* the same social stratum is examined, but the young artist is a more powerful character than poor Emile; his pursuit of his destiny is conscious and deliberate and he succeeds in mastering his own fate. The struggle of the artist, first against the bourgeois suspicions of his own people, his career as a student in Paris, and his painful groping toward the discovery that only by conforming to the soil of his father can he fully realize himself—such is the story.

What is of most interest in the work of C. F. Ramuz is its analysis of the French Protestant mind, and the expression in literature of an element whose absence from the literature of France must always seem a loss to English readers. M. André Gide, it is true, betrays his Huguenot origins in his writings, but only the Swiss have produced a literature in which Protestantism is an influence as all-pervading as in English. M. Ramuz has admirably preserved the Protestant note which, coupled with the familiar idiom of the country people in which he writes, lends a piquant contrast to his novels as compared with the very different atmosphere of French fiction. If the desires of the flesh are by no means a negligible part of his drama of Swiss life, how subdued and uneasy these sinners are! They have none of the abandon, or the frank animality, or the self-conscious ecstasy, of the people described by Maupassant, Flaubert, and the Goncourts. Aline and Aimé Pache, and Emile Magnenat have the inhibitions of the Calvinistic tradition in their souls. They take their pleasure as sadly as the traditional Englishman. The puritan suspicion of joy pervades the communities of town and country of which M. Ramuz has made himself the interpreter. The rhythm of folk-speech alternates with that of the Bible. In *Les Circonstances* we read:

On va longtemps dans une vallée et marcher est peut-être dur; toutefois il y a des pentes couvertes d'arbres, de la mousse, des sources fraîches, on peut se dire: "ce sera plus beau de l'autre côté." De sorte qu'il reste quand même un peu de joie au fond du cœur, laquelle excite à avancer. Mais on sort, on trouve une plaine de sel, et sait qu'aussi loin qu'on pourra aller ce sera toujours cette plaine, cette même stérilité: qu'est-ce qui nous reste? Plus rien.

The same Biblical note is heard in *Aimé Pache*, in a love scene which is quite the farthest removed from all that we are accustomed to expect in French fiction:

D'autres sont entrés dans la mort; moi j'en sors, et je me lève avec elle à la vie. Comme au temps d'Eve avant la faute,—car, toute idée de faute etait écartée d'eux. Ce fut comme au temps d'Eve couchée sous le palmier, et Adam est couché pres d'elle, et ils n'avaient point la notion du mal. Les biches venaient boire, elles étaient sans crainte. Il disait: "Es-tu là?" Elle répondait, "Je suis là." Et il reprenait: "Es-tu là?, et je sais bien que tu es là, mais répète-le-moi quand même, pour que ta voix soit aussi avec moi." Et elle disait: "Je suis là."

The style of M. Ramuz is colored by this inevitable Protestant influence which is so unlike the movement of the French prose of France. Add to that his deliberate cultivation of popular Swiss speech, which has a harshness and a lack of grace at times intolerable to the ear accustomed to the finely polished instrument of cultured French. His critics have not hesitated to warn M. Ramuz of the risk he incurs of forgetting the definite limitations of his method, and passages of an incredible slovenliness have been cited against him. In this respect his last four volumes show him to be impotent, but they have marked a new phase in his development. *Le Règne de l'Esprit*

Malin, Les Signes parmi Nous, and *La Guérison des Maladies,* were all three published by the group of *Les Cahiers Vaudois,* and to them may be added his *Terre du Ciel, La Séparation des Races, Passage du Poète* and *Présence de la Mort,* which are in the same manner. These stories are of a mystical rather than a realistic character, and suggest at times the apparently ubiquitous influence of Claudel. But M. Ramuz is faithful to his Swiss peasants, and what he gives us, for instance in *La Guérison,* is a sort of Protestant Claudelism. One prefers the human tragedy of *Aline* to the mystico-religious study of the miracle-working Marie who takes to herself the diseases of the village, until the unsympathetic authorities remove her to hospital. In *Les Signes* the author essays to give the air of mysterious portents to the threat of two sinister events, which throw their shadow over a prosperous community in war-time. The one, which is never named, is an epidemic of "Spanish influenza," the other is "bolshevism." M. Ramuz gives a vigorous and graphic description of the outbreaks of industrial warfare, but, in the end, he rolls the clouds by most conveniently, and leaves his community in the happiest of circumstances.

Terre du Ciel is a characteristic novel of his later manner in its combination of scrupulous realism in the portrayal of manners with a charming element of legend and folk-lore, testifying once more to his preoccupation with the spirit of the Vaudois countryside. Ever since *The Reign of the Evil One* an element of satire has been perceptible in his work, and here it peeps forth at the very basis of his story. The whole fable is essentially a legend, whether drawn from actual folk-lore or conceived out of the author's own imagination, telling how paradise seems to the rustic adventurers who suddenly find themselves in heaven, and deriving a peculiar savor from the style in which it is cast. C. F. Ramuz has always written a remarkable French, compounded of archaisms, folk-speech, and the idiom of his country, which differs markedly in rhythm and phrase from that of France. *Terre du Ciel* is a typical piece of his prose, awkward and lumbering, but powerful, with the movement of bodies that have been bent over the plough and are no longer supple. It is the writing of one who seems peculiarly fitted to express the mind and interpret the imagination of the peasant, who has never been completely expressed in French literature.

GERMANY

EXPRESSIONISM WITHOUT TEARS

I

WHILE Expressionism has been invading every branch of the arts, the explanatory literature on the subject has been conspicuously absent. We have had much comment and exposition in English, but no satisfactory theory and analysis of the principles underlying a development now familiar to movie fans and first-nighters no less than to connoisseurs of sculpture and painting. In German there is, of course, an already voluminous literature of Expressionism, almost entirely untranslated and for the most part unintelligible. The art of concise self-expression does not appear to be a virtue of the theorists of Expressionism.

In all the clashing array of their Teutonic polysyllables, let me give at random the titles of a handful of representative works: *Expressionismus und Architektur, Eindrückskunst und Ausdrückskunst in der Dichtung, Die Expressionistische Bewegung in der Musik, Die Bühnenkunst der Gegenwart, Natur und Expressionismus, Über Expressionismus in der Malerei,* and *Naturalismus, Idealismus, Expressionismus.* Here we find every phase of the movement with its learned exegesis, whether it be in painting, sculpture, drama, architecture, music, or literature. In this mass of commentators is there one who has provided the layman with a clew to guide him through a maze whose lines include phenomena apparently as far apart as Kandinsky and Schoenberg, *The Cabinet of Dr. Caligari* and *Masse Mensch?* There is one little book, scarcely a hundred and fifty pages of text, which deserves, at this point, to be introduced.

The work in question is concisely entitled *Expressionismus*, and the author is Hermann Bahr, novelist and dramatist, whose charming comedy, *The Concert*, may still be remembered by those who saw it in the somewhat denatured version played by Leo Ditrichstein. This is, within its limits, which do not include literature and the theatre, the clearest analysis of a movement usually obscured by the metaphysical dissertation of its friends.

Bahr began his career in the late eighties as a Naturalist, and his attitude toward the subsequent evolution from Impressionism and Symbolism to Expressionism is one of rational understanding. He is neither the high priest of a cult nor the outraged philistine of culture. He begins, indeed, with an amusing picture of the aforesaid philistine, who is determined not to be as foolish as his predecessors. The latter belonged to the type of "I don't know anything about art but I know what I like." The modern philistine remembers how Wagner was hissed, how Napoleon III indignantly turned his back on Manet's first publicly exhibited picture, how even Mahler and Strauss were denounced as mad. He does not want to appear as foolish, but instead of acquiring taste he has merely acquired fear. His relation to art rests upon fear, fear of being wrong.

Whatever pleases him, he regards as inartistic, precisely because he likes it. . . . If he must admit that something pleases him, then it must certainly be something he does not like. He knows it is a work of art, if he dislikes it. Art is what disturbs him, offends him, and seems hideous. Then he says to himself: that has exactly the same effect on me as Wagner, Ibsen, and Manet had on my parents, so in thirty years it will be recognized, and I do not want then to look like a fool!

Such, in Bahr's view, is the basis of our modern desire for whatever is new. But the Expressionists have succeeded in upsetting this ingenious equilibrium of the up-to-date philistine. At last there are works of art which arouse his indignation, but this indignation is moral, not artistic, since fear has long since taken the place of taste. It is not the taste of the spectator which revolts at pictures by Kandinsky or Marc Chagal, but his moral sense. He objects to swindlers! One does not perhaps mind being told by an expert that what looks like the picture of city roofs in a fog is a portrait of a lady with a mandolin, but one does resent the programmes and manifestoes which announce, not merely a new art, but a new religion and a new philosophy. Bahr agrees that "a programmatic artist" is a dangerous fellow, but it is not the business of artists to theorize but to create.

He calls the new painters all Expressionists, though they themselves would repudiate the term, consisting as they do, "of innumerable little sects which execrate each other." He does so for the reason that they have certain fundamental ideas in common. They turn away from Impressionism and against it. If there is any trace of realism in an Impressionistic work, they repudiate it. They unite in strenuously opposing everything that we expect of a picture if we are to accept it as a picture at all. Here the Expressionists and their opponents agree, for the latter assert that the former have done violence to truth, reality, and perception, and the former cheerfully admit their denial of everything that has hitherto been generally regarded as the essence of painting.

The history of all painting is the history of seeing. Technic changes when vision changes, and only because it has changed. Technic changes in order to catch up with the changed manner of seeing. But man's vision is determined by his relation to the universe . . . so the history of all painting is the history of philosophy. As soon as we learn to distinguish between the interior and exterior world, we have to choose between certain alternatives.

We may either take flight from the world within ourselves, or from ourselves out into the world, or we may hover on the border line between the two: these are the three attitudes which man may assume toward phenomena. In primitive times the first of these three was man's choice. He fled from nature and created an art that was unreal and unnatural. The Greeks brought mankind back to nature, and found divinity not in the depths of the human soul but in the heart of nature. They created the classic man who felt himself to be an integral part of all nature. In the Impressionist Bahr finds the perfection of the classic type, for he goes a step farther and omits man's share in the appearance of things lest that appearance be thereby distorted.

A sharp distinction is drawn by Bahr between the physical and the mental vision. "The eye of the body is passive toward everything; it receives, and whatever is impressed upon it by external charm is more powerful than the activity of the eye itself, more powerful than what it grasps of that outward charm. On the other hand, the eye of the mind is active and merely uses as the material of its own power the reflections of reality." In the rising generation, Bahr continues, "the mind is strongly asserting itself. It is turning away from exterior to interior life, and listening to the voices of its own secrets; it again believes that man is not merely an echo of the world, but its creator, that he is as strong, at least, as it is. Such a generation will repudiate Impressionism and demand an art which sees with the eye of the mind. Expressionism is the natural successor of Impressionism, again one-sided, again denying one side of human nature: again a half-truth."

Bahr compares the Expressionist painter with the musician, of whom we do not ask that he shall reproduce sounds heard in the outside world, but that he shall produce out of himself what he hears within himself. Expressionist painting is "eye-music." In order to have such vision one has merely to conceive of an object so powerfully that it impresses itself upon the eye. "As soon as the waves of our inner life beat upon the eye, we *see* our inner life, as we *hear* it when its waves strike the ear." Impressionism made our vision purely passive and receptive, an ear, so to speak, while Expressionism has made of it a mouth. "The ear is silent; the Impressionist did not allow the soul to speak. The mouth is deaf; the Expressionist cannot hear the world." Both Expressionism and Impressionism are alike in that they lack "the ever-living tie that unites the eyes of the body with those of the mind." That ideal combination has existed "in individual great masters, in isolated works, which have always been misunderstood, but it has never been achieved by a whole epoch."

The attitude of the general public toward Expressionism in all its forms becomes more easily comprehensible in the light of this theory of mental and physical vision. "When painters in whom the eyes of the mind are dominant present their work to a public that is accustomed to rely upon the eyes of the body, or vice versa, there results an inevitable confusion. Those who have never observed their own vision are inclined to regard the eyes as windows through which the world penetrates. Furthermore, we have been educated in classic art, an art which is turned outward and draws into itself the exterior world. Impressionism is simply the last word in classic art, perfecting and completing it by increasing to the maximum our power of external vision while suppressing as much as possible the faculty of interior vision."

The Expressionist describes what he sees within himself, and it is no criticism of that vision to say that it represents nothing that the spectator has seen in the real world. The Ninth Symphony is not a conglomeration of sounds heard in actual life, but the notation of harmonies in the soul of Beethoven and audible only to his ear.

Like all critics and commentators who have shown any real comprehension of Expressionistic art, Hermann Bahr sees in it the inescapable expression of this age of transition. Man is again in search of his own soul; he is in revolt against the passivity which has made him a mere tool of his own work, an instrument of the machine age. "Never was there a period shaken with such horrors, such mortal terrors. Never was the world filled with so deathly a silence. Never was man so small, never so terrified. Never was joy so elusive, and freedom so near unto death. Now our need cries out. Man cries out for his soul. The age is one vast cry of need, and art has joined in the cry, shouting into the darkness for help, for the soul. That is Expressionism."

The circumstances explain the drastic methods of Expressionism. The conditions approximate to those of primitive man. "People hardly realize how close to the truth they are when they make fun of pictures and say they look as if they had been 'painted by savages.' The industrial era has driven us back to barbarism . . . and we must be barbarous if the future of humanity is to be saved from our fate. As primitive man crawled into himself out of fear of nature, so we are in flight from a 'civilization' which destroys the human soul." Primitive man discovered in his own courage a weapon of defence against the dangers and terrors that beset him. Similarly, "we have found within ourselves an ultimate power that cannot be destroyed, and in our fear we have drawn upon it, and set it against 'civilization,' holding it tremblingly before us. It is the sign of the unknown within us, on which we rely to save us; it is the sign of the imprisoned spirit trying to break its fetters; it is the cry of alarm of all terrified souls—such is Expressionism."

II

The gentle and persuasive method of a Hermann Bahr in expounding the theory of German Expressionist painting is far to seek in the writing of those who have interpreted the literature and drama of the movement. The Poetics of Expressionism lack conspicuously the sublime simplicity of Aristotle; they are violently iconoclastic or incredibly metaphysical—rarely clear and intelligible. Perhaps one of the chief reasons for this is the fact that, while Expressionist painting and sculpture have found impartial interpreters, that is to say, men like Bahr, trained, professional critics, literature and drama have mainly relied upon the expositions of poets, novelists, and playwrights.

These gentlemen, needless to say, combine the rash enthusiasm of the uncritical mind with the passionate desire to write their own apologia. Apart from these, we have the professors, who have juggled impressively with the terminology of metaphysics, compared with which the style of Kant's *Critique of Pure Reason* is as limpid as that of an American publicity expert. If any of the quotations I may make seem to lack definiteness, I solemnly invoke the peculiar quality of the Teutonic texts, which appear, if anything, rather simplified in my translations.

The first principle of the new Poetics is that before Expressionism there was nothing. Otto Flake, one of the leaders of Expressionist fiction, has declared that, without Expressionism, he cannot conceive art. "I look at a Renaissance picture, a Dutch, or an Impressionist canvas, and I discover that I cannot

and will not see such things again." Another theorist
remarks, in the characteristic jargon of the school,
that "Expressionism was essentially a revolution on
behalf of the elemental. . . . Nothing is more pure,
more moral, more ethical than the representation of
elementals. The elemental has no truck with compromise. It exists in, for, and of itself; it is." The
elemental can be reached only by way of the abstract, by emancipation from the surrounding world,
from the chain of cause and effect, from everything
that phenomena in time and space have made of
man. Consequently, the Naturalists and Impressionists are scorned, because they professed to explain
man by reference to his milieu, his heredity, to his
appearance under the influence of light and air.
Franz Werfel, one of the most notable of the dramatists, has elaborated the dogma that it is not the
world that makes us, but it is we who create the
world. "The world," he says, "begins in man, and
nothing is more beautiful than to live through the
time when the world is born for the first time, the
age of the Primitives, the childhood of nations and
individuals."

Wedekind, who is admitted to be the precursor of
the Expressionistic drama, embodied in *The Awakening of Spring* the tragedy inherent in this conception
of the universe. That tragedy begins when the dis-
crepancy between the subjective and objective world
is realized, when what is created and existing confronts the potential creator, the man in the act of
willing and becoming. This divergence between the
two worlds is the thesis of Hasenclever's play *The
Son*, where the boy revolts against the father, and in
Otto Flake's novel *No and Yes*, in which the contrast is conceived as between the spheres of contemplation and of action. The dilemma is resolved for
the Expressionists by affirming the will to action,

the will to become. In Nietzschean parlance, they are Dionysians. Thus Werfel prays: "Come, Holy Ghost, thou Creator, and smash the marble of our form." In the words of another exponent of the theory, "One cannot say that Expressionism sets content above form. It turns the form into the content. The external is intensified and the elemental triumphs over the chaos that has reigned before."

What is this elemental? It is movement, and so it is claimed that "Expressionism has discovered movement, and knows that even the quietness and poise and the vast inertia of the world and destiny are simply movements." In the last analysis, it is merely the recognition of an aboriginal form when the Expressionist says of his universe: In the beginning was movement, "for the word is movement, and in the beginning was the word!" The verb is the word that expresses movement and so Werfel concludes that "in poetry the burden of movement is thrown upon the verb," from which it follows that there will come a "de-substantivization" of the world, "an era of verbs, of change, when reality is dissolved and leaves the substantive to dwell in the verb. When that time comes, to bloom will be more real than a flower, and the eye will have less reality than smiling, weeping, looking." All this is quite simple when it is understood that verbs are the Essence of Expressionist poetry. Nine to a single sentence is not unusual!

Since the universe, by definition, is subjective, a projection of the ego, there are no types in the literature of Expressionism, only individuals. Every life is a unique event, and is complete in itself. Contrary to the classical conception, the Expressionists hold that there can be no eternal verities embodied in representative human figures. Expressionism is the revolt of the individual against the similar and recurrent. Therefore this literature is esoteric. Werfel proclaims the all-too-convenient fact boldly. "Literature will become more and more esoteric, and will live in circles, groups, and coteries, because it can no longer bear the panbureaucratic existence of social abstraction." Another of the initiated says: "Poetry is an expression of the esoteric, by a small circle for a small circle." Logic and psychology are superfluous, for these presuppose a certain homogeneity.

"Cast to the winds motives, logic and justice. Write plays full of illogical surprises, of unjustifiable circumstances"—such is the exhortation addressed to the Expressionist dramatists by an adept. It may relieve the minds of those who have had a foretaste of this most popular branch of Expressionistic art. The poets have never reached the wide public which knows the work of Georg Kaiser, Hanns Johst, Franz Werfel, Fritz von Unruh, Walter Hasenclever, and Ernst Toller, to mention names which have reached even the English-speaking world. The novelists such as Alfred Döblin, Kasimir Edschmid and Otto Flake have not even penetrated to those self-consciously modern reviews in London and New York where their work would more naturally have a place than that of the relatively venerable warriors of the older generation whose names are so proudly listed in incongruous company. The Expressionist drama, therefore, deserves particular mention in such an essay as this.

To Wedekind, and the later Strindberg of *Towards Damascus*, the theatre of Expressionism is usually traced. The first Expressionist play in Germany was *The Beggar*, by Johannes Sorge, which appeared in 1912, and just before the war submerged the whole Expressionist movement in a swamp of pacifism, from which it has not yet entircly disengaged itself. Hasenclever wrote *The Son* and Kaiser, *The Burghers of Calais*. Georg Kaiser's *Morn to Midnight* dates from 1916, and the bulk of the plays belong to the period of the war and its aftermath. Prior to that the drama of Expressionism, while presenting the essential features of the species, was more or less comprehensible. Sorge's pioneering work, *The Beggar*, is marked by the now familiar combination of realism and symbolism, and by the then technical innovation whereby groups of characters are made to appear and disappear by the manipulation of lights, while verse and prose are intermingled in the course of the dialogue.

The comparative simplicity of the early Expressionists is gone. Now we have chaotic and amazing fantasies, where the real and imaginary, the profound and the trivial, the articulate and the inarticulate, jostle each other, and it is left to the producer of genius to infuse some unity and meaning into the chaos. The logical end of such plays is the film, and that, in effect, is what Hasenclever calls *The Plague*, although that description might equally well have been applied to Kaiser's *Noli me Tangere*, and other ecstatic explosions of the subconscious. The dramaturgy of this recent body of Expressionist literature, very naturally, is itself arcane.

Max Freyhan, a daring pedagogue, undertook to explain these mysteries in a course of lectures in Berlin, which are now available in book form. I know of no other work so resolutely comprehensive and so persistently incomprehensible as this now standard tome. The author's survey covers every important dramatist: Fritz von Unruh, Georg Kaiser, Carl Sterheim, August Stramm, Ernst Toller, Franz Werfel, Reinhard Goering, Hanns Johst, Walter Hasenclever, Oskar Kokoschka, Anton Wildgans, Rolf Lauckner, Paul Kornfeld, Ernst Barlach, Reinhard Sorge, and Hermann von Boetticher. These are the names which will doubtless occupy the prophets of the theatre of to-morrow for some years to come. Kaiser has been performed by the Theatre Guild, which has also done· Toller's *Masse Mensch*, while the latter's *Maschinenstürmer* has been produced in London. What, then, has their learned exegetist to tell us of this army that has besieged the modern theatre, and made a substantial breach in the wall of tradition?

The author divides drama into three kinds, which he calls dynamic, ecstatic, and synthetic. The first is concerned with "the reality of power," the second with "the reality of ecstasy," and the third with "collective reality." Having established these categories, he then sets forth in elaborate subsections the development of the principle involved. For example, the principle upon which the "ecstatic" drama is based is Nietzsche's doctrine of Apollonian and Dionysian. The Dionysian spirit is then considered as the denial of logic, illustrated by Rudolf Panwitz's *Liberation of Œdipus*; as an ethic, illustrated by such plays as Werfel's *Spielgelmensch*; as style, illustrated by Hasenclever's *Antigone*; and, finally, Hasenclever's *People* is analyzed as "the exaggeration of the principle." This schematic system is applied to all three categories, and the modern German drama is neatly and finally fitted into these pigeonholes, every play being labelled according as it is dynamic, ecstatic, or synthetic.

Obviously, such a piece of critical prestidigitation leaves much to be desired in the way of specific explanation and analysis. The professor is prodigiously abstract and metaphysical, but his hierophantic utterances are so characteristic of the mood of German literature since the war that I will endeavor to summarize them. The dynamic drama is the expression of an age intent upon money-making and action; its source is in Wedekind's *Lulu* and

Marquis of Keith, a prostitute and a swindler. "The pulse of modern unrest was too irregular, greed and desire were active and insistent, the mechanism of civilization enslaved and debased us—all this demanded its own speech and rhythm, demanded the realization of its own curse and fate in drama; it wanted to bubble up and break out, threatening and terrible, in drama, and so, out of this inner necessity the dynamic style becomes more and more absolute, the will and expression of a dramatic art."

In the ecstatic drama "the soul of the period sought another liberation, the road to another redemption. . . . An intoxication seizes mankind, ecstasy draws us on; once again bard and seer shall prevail after the despotism of the word, the devastating victory of knowledge and science. There shall be love and brotherhood and radiant happiness. . . . Europe, the world . . . are summoned to the service of mankind." "Since the naturalistic period the drama had passed through various stages of reality. In the first it had learned to observe reality, to describe a milieu, to project living human beings. Then, however, it had drawn within its scope many other kinds of reality; it had thought in symbols, given wings to energies, nihilistically denied reality, or taken flight from it to ecstasy. The world and the reality of drama are more than one world, one reality. From that conviction, from that feeling, emerged the drama of synthesis. This includes within each other many degrees of reality, changes the register without warning, or lets it gradually mount, swell out, and rise to the highest diapason."

The comprehensive sweep of this drama, its elevation from the lower to the higher forms of reality, indicates it as the medium of expression for an age "that is asking again what is the aim and meaning of life, why man is wicked . . . and is seeking God."

But it can achieve its end only if "in all the categories it employs, realistic, lyric, and dynamic, these realities are entirely conceived within the resources of realistic, dynamic, and ecstatic art, if each of these forms of reality is represented according to its own laws and character, and if the rhythm is raised to the point where it can transpose and transform one reality into another." Such are the sage exhortations of our guide through the maze of Expressionistic drama. His optimism is not so excessive as his learning, as this conclusion will show.

"Are we," he asks, "as fortunate as the generation of thirty years ago? Will a genius come to our drama, and may we, too, say: *habemus poetam?* We have a drama which claims its own laws, and we have true poets whose visions are created within these forms, and who express the meaning and aspect of the age. Naturalism had Gerhart Hauptmann as its prophet and leader. The drama of to-day still lacks this one mind summing up within itself all energies. . . . If this drama of the younger man has not yet found its protagonist, if everything is as yet in the process of developing and becoming, . . . still the movement, the struggle for form, the rebirth of the metaphysical, God-seeking man, are an augury, a promise of new changes and resurrections, and the never-ending road along which the soul makes its pilgrimage in search of itself."

III

When one turns from the theory to the practice of Expressionism, one begins to understand, not perhaps the vagueness of the theories, but why they are vague. As I have pointed out, the poetics of Expressionism lack simplicity. Some declare that Expressionism is movement, "for the word is movement,

and in the beginning was the word." Others contend
that Expressionism "sets content above form. It
turns form into content. The external is intensified,
and the elemental triumphs." Finally, there is the
exhortation to "cast to the winds motives, logic, and
justice, write plays full of illogical surprises, of unjustifiable circumstances."

Those who have tried to reconcile such theories
with the specimens of Expressionist drama which
have been shown in New York will probably have
wondered whether, after all, Georg Kaiser's *From
Morn to Midnight*, Elmer Rice's *The Adding Machine*,
John Howard Lawson's *Processional*, realize the full
intention of this particular form of dramatic art.
The truth is, they do not. They represent a step
further than Eugene O'Neill's *The Hairy Ape* in the
direction of Expressionism, but the American theatre
has yet to see this form of drama in its purest and
most logical expression. Georg Kaiser's *Morn to
Midnight* represents merely a stage in the evolution
toward Expressionism of a dramatist who had previously established his reputation in other forms; and
his case is, to that extent, comparable to Eugene
O'Neill's. Mr. Rice is more advanced in his technic—Mr. Lawson considerably less so—but in order to realize the distance which lies before them,
one must compare them with the younger German
dramatists.

The complete Expressionist in literature belongs
to the generation that was just becoming articulate
when the Great War began: the poets, Ivan Goll and
Alfred Wolfenstein; the novelists, Kasimir Edschmid
and Alfred Lemm; and the dramatists, Walter Hasenclever and Oskar Kokoschka. Here we find the new
technic almost untrammelled by the old conventions; and, in consequence, a literature which started
at the point where the later converts to Expression-

ism, and its disciples outside Germany, usually stop. The outstanding figure in this group is Walter Hasenclever, poet and dramatist.

Hasenclever has written a thumb-nail sketch of his own career, which is so characteristic that it is worth quoting: "I was born on the 8th of July, 1890, at Aix-la-Chapelle, where my name is still anathema. In the spring of 1908 I graduated, went to England, and studied at Oxford. There I wrote my first play, and won the cost of printing it at poker. In 1909 I was in Lausanne, and afterward came to Leipzig." There he came into contact with a group of the younger writers, and "soon surpassed his masters." Then he went to Italy and "frequented doctors."

In 1913 his first book, a volume of poems, appeared under the title of *The Youth*, followed, in 1914, by his first drama, *The Son*. He served in the war as "interpreter, caterer, and kitchen-boy," and wrote out of those experiences his second book of verse, *Death and Resurrection*. A year later he published a pacifist tragedy, *Antigone*, which was followed by *Mankind*, *The Saviour*, *The Decision*, *Beyond*, and *The Plague*. Of all these the two last-mentioned have appeared in English. *Beyond* has been produced by the Provincetown Players and *The Plague* was published in *The Smart Set*. It was described by the author as "a film," and has been seized upon by the critical opponents of Expressionism as the logical culmination of Expressionistic drama.

Before jumping to that rash conclusion, however, let us see what Walter Hasenclever has accomplished within the limitations of the drama proper. Most of his plays have been produced in Germany, and they have aroused considerable interest and discussion. His work for the theatre, therefore, is not theoretical but practical; and, as it shows, at its best, the highest achievement of the Expressionistic drama, the claims of the school may fairly be tested by it.

His earliest important play was *The Son*, a five-act drama, which has acquired in Germany the significance of a manifesto. Its theme is essentially that of the whole philosophy of Hasenclever's generation, the revolt of youth, the conflict of father and son. Out of the simplest situation, the rebellion of a son against parental authority, the dramatist has made a play of remarkable intensity and technical originality. The plot merely follows the adventures of a young man who fails in his examination, defies the tyranny of a stern old-fashioned father, is initiated into the ways of physical love by an expert, is recaptured by the police, and, grown conscious of his own identity by experience, resolves to murder his father, but is saved from parricide by the latter's sudden death during their supreme altercation.

The novelty lies in Hasenclever's development of the various situations. Thus, when the Son contemplates suicide and asks his tutor to leave him alone, the latter asks him what he proposes to do. "Indulge in a soliloquy," he replies. "There was a time when this was laughed at, but I have never seen any harm in kneeling to my own pathos." Again when he recites the long verse monologue on suicide, the author reminds us, through the mouth of one of the characters, that the Son has just plagiarized *Faust*. There is a consciousness of the art of the theatre in the characters themselves which gives a peculiar quality to the scenes. In moments of exaltation the verse form is used, and music plays an important rôle, as when the Mephistophelian figure of the Son's Friend entices him to freedom with the assistance of the Ninth Symphony. The song of the Marseillaise, in its turn, is employed when, on Freudian principles, the King becomes a symbol for the Father and this drama of the Œdipus complex moves toward its climax.

Hasenclever's *Mankind*, a drama in five acts and twenty-two scenes, is the most perfect example of Expressionist drama. In it are found all the elements of the new technic and almost nothing of the old, neither of the realistic nor of the romantic theatre. Intense, colorful, and with a powerful dramatic unity, in spite of the apparent incoherence of theme, which is nothing short of the life of man, this play passes over into the domain of the cinema but transcends the art of the screen.

Unlike *The Plague*, it is not a film; it is a stupendous drama. In inverse ratio to the verbosity of the theories of Expressionism is the brevity, the taciturnity of its best poetry and drama, and in this respect alone Hasenclever's *Mankind* is remarkable. One word or two, seldom more, is all that each character contributes to the dialogue. Yet no painful effort is required to supply the missing logical and conversational links to complete the sense. Hasenclever does not set down his ideas in a series of ill-digested lumps, to which one must give shape by dexterous ingenuity. The superfluousness of verbal realism on the stage has never been so effectively demonstrated.

In order to appreciate this peculiar feature of the play, quotation would be necessary, a brief synopsis of the play is indispensable. The scenes move from a cemetery to a café, then to a gambling-den, to a fortune-teller's, to the study of a specialist for venereal diseases, to the opera, to maternity ward, to a court-room, and to a madhouse. The action takes place among gamblers, thieves, prostitutes, criminals; in the world we live in, and outside of time and space.

As the play opens, Alexander, the central charac-

ter, returns from his grave to the world, to atone for
all the suffering he has caused during his previous
existence. When he encounters a man who declares
himself a murderer, Alexander takes from him a
sack containing the victim's head, and the murderer
descends into the grave. Henceforth Alexander goes
through the world on his journey of expiation and
atonement bearing with him this sack as a burden and
a warning. First he becomes a waiter, and then he
appears in different forms through the twenty-two
scenes which lead him back to the grave. There he
can return only when some sacrifice is made for him,
as he himself assumes the guilt of the unhappy in each
place through which he passes. Finally the murderer
rises from the grave and gives his place to Alexander
from whom he receives back the sack, now empty
as a sign that the work of atonement is complete.

The outline of such a play cannot be given, because the dramatist himself has reduced it to elementals; and its scenes are the whole panorama of
human life and yearning, of civilization and its
institutions, of poverty and vice. Each phase of
existence has its type, made visible in essential outline, and speaking only the key-words of the character. The gambler cries "bank," the worker
"strike," the prostitute "silk," humanity "money,"
and the judge "death sentence." Through this chaos
of passions and suffering goes the seeker with out-
stretched arms, crying "Love," "Who am I?" "I
seek myself," "I will atone," "All are murderers."

As I have already stated, hostile critics regard the
cinema as the logical goal of Expressionistic drama;
and when Hasenclever described *The Plague* as "a
film," they rejoiced in their own wisdom. *Mankind*,
however, must be regarded as the vindication of his
method, for here is drama which, while calling for
the producer of genius and imagination, nevertheless

derives its essential interest from the living humanity of its scenes and characters.

In its frank recognition of the fact that, in writing for the theatre the barest indications are sufficient to secure effects which can be described only at the cost of many words, the play is an interesting revolt against the opposite tradition as elaborated by Shaw and the dramatists of that school. Clearly there are limits to this method, and Hasenclever himself did not attempt to express the drama of *The Son* in brief notation. Even if *Mankind* be regarded as a scenario, it would mark an important advance for the cinema which has not taken kindly even to that elementary form of Expressionism associated in the popular mind with the angular fantastic settings and irregular lines of *The Cabinet of Dr. Caligari*.

As it is, however, Walter Hasenclever has made a real contribution to the Expressionist theatre. He has kept strictly within the limits assigned to this form of drama by the theorists, and he has achieved the perfection of its special technic. Until *Mankind* has been seen on the American stage we may refrain from wasting our astonishment or our indignation upon lesser wonders.

SCANDINAVIA

GEORG BRANDES

"IT was difficult to account for the repulsion and even terror of Georg Brandes which I heard expressed around me whenever his name came up in general conversation," wrote Edmund Gosse in that charming volume *Two Visits to Denmark*, where he has recorded his first impressions of his great Danish colleague. With characteristic discretion, Sir Edmund waited nearly forty years before he published this account of his pilgrimage to the Denmark of that "Transition Period," whose herald and man of destiny Georg Brandes was designed to be. It was in 1874 that the English critic first met "a tall, thin, young man—he was then just thirty-two, and looked less— gentle and even mild in appearance, pale, with a great thatch of hair arched over a wide forehead." Such was the youthful Brandes, whose name was a portent of evil in all respectable society, "a Jew," as Gosse says, "an illuminated specimen of a race little known at that time in Scandinavia, and much dreaded and suspected." Moreover, he was "an angry Jew, with something of the swashbuckler about him, shouting that mental salvation was impossible without a knowledge of 'foreign devils' like Taine and John Stuart Mill and Schopenhauer."

The circumstances of that meeting were typical of Georg Brandes, who "looked bored at being disturbed, and bit the feather of a pen rather querulously," but, as soon as he heard the name of his visitor, he led him in, plied him with many questions, and immediately engaged him in a discussion on Swinburne, whose *Songs before Sunrise* Brandes had just been reading. The book was then a recent and much-debated work, and it was characteristic of the whole career of the Danish critic that it should be already on his table, and that he should at once plunge into a conversation about it, when chance brought a compatriot of the poet to his door. A few years later a German caller might have found the same critic engaged upon a volume entitled *Beyond Good and Evil*, by an obscure professor, whose discovery is only one of the many acts of critical alertness and discrimination to the credit of Georg Brandes. One can hardly think of him at any period of his great career when a visitor would not have found him surrounded by books, yet never buried in them but abreast of them all, in spite of their multitude, and very much alive to the significance of the newest of them.

When I first entered Georg Brandes's study I had no sooner declared my nationality as Irish than I was met by the shrewd query: "A real Irishman or a Unionist?" And in a moment it was clear to me that, for all his absorption in European literature and politics, Brandes had found time to acquire a more intelligent conception of the Irish political situation than most people outside Ireland itself. When he heard that I had lived in America, he produced from the chaos of books and papers on his table a volume of H. L. Mencken, at that time little more than a vague name to more than a handful of Americans, and very soon we were discussing a group of American writers who are nowadays as representative as they were a few years ago obscure. The freshness of mind, the intellectual vigor, the indefatigable curiosity where art and ideas are concerned, of this veteran of European culture, were the attraction of many conversations, and remain a memory of which I am proud.

When a critic achieves a world-wide reputation

there is more occasion for wonder than when a poet, a dramatist, or a novelist reaches out beyond the limits of his own borders. When that critic is a citizen of a country with only two and a half million population, whose language is rarely studied by foreigners, the phenomenon is all the more remarkable. And when one finds that critic, long after the Scriptural span of life, still the dominating and challenging figure of his nation, the case is obviously one of unusual distinction. Such is the position of Georg Brandes to-day. There has been no figure in literature like his since Taine, but unlike Taine his language has no international currency. Indeed, it is a curious fact that almost nothing of Brandes is available in French. Even his *Main Currents* has never been translated in France, except the one volume on the *Romantic School,* and a small volume of his essays is the only other book of his in French. Nevertheless, his name stands out to-day as one of the great survivors of an era when "good Europeans," civilized men of cosmopolitan and international culture, were less rare than they have become since Europe began her march back to mediæval-ism, that period when, as Schopenhauer said, "fists were more exercised than brains." In the Scandinavian countries, moreover, there is discernible something of the spirit which Gosse noticed when Brandes was mentioned in 1874. My own conclusion was that Denmark is divided into two parts, those who are with Brandes and those who are against him. It is a testimony to the youthfulness of his old age that one can still upset the equilibrium of a literary gathering in Copenhagen by a show of more than lukewarm interest in him.

Fifty years ago it was the elders who resented him, now it is the orthodox youth, the strange generation of precocious conservatives which is as characteristic of the new Europe as the Senegalese troops in Goethe's house at Frankfort. Recently I noticed an echo of old yet current Danish controversies in an article on Scandinavian literature in an American review, where the writer declares that "it is a pity that Georg Brandes has stood before the outside world as representative of Danish intellectual life." It seems he is too "negatively nationalistic," he lacks "warmth and geniality," in short he is not a typical householder. Similarly, I suppose Shelley was not as representative of England as Horatio Bottomley. Mr. Moritzen, an enthusiastic admirer, and the only, if rather inadequate, biographer of Brandes in English, does not seem to be aware of the intensity of feeling in Denmark on this subject. Official recognition largely at the hands of men who had grown up with him, a generation moulded by the ideas of which Brandes himself was the prophet, does not present the contrast with his treatment as a young man which Mr. Moritzen emphasizes. Even after the war, when Denmark had recovered from her illusions about the Allies and her terror of Germany, which had combined to turn opinion against Brandes because of his logical, and clear-sighted attitude of neutrality, I noticed everywhere a resentment against him. It seemed to me little more rational than an almost subconscious jealousy.

The life of Georg Brandes has been one of challenge and combat, of criticism that is creative and constructive, and the record of his accomplishment is the final answer to his opponents. As the intellectual mentor of his own country he can claim for his disciples such men as Holger Drachman, J. P. Jacobsen, Erik Skram, and Sophus Schandorph, and as the interpreter of Scandinavian literature abroad he can point to his championship of Kielland, Strindberg, Ibsen, Björnson; his writings on Oehlenschlaeger,

Holberg, and Andersen. There is hardly a writer in the Scandinavian countries, from Holberg to Johannes V. Jensen, about whom he has not had an effective and timely word to say. He translated John Stuart Mill; was the first to recognize Nietzsche; and his studies of Renan, Taine, Lassalle, and the French Realists, his classical study of Shakespeare, show him as the intellectual bridge between Scandinavia and the rest of Europe. His *Main Currents in Nineteenth Century Literature*, of which the first volume was written before the author was thirty, remains, of course, as the finest monument to his peculiar genius and its most typical expression.

Mr. Moritzen, however, has an adequate, if inarticulate conviction of the importance of his subject. In his *Georg Brandes in Life and Letters* he never commits such amazing *gaffes* as Professor Hjalmar Boyesen, who reproached Brandes with having "discredited himself by his open sympathy with anarchism," and says, "nowhere has he unmasked so Mephistophelian a countenance as in his essays on Luther and on *an obscure German iconoclast named Friedrich Nietschke!*" Mr. Moritzen recognizes in Georg Brandes "a missionary of culture," as Nietzsche once called him, to the great indignation of Brandes, who denied the epithet, "because I have never seen a missionary who did not moralize." The repudiation of such a phrase reveals the quality of the man, whose life has been consecrated to the liberation of the mind, to the championship of freedom, but who has kept himself singularly free of the cant of liberalism. But the freedom he set out to achieve for himself and for others was intellectual liberty, the only kind which has ever meant anything permanent in human history. His doctrine and his life have been those of "a good European." Just as he so aptly coined the term "aristocratic radicalism" to describe Nietzsche, so the Nietzschean ideal of the good European has been perfectly realized by Georg Brandes.

It is interesting to compare the writings of Georg Brandes and Benedetto Croce where their subjects coincide, as for instance in *Main Currents* and *Poesia e Non Poesia*. The title of the latter work by no means suggests what the book is, namely, a fragment of a study which might have been an Italian counterpart to the great work of Brandes. In his preface Croce explains that he had intended to "re-examine the literature of the Nineteenth Century," in order to bring out "conclusions still implicit in the writings of those who have discussed it, or to demonstrate other conclusions more exactly, or to confute current prejudices, or to propose some new judgments, but especially to keep in mind pure literature which—in spite of the ease with which the fact is forgotten by those whose business is criticism —is the real concern of criticism and literary history." Apparently these essays are all we shall see of this projected work, for other studies have made the realization of Croce's original plan impossible. As it stands, however, the book consists of a series of provocative chapters on such figures as Alfieri, Schiller, Scott, Stendhal, Manzoni, Balzac, Heine, George Sand, Musset, Baudelaire, Ibsen, Flaubert, and Maupassant. Brandes stopped his survey at the middle of the century, but within the limits where their work coincides both he and Croce necessarily discuss the same writers.

In the eyes of both their admirers and their detractors Brandes and Croce usually pass for the opposite extremes of critical method and attitude. The Italian stands for pure æstheticism; the Danish critic is accused of propaganda. Here in America, it is true, Croce is denounced as a subtle immoralist, but his crimes are more elusive than those with which the political radical, Georg Brandes, has been charged. *Main Currents in Nineteenth Century Literature* has been described by orthodox thinkers as an elaborate, prolonged, and utterly ruthless indictment of all the ideals and conventions of bourgeois society. Croce is credited with being solely concerned about the intrinsic artistic qualities of the works he has studied.

If life were not so short, one might begin again the eternal debate as to which of these two attitudes is right in a critic of literature. I prefer to point out the rather more interesting fact that, whatever the æsthetic theories of a critic may be, it is his practice that counts. In this case, as in most others, it would be difficult to show just wherein Croce's final estimate differs, in most cases, from that of Brandes, or wherein their judgments were actually governed by their politics. Just as some English and American novelists discourse airily and metaphysically about style, but produce works of their own remarkably similar to dozens of others, and quite unlike their theoretical ideal, so Messrs. Croce and Brandes agree in their judgments so often that I am left colder than ever by the disputes of the schools they are supposed to represent.

Their treatments of Walter Scott and George Sand supply two good examples of this similarity of judgment. Brandes is supposed to have belauded George Sand because she was in revolt against the conventions of her sex. It is true, he gives a more or less sympathetic account of her ideas on the subject of love and marriage, while Croce does not, but both critics see the artistic worthlessness of that part of her work and agree that the only books which deserve to survive are the simple idyllic studies of peasant life. So far as Scott is concerned, Brandes sums him up by saying that he is the kind of author whom "every adult has read and no grown-up person can read." Croce also describes his work as unreadable, but ends with an appeal for mercy, on the ground that a writer who delighted our parents and grandparents "does not deserve harsh treatment from their children and grandchildren." Oh, æstheticism, where is thy sting? Oh, propaganda, where is thy victory? A critic must still be judged by his appreciation of specific works, and not by the theories which evolve *in vacuo*. Whether in their treatment of the illustrious dead or of their contemporaries, neither Brandes nor Croce diverges from the all-too-human principle of personal taste and emotion, for that, in the last analysis, is the only basis of literary criticism. It then becomes a question of the quality of the mind employed, and this can never be disguised by æsthetic faith or propagandist good works.

JOHAN BOJER

JOHAN BOJER is one of the foremost contemporary Norwegian novelists, and his peculiar talent lies in his psychological studies of peasant life in which the figures of rural society lend themselves to an analysis as profound as any that has been made of more complicated existences. That powerful work, *The Power of a Lie*, as merciless and sardonic as life itself, has long since been accepted as a masterpiece of novel dissection, an extraordinary exposition of the human capacity for self-deceit, culminating in the dependence of an entire community upon a profound belief in a lie. The English publisher of the book was apparently so scared by the uncompromising detachment of the author that Mr. Hall Caine had to preface the novel with the most ludicrous introduction ever associated with a great work, a laborious plaint against Bojer's failure to punish the wicked and reward the virtuous.

Just as in *The Power of a Lie* the novelist declined to destroy his effect by interfering on behalf of the victim of untruth, so in *The Great Hunger* he steps aside and allows the worst to happen, without once intervening on behalf of his central figure, Peer Holm. Holm is the illegitimate child of a wealthy officer in the army, whose sudden death leaves the boy without the help which had been generously provided for him. After years of hard work and obstinate determination to rise above the stigma of his birth, Peer Holm becomes a famous engineer and makes a fortune as a constructor of river works and railways in Egypt and Abyssinia. His return to Norway finds him sated in his great hunger for power and wealth, but hungry for happiness, which he finds in marriage and a life of contentment amongst his own people. But the spur of ambition goads him eventually, and in a concatenation of disasters his happiness and wealth are lost. Finally he is described as finding peace as a humble village blacksmith, shorn of all his splendor, social and scientific, but unbowed in spirit by the blows of adversity. The reader is left with a reminder of the symbolic opening chapter, in which Peer and his boy companions sail out to fish in deep waters, but catch a great shark from which they do not escape without injury. The adventure of life is somewhat similar for Peer Holm, and the prize of his ambition is wrested from him at painful cost. The book cannot be compared to *The Power of a Lie*, except for the first half, in which the author's power of temperamental analysis, and his vivid pictures of humbler life, by the sea and in the city, show their accustomed quality. But *The Great Hunger* trails off into a moralizing tale of the vanity of human wishes which seems very commonplace after that earlier novel of the finest realism. Mr. Hall Caine would have rejoiced on this occasion had he been invited to the writing of a more congenial preface.

It is more than five years now since *The Great Hunger* brought Bojer the success in this country to which his fame in Scandinavia and Germany entitled him. With Hamsun he had long been recognized as one of the two most important figures in Norwegian literature, but the English-speaking world has been slow to welcome him. In neither instance were the pioneering efforts of their English publishers rewarded, for it was not until the reissue of *The Power of a Lie* that this work, first translated in 1908, secured the attention now lavished on all his works, good and bad. Knut Hamsun has not had the same good fortune. The early translation of *Hunger*, in 1896, and *Shallow Soil*, in 1914, were rescued from oblivion when *Growth of the Soil* obtained its unpredictible success, but neither these nor subsequent works have equalled the vogue of that deservedly successful masterpiece. Johan Bojer's works were also resurrected. After *The Power of a Lie* came *Our Kingdom*, a work which first appeared in 1912 as *Treacherous Ground*. With its title accurately translated, the book enabled a public which judged Bojer entirely by *The Great Hunger* and *The Face of the World* to revise its conception of the author. *Our Kingdom* belongs to the order of *The Power of a Lie*, and is more typical of the work upon which his fame rested than the two books which established him with the English-speaking world.

Like his earlier untranslated novels *Our Kingdom* is a powerful psychological study in a realistic setting of peasant life. Readers of *The Great Hunger* got a taste of this quality of realism in Bojer's work in the first portion of that novel, which afterward trails off into a vague exposition of the hollowest moralizing "philosophy." At his best the author is objective, dispassionate, and ruthless in his analysis of character; he is innocent of the uplifting aspirations in which his later work is invariably involved. Erik Evje in *Our Kingdom* is a figure drawn by the hand which revealed Knut Norby in *The Power of a Lie*. Bojer describes him with the same impartial desire to achieve the notation of a complex human type, and with the same naturalistic skill he portrays the life of the rural community upon which Erik Evje brings ruin and death. The "treacherous ground" upon which Evje's hopes are built is his character, whose unstable foundations are like the quagmire that eventually swallows up the homesteads erected on the land he only half reclaimed. Those who are not in search of any hortatory message or spiritual philosophy will find in *Our Kingdom* those qualities of psychological truth and realistic objectivity which are characteristic of *The Power of a Lie*. These two earliest translations are the most important. If the popularity of the later volumes brings to the others the success which they missed at first the Bojer "boom" will have justified itself and . . . the cynical.

Johan Bojer's *Life* may be regarded as marking the transition from the earlier manner of *The Power of a Lie* and *Our Kingdom* to the mood of those later novels, *The Great Hunger* and *The Face of the World*, upon which the author's popularity rests. *The Power of a Lie* is not the sort of book which arouses popular enthusiasm. It does not lift its creator into the charmed circle of the purveyors of "gladness," of that benign optimism which is as soothing as a marsh-mallow sundae and as eagerly consumed by the connoisseurs of such things. It is only necessary to read Hall Caine's ingenuous preface to that sardonic masterpiece to understand why *The Power of a Lie* was neglected until the "boom" following *The Great Hunger* brought all Bojer's work into prominence.

As might be expected in a transitional work, *Life* alternates between the pessimistic realism of the early Bojer and the rather vague optimism which permeates his later writings. The book was written on the novelist's return to Norway after a period of foreign travel, and the dominant note is one of pleasure in the natural beauty of the northern countryside, and of the joy of living as reflected in the native festivals, sports, and dances. There are passages full of the zest of life amid fiords and snow-fields, of a craving for the delights of health and sunshine. But the joy of living is not the only motive. Against the light and gaiety of General Bang's circle, Bojer sets the drab existence of Holth, the poor schoolmaster, and of Captain Riis, the broken-down military officer, whose gloomy days are filled with hatred and envy. Riis attributes his failure to the general, his erstwhile comrade, by whom he has been left behind in the race for success. Astrid Riis is the victim of her father's embittered and poverty-stricken isolation. She is the household drudge, and must lie and scheme to escape from the miserable home to the happy world outside which is calling her.

When Inga Bang and Astrid become friends, the latter learns as a guest to appreciate the kindly simplicity of General Bang, whom the captain has always represented as a monster of malice and selfishness. Astrid does not dare to confess to her father that she is a friend of the Bangs, and time slips by while she moves to and fro between these two opposed and contrasted worlds, her home and that of Inga and her brother Reidar. It is the latter chiefly who drives her to prolong an elaborate deception and is the unwitting cause of her ruin. Astrid loves him, but is afraid to acknowledge a feeling which would involve a proposal to unite her family with that of her father's worst enemy. She drifts into a sentimental relationship with the wretched Holth, who comes, like herself, from sordid domestic misery to bask in the warmth of the prosperous lives of their common friends. In a momentary aberration of the senses, with the image of Reidar in her soul, Astrid yields to Holth. Then, when the miracle happens, when the family feud is buried, and she is married to Reidar, she goes out to die by her own hand, as her mother had done before her, also a victim of the craving for life and happiness.

The dual motive in the contrast between Captain Riis and General Bang and their surroundings is a reflection of the conflicting moods of Johan Bojer at this stage of his development. There is a wavering, indecisive quality in the conception of this story. The life and tragedy of Astrid Riis are obviously the main theme, but the theme does not harmonize with the general tone of the narrative, with its joyful consciousness of life and beauty and movement. Moreover, the fate of Astrid lacks that inevitability which alone would justify her tragic end. Bojer, who so wonderfully analyzed "the power of illusion," fails absolutely to convince the reader of the particular form of self-deception which caused Astrid's misfortune. A situation so inconceivable as the relationship between Astrid and Holth, with Reidar in the Freudian background, demanded more of the novelist's persuasive art than Bojer has given. Throughout the whole book there is a perceptible contradiction between mood and idea. The idea has its roots in the pessimistic realism of the author's earlier manner. The mood is one of tempered optimism, it is true, but that of optimism, nevertheless, which is now so characteristic of Johan Bojer. *Life* is a work of transition, and its indecisiveness must be attributed to the fact that he had not yet adopted definitely that philosophy whose uplifting sonorousness has proved so irresistible.

AN UNMELANCHOLY DANE: GUSTAV WIED

THE Scandinavian theatre has come to be associated in the minds of the English-speaking public with problem plays, earnest, often incomprehensible dramas, which are usually denounced at first as "morbid" and "obscene" and finally buried in the consecrated ground of what is vaguely termed radical literature. There, when not entirely forgotten, they are occasionally exhumed by class-conscious intellectuals to serve as the pretext for some social thesis, or to fill the programme of a literary theatre. Although the comedies of Ludvig Holberg exist in several English versions, and his name was duly mentioned in connection with the Molière tercentenary celebrations, it would be rash to suppose that the work of the "Danish Molière" is very widely regarded as a proof of the existence of the comic spirit in Scandinavian literature. Holberg, I suppose, is the legitimate prey of the college classrooms. Nothing has been translated of Schandorph, the great humorist of that famous group of "transition men," whose leader was Georg Brandes in the seventies and early eighties, the group which included Holger Drachmann, J. P. Jacobsen, and Erik Skram, and laid the foundation of modern Danish literature. Thus we come to the successor of Schandorph, the inheritor of the comic tradition bequeathed by Holberg, the quintessential Dane, Gustav Wied.

It is not a mere coincidence that the comic spirit in Scandinavian letters has expressed itself in Danish rather than in Norwegian and Swedish literature. As every guide-book insists, Copenhagen is the "Paris" of the North, and the prevailing tone of its intellectual and social life is one of amused tolerance and happy scepticism, the mood of a people mercifully freed from the illusions and ambitions that harass other nations. Problems which exist elsewhere seem to have solved themselves in Denmark, leaving the country with a mind at ease, almost untroubled by the panicky fears of privileged imbecility, on the one hand, and the ever-hopeful aspirations of tearful radicals, on the other. In such an atmosphere humor and satire flourish, and healthy mockery drives away the bogies that haunt the uneasy dreams of contemporary democracy. Gustav Wied is the personification of that Danish wit, that ironic laughter, which makes Copenhagen irresistible to those who know it is as a refuge from the humbug of latter-day prophets.

Just as most Parisians come from the provinces so this typical Copenhagener was born at Holmegaard, on the island of Lolland, on the 6th March, 1858. He died in Copenhagen on the 24th October, 1914, thereby disturbing the chronology of the following biographical summary which Wied once published:

I came into this world quickly and easily on the 6th March, 1858.
Confirmed, 1873.
Bookseller.
Failed at matriculation, 1880.
In a lawyer's office, 1881.
Failed again, 1882.
Tutor, 1883.
One day in the "Blaagaard" training-college, 1884.
Graduate, 1885.
Cand. phil. 1886.
Gave lessons by the hour, 1887.
Poet, 1887.
Play hissed off the stage, 1890.
In jail, 1891.
Married, 1896.
Raised children, built a house, and will finally die on the 12th April, 1927, deeply regretted by sorrowing friends and relatives.

Except for the final paragraph this is an accurate outline of Wied's history, and little remains to be said of his personal life. He was a child of fifteen when he became apprenticed to a bookseller. "There," he says, "I sold books and pens and had to deliver parcels in the city, pushing a handcart. This wounded my sense of dignity in the highest degree." His repeated failure to pass the *Abiturienten* examination—corresponding roughly to matriculation—he ascribed chiefly to his inability to write a satisfactory composition. "And to this day," he adds, "I am often uncertain where a comma should go, and where not." The period spent as a tutor on a country estate was always regarded by Wied as one of the happiest in his life, although his conception of the art of tutoring was characteristically unorthodox. "In my opinion it does not matter so much whether children learn anything, as that they should be happy at their lessons."

When he came to Copenhagen, Wied earned his living by teaching "at ten cents an hour." This lasted for five years, and then he began to write.

I ought not to have done so, at least not in the way I did . . . for the police . . . really, it is dreadful for me to confess it— I assure you it was the darkest period of my life, and I am horribly ashamed of myself— But I must confess it: the police put me in jail, me, who had myself been a guardian and protector of youth. And there I sat, sad unto death. Yet, it was just that little . . . accident which made "something" of me.

While I sat between those bare walls I resolved to turn over a new leaf, as soon as ever I regained my freedom, I decided to take a course in orthography, and strain every effort to write my books in such a manner that the Pope himself could give them to his sisters as Christmas and birthday presents.

That is what I resolved to do. As a matter of fact, it would have been better to have given up writing altogether. But I *couldn't* do that. And so here I am, forty-six years old, with a wife and children of my own, living between a church and a lunatic asylum.

How strange life is!
Therefore I pray to God every day that I may not "preserve
my intellectual faculties to the end," as the obituary notices
say. After all, one is entitled to some rest.

It is hardly necessary to emphasize the irony in
Wied's account of himself, and to say that his novels
and plays have been a continuous laughing protest
against the seriousness of life. After two youthful
efforts, *En Hjemkomst* (1889) and *Silhuetter* (1891),
which provoked in the author the expression of
"regret" which I have quoted, Gustav Wied began
to write that series of novels, plays, and stories which
have placed him in the front rank of contemporary
Danish literature. His first play, *A Homecoming*,
was a typical essay in the manner of Strindberg,
under whose influence the young playwright came
when the Swedish dramatist's works were produced
in Copenhagen. Wied threw himself actively into
the fight to secure Strindberg a hearing, and actually
took part himself in some of the productions. His
own success began in 1895 with an autobiographical
novel, *Ungdomshistorier* which might be rendered
into English as *In the Days of Youth*, and the next
year came his first successful play, *Erotik*, which was
also the first of those *Satyrspil*, dramatic satires,
which he afterward collected into several volumes,
that are regarded by many as his most characteristic
work. The most notable of these are *Byens Stolthed*
(*The Pride of the Town*) a sardonic exposure of the
morality-mongers; *En Mindesfest* (*A Commemora-
tion*), in which a husband and a friend of the former's
dead wife recall the memory of the dear departed
over an exquisite dinner and under the influence of
good food and choice wines celebrate a remarkable
mourning. Schnitzler has done nothing better of this
kind.
The list of Gustav Wied's works is extensive, in-

cluding more than thirty volumes, of which nothing
is known in English. His important novels, *Slægten*
(*The Race*), with its sequel, *Fædrene æde Druer* (*The
Fathers have Eaten Sour Grapes*), *Livsens Ondskab*,
Knagsted, and *Pastor Sørensen*, a series whose title,
adapted from the first volume, might be *Life's Little
Malignities*, are famous all over Scandinavia and
Germany. Also worthy of mention is that curious
book, *Dansemus* (*Dancing Mice*), a novel cast in the
form of short scenes, in which the action is explained
by the dialogue, and the narrative thread sustained
by the passages corresponding to the stage directions
in a play. It is a most interesting and successful
experiment in fiction. The cumulative effect of this
series of pictures of life in Copenhagen is exceedingly funny, for Wied just flashes the light of his
lantern for a moment on each place, like a good-
humored Diogenes in search of the ironies of the
social order. The meeting of "the Cabinet," whose
members have an average age of ninety years, to
consider the charge of immorality brought against
the Minister of Religion, is as amusing as the arrival
home of a newly married couple of which the husband suffers from shyness. Everywhere the irreverent wit of the sceptical Dane plays effectively.

Of all this work only one play has been published
in English, *Et Opgør* (*The Reckoning*), which appears
in a recent anthology under the strange title *Autumn
Fires* and is listed as a "Swedish" play! It was
performed by the Provincetown Players as a tragedy
more or less, but is, in fact, a typical example of
Wied's manner of reducing the "problems of sex"
to an absurdity, as when, in this piece, the two an-
cients in the Old Men's Asylum squabble about
trifles, but are united after one of them learns that
his child is not really his, that his wife had been un-
faithful, that his friend is the boy's father. The note

of mocking disillusionment becomes almost Shavian in this little play, with its failure to emphasize the heroics of adultery, its realistic perception of human emotions as distinct from conventional attitudes.

When Gustav Wied published *Silhuetter* at the outset of his career, he wrote as its motto: "Let us have no solemn antics. After all, we are only human!" The phrase well describes the mood of all those charming *Satyrspil*, of which "$2 \times 2 = 5$" is admittedly the most famous. It appeared in 1906 under the title, *Ranke Viljer* (*Steadfast Characters*), but the subtitle, "$2 \times 2 = 5$," a phrase of Paul Abel's in the last act, has become more famous both in Scandinavia and elsewhere on the continent of Europe. The play might be translated as *Men of Principle*, for the aim of its satire is our tendency to dress up the desires and weaknesses of human egotism and ambition as the expression of the loftiest principles. Paul Abel is Wied himself, and his ability to laugh at his own foibles is one of the most charming traits of his work. The author is the antithesis of Ibsen, whose *Pillars of Society* deals with the same theme, for Gustav Wied does not look at society and its hypocrisies with the stern eyes of a judge, but with the mocking glance of a born satirist. He is, however, not a satirist of the order whose "indignation makes verses," for one feels that his occupation would be gone, were nothing left for his mockery. He is never indignant. As he once wrote, "the only real joy in life is irritating one's neighbors," and again: "We mortals have a choice before us either to bow the knee reverently before life, or to laugh at it until our sides ache—I have chosen the latter."

With the exception of Gustav Esmann, who deserves to be better known in this country, Wied is the only Scandinavian writer of his generation whose work is dominated by the irresistible force of the comic spirit. In spite of its occasional crudities, its lapses into mere burlesque, it represents a healthy reaction against the exaggerated cult of the ego, and the solemn preoccupation with spiritual and social problems which the influence of Björnson, Ibsen, and Strindberg undoubtedly fostered in the literature, first of Scandinavia and then of continental Europe. With a malicious flash of laughter in his eyes Wied likes to snatch away the mask from the faces of pompous humbugs, to emphasize the human—all-too-human—element in all of us, from Chamberlain Hamann to Miss Othella Lustig. His satire ranges from the highest in the land to the humblest, and is based upon the theory that "men differ from animals chiefly in so far as they make a great fuss about themselves." "He sees the world dancing to the tune of a higher hurdy-gurdy" and nowhere is that dance more diverting than in "$2 \times 2 = 5$," the most popular and successful of all his plays.

J. ANKER LARSEN

When the famous firm of Scandinavian publishers, Gyldendal, offered an award of 70,000 kroner—an interesting problem in mathematics was raised. There are about two and a half million Danes, and half a million Norwegians, so the statistically minded can work out for themselves what amount an American or English publisher—with the whole English-speaking world to draw upon—would have to offer to compete proportionately with this award. Add to this the strange appetite of Scandinavia for tenth-rate English and American fiction, and the fact of the prize being won by J. Anker Larsen's *The Philosopher's Stone* becomes more inexplicable than even literary prizes usually are. The book has no elements of wide popularity, and the author was respected by the few as a distinguished craftsman rather than known to the many as a writer of fiction.

When I knew him he was the stage-manager of the Dagmar Theatre in Copenhagen and the part author of a number of successful plays, about which he always maintained a discreet silence. It was understood that one should no more discuss these plays than one should talk of ropes in the house of a man who has been hanged. They were simply a lucky source of income to a distinguished literary artist who had published five charming works unknown to more than a handful of readers who appreciated them, and who had been a prompter in a country theatre at Aarhus and a proof-reader in Copenhagen before he simultaneously made his début, in 1905, as an actor and an author. In the latter capacity his specialty was playing the parts of "little old men from the country," and, as he has stated to the press, he wrote his books "when there was no demand for old men of rural parentage, or when another stage-manager was at work." In this fashion he produced his first volume of short stories in 1905, *Livets Ubønhørlighed*, which was followed in 1908 by a second collection of longer stories, entitled *Landsbyens Magdalene*, a novel called *Pinsesolen*, another book of short stories, *Menneskeøjne*, and, finally, *Bugten*. Common to all these works is the author's predilection for studies of rural life and character, and a tender, playful fancy which one found in Hans Christian Andersen—that peculiar power of evoking the poetry in simple, familiar things which is a national trait of Danish literature. Their charm lies in the atmosphere and in the manner of telling rather than in the substance of the stories themselves.

Each of these books is short and neither of the novels is full-length, or, properly speaking, a novel as the term is generally understood. They present, therefore, a contrast all the more remarkable with the work which gained the Gyldendal prize, for any three of them would not bulk as large as that imposing tome of more than 500 closely printed pages. And it is not only in mere number of words and dimension of page that *The Philosopher's Stone* is a bigger and more substantial achievement than anything Anker Larsen has hitherto written. The title—characteristically—is taken from Andersen's fairy-tale of the same name, but the book is far removed from those poetic and idyllic studies of Danish country life which seemed to be the author's chief preoccupation. It is a profound, philosophic novel, with the religious instinct in man as its theme, and as variations upon that theme the strange pursuits of the human soul in its search for religious expression. In describing how he came to write the book, how his business in the theatre and as a playwright made it impossible for him to concentrate on a lengthy and ambitious work, and how the offer of the prize decided him to take a year's leave of absence, Anker Larsen says:

> The beginning of *The Philosopher's Stone* dates far back. It grew out of my interest in the psychology of religion. . . . My opinion was—and is still—that in this new science there exists a possibility of "penetrating to those regions of the human mind whence religions originate." It was my first conviction that, by following religious feeling from its source and studying its course and ramifications, it would be possible to discover that it was the same "water of life" that courses through all religions, and that all the different forms of faith might be compared to the vegetation growing in various places along the banks of the river and drawing its nourishment from it. In other words, there is only one religion, as there is only one God.

With this guiding idea the novelist works over a large canvas, filled with various types, and his narrative wanders almost as far afield and as erratically as Wassermann's in *The World's Illusion*. There is the same absence of logical plot, the same teeming variety of life and experience. But *The Philosopher's Stone* is essentially Danish, in its scenery and characters, in its portrayal of every phase of Danish life in town and country. In his delineation of rural types Anker Larsen's accustomed skill is apparent, and his poetic imagination finds characteristic expression in the early chapters of child life. The protagonists are Jens Dahl, the Lutheran minister's son, and Christian Barnes, the curate's child, each representing a type of religious mind. Jens is a natural mystic, whereas Christian has from the beginning a leaven of scepticism, but his mind does receive the dogmatic imprint. While we are shown Jens as a little boy gifted with a mysterious power of communion with nature, we see Christian becoming aware of the deliberate artifice in his father's eloquence as an orator of sermons for the dead. When his mother falls desperately ill the bereaved husband proceeds unconsciously to work up the situation into an impassioned funeral address.

The two boys gradually get rid of all dogmatic religion, but they study theology at the university. Jens Dahl's search is for a faith that will give him back the dreams and innocent security of childhood, and he passes through all the phases of latter-day mysticism, ending with theosophy, of which there is an elaborate exposition betraying the author's strong personal curiosity concerning this belief. This interest I discovered in Anker Larsen the first night we talked together, for we talked at great length about the poetry and philosophy of Æ., whose mystical experiences are paralleled by those of Jens Dahl, which have an authentic note. Against the impulse toward mysticism Jens has nothing to set but sexual desire, which takes in him the form of a blind attraction toward woman as a sex rather than to the individual woman. His disillusionment leads to his death by drowning. Christian, on the other hand, after a period on a ranch in America, returns to Denmark ready to take his place in the real world. As a Danish critic points out, "he is a cured visionary, just as his friend is an irretrievably lost one."

It is impossible to outline the story of a work so packed with incident and ideas and people as *The Philosopher's Stone*. The background of diverse human characters is fascinating; Holger Enke, the village failure, who as a criminal and worker personifies the blind instinct of religion, kept alive by an eternal recurrence of sin, punishment, and repentance; the mysterious interlocutor called "The Candidate," whom one has met in other works of Anker Larsen's and who is the ironist, the commentator, holding in his hands the threads of all the experiences through which the characters pass. The gallery of women, too, is drawn with fine feeling and skill: Tine, who almost leaves her husband for Jens; Miss Hansen, a characteristic example of the Danish unmarried mother, and her daughter Helen, whom Christian Barnes eventually marries. The religious discussions, the debates on marriage, the analyses of different experiments in the art of living—all these elements combine to make a book of real originality and great interest. The internal struggle of our age, rather than its outward manifestations of disquietude, is contained within the limits of this story. A "deeply religious, atheistic mystic"—to quote his play-writing collaborator and friend, Doctor Egill Rostrup—J. Anker Larsen has written a modern epic of religious unrest.

POLAND

WLADYSLAW REYMONT

WLADYSLAW STANISLAW REYMONT has been dragged once more from the obscurity which seems to be his fate in English translation by the award of the Nobel Prize for literature. The first volume of his four-part peasant epic, *The Peasants*, had been published for several weeks without attracting much attention when the news was sent forth that Sienkiewicz had a successor in the roll of Nobel Prize winners. At once there was the usual scramble to obtain some facts about the illustrious unknown whom the Committee of the Swedish Academy had selected in preference to Thomas Hardy, Georg Brandes, Benedetto Croce, Thomas Mann, or any of a dozen other writers of the first rank of whom the world has heard. So dim was the twilight in which this Polish novelist dwelt, so far as American and English readers are concerned, that the press appeared to be laboring under the illusion that he had but recently begun to be published in English. Yet in 1920 one of his most important novels, *The Comédienne*, was issued in New York. His first appearance in book form in English was in 1916, when Else Benecke and Marie Busch included him in *More Tales by Polish Authors*, and in 1921 the same translators secured for two fragments of *The Peasants* the consecration of inclusion in *Selected Polish Tales* in the Oxford University Press's famous series of "The World's Classics." An extract from Reymont's great novel of industrial Poland, *The Promised Land*, was published in 1921 by Paul Selver in his *Anthology of Modern Slavonic Literature*.

Such, apart from selections in magazines, is the

work of Wladyslaw Reymont which is available for readers of English, a meagre portion of the total of twenty-eight volumes of fiction with which the author is credited. In French only an extremely abbreviated version of *The Peasants* appeared as a serial in the *Revue de Paris* many years ago, but his major works have long since passed into German, where such fame as Reymont enjoyed outside his own country was founded upon the masterly German translation of *The Peasants*. This work, with its two-volume counterpart *The Promised Land*, together with *Ferments*, *The Dreamer*, and *The Comédienne* constitute all that any but the most voracious and indefatigable foreign reader will need to arrive at a conclusion concerning the merits of Wladyslaw Reymont. Only the two last-mentioned books are novels of ordinary dimensions. *The Promised Land* and *Ferments* are in two volumes and rival *The Brothers Karamazov* in length, while the four monstrous tomes of *The Peasants* run to at least four hundred thousand words, *Autumn* being the shortest. Reymont shares with his predecessor Sienkiewicz the Polish weakness for diffuse and leisurely narrative, without attaining, however, such heights as the famous *Trilogy* in thirteen volumes, which has not prevented Sienkiewicz from becoming the most popular of all translated authors in modern literature.

It is not likely, however, that Wladyslaw Stanislaw Reymont will ever rival Henry Sienkiewicz in the affections of the plain people; he is just a little too good a literary craftsman to produce anything that could compete with *Quo Vadis*, and neither *The Peasants* nor *The Promised Land* has that Dumasesque quality of picturesque historical entertainment which gave *With Fire and Sword* and the rest of the *Trilogy* an interest entirely apart from the patriotic enthusiasm to which the work could appeal in Poland. Like his more notorious contemporary Stanislaw Przybyszewski, Reymont was born in 1868 and belongs with the author of *Homo Sapiens* to the literary generation which is known as *Young Poland*, the successors of the Romantic era of Kraszewski, Prus, Orzeszko, and Sienkiewicz—to mention only those translated into English. This is the generation which began to write at the beginning of the present century, and which has produced an interesting group of writers as little known to the English-speaking world as Reymont himself: Stanislaw Wyspiansik, a dramatist of such curious power that his *Wedding* has even been translated into French, and two novelists, Waclaw Berent, of whom nothing exists in English, and Stefan Zeromski, who has been translated by Else Benecke and Marie Busch. Zeromski is regarded in Poland as the successor of Sienkiewicz, and a recent authority on Polish literature, Doctor Roman Dyboski, says of him: "If any Pole is asked who reigns supreme in the Polish novel today, one name alone can leap to his lips—that of Stephen Zeromski." This interesting fact would seem to have escaped the attention of the Committee when it turned to Poland for an author worthy to receive the Nobel Prize for literature.

Reymont is a self-taught peasant of the stock which peoples his rural epic. He was born at Kobiala Wielka in what was then Russian Poland, of poor parents who could give him only such education as was offered by the village school. As a boy he tended the flocks, and as he grew up his circumstances compelled him to earn his own livelihood as early as possible. He tried farming, and twice followed the stage; he was a railway employee and even served to no purpose a novitiate with the Paulist Fathers at Czenstochowa. It was in 1893, while he was employed as a railway official, that he began to write short stories which showed him to be a realist under the influence of Zola and Maupassant, and he was accused, in the fashion of the time, of being a "decadent." *The Comédienne*, however, his first novel, appeared in 1896 and marked a considerable ripening of his talent, in this study of the ardent, eager quest of a girl hungry for fame and beauty who fails in the theatre and ends comfortably in the resignation of perfect philistinism. He drew upon his own experiences in the minor theatrical worlds and filled his picture with vivid figures from the underworld of strolling players and bohemians of various kinds. From his early life and his career as a railway official he then drew the material for *Ferments* and *The Dreamer*. The latter is probably the most biographical of his novels, relating the life of a poverty-stricken gentleman, Joseph Pelka, who is obliged to work in the ticket-office of a railway-station, where the perpetual stretching out of hands for tickets irritates him and at the same time arouses in him dreams of travel. He reads of foreign lands and travels in imagination, until one day he steals money and takes flight to Paris. There the dreamer soon discovers that the realities of a life of leisure abroad are not what he fancied. His Polish mistress suspects him of being a criminal of some sort and she abandons him. In his boredom he goes from station to station watching the ticket-sellers at work and finally commits suicide by allowing an express-train to run over him.

The novel was a study of a typically restless, exalted Pole, true product of a country which lived upon visions and memories, and strove incessantly against Russian censorship and despotism and German discipline as obnoxious to the Polish temperament as Czarism. Fear of the censorship undoubtedly weakened the force of *The Promised Land*, a crowded picture of industrial life in Lodz. He shows a land flowing, not with milk and honey, but with wealth for the Jewish and German capitalists and with blood and tears for the Polish proletariat; the fierce plundering of ruthless exploiters, the jungle morality of a social order founded exclusively upon gain, and foundering upon snobbishness and reckless self-indulgence. It is a book which will remind readers of Zola's *Germinal* as the vast, turbulent, swarming picture itself is completely influenced by the Naturalist technic. Its weakness lies in the author's failure to develop effectively the contrast between the exploiters and the exploited, a contrast which is discreetly suggested in deference, obviously, to the susceptibilities of the censorship. His analysis is in parts excellent, but his synthesis is weak; he is without fundamental ideas, and the book best serves as a mirror of external circumstances.

Reymont was not really interested in the fate of the industrial worker, but all his instincts brought him close to the worker on the land, and the epic breadth of *The Promised Land* was an earnest of what he was finally to accomplish in *The Peasants*. With such minor efforts as the two thrillers, *The Vampire* and *Opium Smokers*, we need not delay. A lengthy historical novel, *The Year* 1794, marks his failure to do the inevitable three-volume romance, in the Sienkiewicz manner, of the former grandeur of Poland, this time at Grodno, during the last year of the independent Polish parliament. His theme is the contrast between the refined world in the whirl of its enjoyments and the masses whose patriotic remnant saved the ark of nationalism in the flood which overwhelmed and destroyed old Poland, when Kosciusko fell. Reymont has not, as I have said, the picturesque facility of a Sienkiewicz, and when he does not entirely possess and dominate his material there is no compensation in the shape of mere narrative entertainment as Dumas understood it. This novel is one of the least successful of Reymont's works.

His most successful is *The Peasants*, which is not so much a novel as a prose epic, elemental, undidactic, and primitive, full of a natural poetry, narrating the life and adventures of a village rather than telling the story of a hero and heroine. The very order of the volumes is significant, for the rural year begins in autumn, and ends in summer with the harvesting which is the final splendid picture upon which Reymont closes. His four parts are not dictated by artistic considerations; they are not four acts of a drama, for there is no culminating point in the third volume, *Spring*, which is actually the most monotonous and ineffectual of them all. They are simply the four stages of life as lived by and for the soil. The woman of destiny, the mystic Helen, who is the human pivot about which the village epic revolves, is the traditional figure since Homer, the woman for whom men destroy themselves, the temptress who is herself the victim of love. Yagna comes between father and son, she becomes the scourge of virtue, and is dramatically humiliated and punished in the end. The rivalry of Antek and his father supplies the slender thread of what must be accepted in lieu of a plot, but their story is but an incident in a vast panorama of events.

To compare Yagna to Tess of the d'Urbervilles is misleading, for her tragedy is incidental and almost impersonal, in the sense that the woman herself is never individualized, but simply fulfils her rôle as the element of sex in this ambitious unfolding of every aspect of rural existence in Poland. Reymont is a chronicler, amazingly sensitive to direct impressions, utterly unconcerned with rationalization and analysis. We witness the peasant at every hour of his day, through the four seasons of his year, as he ploughs, sows, and harvests; as he tends his cattle, feeds his family, and transacts his business at the fairs. The eternal acts of all who have tilled the soil from the beginning of time are here, together with all the wealth of local and picturesque detail which fixes these scenes in Poland particularly: marriage ceremonies and quaint superstitions, religious fervor and brutal merrymaking, the revolt of the farmer against the landed gentleman, the revolt of the Pole against the foreign oppressor. At each season the setting, atmosphere, and gestures merge into a harmonious whole, so intimate and inevitable is the bond holding these peasants to the soil and identifying their every movement with the rhythms of nature. The relative flatness of the third part, *Spring*, may even be explained by the fact that in Poland the awakening of spring is not the joyous bursting forth of life, but a moment of crisis, of painful adjustments amongst a peasantry whose labors have not carried them on easily from one harvest to another. It is a transition period of privation.

Even in English it is possible to discern the natural charm and poetry of Reymont's writing, which has been highly praised by Polish critics. His descriptions are marvels of vividness and accuracy, smacking of the soil and revealing direct observation rather than literary cunning. The flavor of the dialogues must be largely lost. The English has not, for example, the power of the German version; it oscillates between inappropriate archaisms and a gentility which is not, I gather, in the text. One serious defect is the unnecessary rendering of names in forms so unfamiliar to our ears as to be unrecognizable. Anna is called Hanka throughout, and Eve or Eva becomes Yevka, as Jacob becomes Kuba. There does not seem to be any method in these renderings, for a girl who is called Nastka turns out later to be Nastusia; Francis varies from Franek to Kranek, and Bartek takes the place of Bartholomew. Yagustynka is a formidable name which occurs frequently where the German translator has found the less alarming Gusche. Yacek, too, seems somewhat exotic for Hyacinth. The vexed question of transliteration arises at the outset in the French form of Ladislas where all previous English translations use Wladyslaw, and I suppose that, even more than in Russian, there are opportunities for endless dispute. Merely as a help to this work in English, however, a reduction in the number of unfamiliar proper names, difficult to pronounce, is desirable.

The position of Wladyslaw Reymont in the literature of Young Poland is a peculiar one, for, apart from his style and his preoccupation with the minor bourgeoisie and peasants, he belongs to the tradition of Sienkiewicz. Young Poland, on the other hand, represented a more deliberate break with the past. There was no school, in the strict sense of the word, but simply a group of poets, dramatists, and novelists who had come together in Cracow, and who, very much like their contemporaries in Ireland, wished to see a literature in which the patriotic will was not taken for the artistic deed. Wyspianski's plays, whose analogy with those of Synge has been noted by Polish critics, the plays and novels of Zeromski, and the revolutionary ideas of Przybyszewski, with the lyric poetry of Jan Kasprowicz, sum up the major achievements of Young Poland. Reymont's connection with this literature was accidental, as all the circumstances of his life were remote from literary movements and the play of ideas. He is not an intellectual, but perhaps for that reason he could better catch the qualities of rural life which he has transferred to *The Peasants*, in a manner which renders that saga of nature a unique, if not an absolutely first-rate work of modern literature.

What may be termed the spectacular element in the revolt of Young Poland against the old traditions is more characteristically illustrated by the career and writings of Stanislaw Przybyszewski, known to most readers in this country as the wicked author of *Homo Sapiens*. Only ten brief years ago this work appeared with the bold superscription: "It is universally conceded that Stanislaw Przybyszewski is Poland's greatest living writer"—a bouquet which has now been transferred by the same hands to the more innocuous Reymont. In that interval, however, Reymont has been smiled upon by the Nobel Prize Committee, whereas Przybyszewski was frowned out of existence by the New York Society for the Suppression of Vice. Since *Homo Sapiens* was withdrawn from the chaste gaze of the American people, nothing more has been done to create an audience for him here except the publication of his four-act play *Snow*. We are evidently not to be surfeited by the works of "Poland's greatest living writer." Another play, in three acts, *For Happiness*, which appeared in *Poet Lore* in 1912, completes the brief bibliographical record.

The life and work of Przybyszewski have been exactly the contrary of everything that we have seen in the case of Reymont. He was born at Logen in what was, at the time, Prussian Poland, but unlike his contemporary under Russian rule he does not seem to have revolted against the language of the alien government, for his earliest writings were in German, *Zur Psychologie des Individuums: Chopin und Nietzsche*, in 1892, and in the following years *Totenmesse* and *Vigilien*. Even his famous *Homo Sapiens* was first published in German, in three volumes, during the years 1894, 1895, and 1896, under the titles *Über Bord*, *Unterwegs*, and *Im Maelstrom*. He studied at the University of Berlin and took his degree of medical doctor.. He edited a German Socialist paper and was an active figure in the literary life of Germany in the early nineties, especially the group which used to meet in Berlin at the "Schwarzen Ferkel": Richard Dehmel, Ola Hansson, Holger Drachmann, and Strindberg. The Swedish novelist's influence is very obvious in the Polish writer's melodramatic misogynism, and in his *Inferno* Strindberg refers to Przybyszewski as "that fine spirit with a streak of genius who dreamed of the highest fame." Most appropriately these two women-haters, who could never make terms with sex, quarrelled and separated because of a woman.

After a couple of years of travelling in Europe, during which he visited Norway and married there, Przybyszewski returned to Poland in 1898, settled in Cracow, and became the head of the Young Poland movement, writing only in Polish, *pour encourager les autres*, so to speak. It was he who founded the review *Zycie—Life*—which was the organ of the new movement, and for two years assembled the writers from whom the Polish literature of to-day was to come, Wyspianski, Zeromski, Kasprowicz, and others. He came as the experienced and most extreme champion of the prevalent theory of art for art's sake, of the Nietzschean morality of individualism, of all the libertarian ideas of a period when the pleasant business of amazing the bourgeoisie had charms which now seem rather faded. Characters like Erich Falk in *Homo Sapiens*, like Gordon in *Children of Satan*, embodied the current ideals of the sex-obsessed misogynist, who was, it seemed, the superman, the seeker after absolute reality, whose mission it was to destroy in himself the atavistic workings of conscience and in society the conventions of outworn tradition, who was to strive after power and æsthetic pleasure as the only and supreme good.

It will be remembered that George Moore, as *Confessions of a Young Man* duly recorded, also expounded that philosophy, to such good purpose that the curious will find his youthful quips solemnly chronicled in a serious work entitled *Nietzsche and Other Exponents of Individualism*, as though the ingenuous Mr. Moore ever gave a thought to the true implications of Nietzsche's teaching and should be counted amongst the initiated. Curiously enough, when Moore came to Ireland, just a short while after Przybyszewski's repatriation, the Nietzschean and immoralist lion proceeded to lie down with the Celtic lambs, so innocent of the wickedness of an epoch which was giving to absinthe and decadent loves what they were giving to build up a national Anglo-Irish literature. The spectacle, as Mr. Moore has not failed to record, touched him so deeply that he toyed even with the idea of learning the Irish language, and produced *The Lake* and *The Untilled Field* in proof of his desire to renounce the heresies of his Naturalist period—to which, it so happens, he has never returned. Stanislaw Przybyszewski also underwent a gradual change of heart when restored to the land of his fathers.

He moved from Cracow to Lemberg in 1900, and then to Warsaw, and in all three Polish centres his influence was exerted and felt. If the whole doctrine of the "ego and his own," of what was called "the Absolute," did not convert his colleagues and their readers into so many Sanines, his anarchic individualism, his passion for art, and his own superb example as a stylist contributed enormously to the emancipation of Polish literature from the two evils of mere utilitarianism and mere patriotic propaganda. The problem which confronted Young

Poland was exactly that which W. B. Yeats, Æ., and the others faced in Ireland during the same period, and if the results of their activities in both countries have not been exactly what the pioneers planned, they have fully justified the faith which gave impetus to the movement from which a new literature has sprung. Przybyszewski modified in time the passionate revolt of his German period, and even acquired the tone of the moralist which is the mark of literatures with an inferiority complex, once they lose the props which are supplied by the convenient and glorious past on which the writers in oppressed countries like to dwell. The theatre attracted him and he began to write symbolic dramas in the Ibsenite, or even the Maeterlinckian manner, and the note of middle-class morality became more and more perceptible. In *Strong Men* he repudiated the amoralism of his youth, and in such plays as *Snow* and the cycle of *The Dance of Love and Death* he tumbled rapidly down what a German critic has called "the steep path of definite philistinism."

It is an ironical circumstance that we should have encountered him only in his early incarnation when it was necessary for the professional moralists to avert our faces—by force—from so wanton a spectacle. Nowadays, if we may believe Professor Roman Dyboski, Przybyszewski is "honored as a literary veteran, though little read," whereas in this country, thanks to the efforts of the Society for the Suppression of Vice, he is avidly read by optimists who hope that the suppression of *Homo Sapiens* was a guarantee of its "lewd and lascivious" qualities, but he is without honor, since even his publisher has conferred his title of greatness, once so proudly flaunted beside the title-page, upon the decorous author of *The Peasants*. Yet, in spite of the Nobel Prize, it is doubtful if Wladyslaw Reymont will meet with the response which would have been Przybyszewski's, had it been possible to continue the translations of works which correspond more closely to the ferment of ideas in the younger generation of American readers and writers to-day. His importance in the evolution of which Reymont was a part cannot be overstressed, and all authorities concur in the view of the Polish critic whom I have quoted when he says: "All who once gathered round Przybyszewski, diverse as may be the ways they may have since gone, carry with them the potent stimulus of the idea which he inculcated. The greatest of them, the painter, dramatist, and national prophet Wyspianski, made the noble and memorable admission: 'Without Przybyszewski, we should all have been nothing.'" From which I conclude that it was an advantage, to Poland at least, that the country was deprived of the self-imposed services of Mr. Anthony Comstock and Mr. John S. Sumner.

CANADA

CANADIAN-FRENCH FICTION

In the spring of the year 1921 Daniel Halévy, the friend of Charles Péguy and collaborator in the now famous *Cahiers de la Quinzaine*, aroused the interest of all the friends of that amazing adventure in periodical literature by launching a series of *Cahiers Verts*, in which the main idea of Péguy's editorship was preserved. Each issue of the series is a complete work by one author, but M. Halévy has adopted the conventional format of the French novel, and is obviously editing a series of books, not a periodical of which every number is a book, as Péguy did. The first work selected by the editor showed that, while thus modifying Péguy's plan, he had retained the tradition of befriending newcomers and of breaking new ground. It was a volume entitled *Maria Chapdelaine: Récits du Canada français*, and the author was Louis Hémon, a name unknown to the vast majority of the reading public in France. This simple and charming story of French Canadian farm life had an irresistible appeal in France, where the literature of rural manners lacks the sense of wildness, of great open spaces and of untamed nature, which informs the narrative of Louis Hémon. The book had been published at Montreal in 1916, in a now rare edition, charmingly illustrated with naïve woodcuts, but it did not have any particular success, and to this day the French Canadians are unable to understand its enormous vogue in France, and in the two English translations which were made of it by rival enthusiasts.

The French peasant, whether revealed in the harsh light of a Maupassant and a Zola, or in the more sober colors of a George Sand or a Gaston Chérau, is exceedingly remote from those exiled pioneers in Quebec and Ontario whose link with France is little more than a memory of ancestors who started on a great adventure only to be forever parted from their mother country. In *Maria Chapdelaine* these authentic Canadians, who refuse that title to any other race in Canada, evoke memories long dormant in France, and the tale of their struggle for existence against storm and snow, of their stand for race and tradition against the overwhelming forces of another dispensation, opens up a new perspective in French literature. The descriptions of nature, the faithful notation of the round of tasks, the joys and sorrows, which make up life in those distant regions, gain an added savor from the idiom of this Canadian French, where sonorous archaisms and barbarous Anglicisms jostle one another in the happiest innocence. It is not surprising that this unpretentious story of a farmer's daughter, who loses an unspoken love through the death of a young guide in a snowstorm, and is then married to the farmer of her parents' choice, should have aroused the enthusiasm of French critics. Here was something as different from the incredible "Far West" of French literary convention as from the studies of rural life to which the public had been accustomed in a country whose agricultural population is probably the most settled, comfortable, and unadventurous in Western Europe. This lonely community of almost forgotten French men and women, speaking a tongue akin to that of Ronsard and Montaigne when it is not perilously like the French of Stratford-atte-Bowe, came as a revelation through the fine work of Louis Hémon, just as the Irish of Synge's plays brought a breath of Elizabethan English and the play of elemental human beings into our modern literature.

The history of French-Canadian and Anglo-Irish literature suggests some interesting parallels. In both cases there is the effort of a racial minority to preserve its national identity. In French Canada the substitution of English for the native language has not succeeded as in Ireland, and the situation is somewhat similar to that of two centuries ago, when Irish was still the medium of literary expression. In Ireland there has been a twofold renaissance, for not only is there a growing literature in Irish, but the Anglo-Irish writers, under the Gaelic influence, have so moulded the language imposed by the conquest that it has become an adequate instrument of national self-expression. Anglo-Irish literature is now known as a distinctive manifestation of the Irish spirit, and quite unlike the Anglicized literature by provincial Irishmen which could never be more than a feeble echo.

The literature of French Canada, like that of Ireland, has been largely thrown back upon past history for its material. It was only after the advent of Standish O'Grady and W. B. Yeats and the group associated with the Irish literary renaissance that attention was diverted from old sorrows and hatreds to a broader and deeper conception of nationality. For the past quarter of a century and more Anglo-Irish literature has been concerned with the legends and traditions of the race rather than with the political struggles which succeeded the classic age of Irish culture. In Canada a similar change was initiated by Philippe Aubert de Gaspé in 1863, when he published *Les Anciens Canadiens*. This epic of Canadian-French history surprised its critics by its absence of rancor. The Abbé Camille Roy, an authoritative historian of Canadian French literature, reproaches him with being too ready to approve of "national resignation" in the face of Britain's victory. That is just the sort of criticism which was brought against the pioneers of the revival in Ireland, but literary jingoism has had to submit to the facts, which have justified the innovators by bringing to them and their country the world-fame denied to the purely patriotic writers who preceded them. Similarly, Gaspé's work attained extraordinary popularity and is one of the few Canadian-French works which have been translated.

Maria Chapdelaine is typical of the literature of French Canada, which has been chiefly concerned with rural conditions, as is the case with Irish literature. The Canadians have to face the same problem as their Irish contemporaries. It is not in the half-Anglicized drawing-rooms of Montreal and Quebec that the native spirit thrives, but in the smaller communities and scattered farms, outside the reach of urban influences. While the drama such as it, in the absence of a folk-theatre, is almost entirely restricted to historical subjects, the novel concentrates on the life and manners of the countryside. The lack of good novelists has been the striking anomaly of Anglo-Irish literature until the strange genius of James Joyce began to realize itself in his powerful studies of the middle class. The Irish have the gift of story-telling, the art of the Shanchie persists, but the novel is neglected, or practised as a pot-boiler.

The French-Canadian novelists have been relatively more numerous, but they have had nothing to show comparable to *Maria Chapdelaine*. Apart from the emulators of Gaspé, of whom Laure Conan is the most important, the majority have studied the rural civilization of the old *habitants* and their successors. The first novel of importance was *Charles Guérin*, which had a considerable vogue in the late forties, but the author, P. J. O. Chauveau, was not familiar with the manners of the Canadians except as they revealed themselves in the half-French, half-English society of the large cities. Its success was mainly due to the fact that he wrote with more care for style than was usual at that period—or since! The typical fiction of French Canada dates rather from Gérin-Lajoie's *Jean Rivard*, which appeared some twenty years later. At last there came a novelist who attempted to write the epic of colonization, the struggle of man against nature on the virgin soil of a new country. There is a peculiar, naïve charm to this novel, through which the practical wisdom of the agriculturalist pierces, even to the extent of notes of interest to farmers! Since then others have developed the theme with less obviously utilitarian intention. The hardships and adventures of the pioneers and backwoodsmen, the great life of the prairies and forests—these are the eternal subjects of the Canadian novelists.

Despite the occasional fine work of such men as Doctor Choquette in *Les Ribaud* and *Claude Paysan* during recent years, and the historical tales of Laure Conan, dealing with the period of the Anglo-French War, the average novel continues to trace the more or less external aspects of the rural communities without any achievement worthy of note. Just before the war a new writer, Hector Bernier, came forward with what promised to be a welcome innovation, *Au large de l'écueil* and *Ce que disait la flamme*, two novels of contemporary middle-class society. Unfortunately, bad writing and an excess of that religiosity with which these transplanted French endeavor to compensate for the delinquencies of the original stock in matters of faith, seriously invalidate their claim to serious attention. *Ce que disait la flamme*, however, has this interest, that it sets forth the problem with which the Irish writers have had to contend, the problem of what is known in Ireland as "West Britonism"; that is, the affectation of the pseudo-English, who hold that what is native is vulgar and inferior.

The flowering of poetry in Ireland has its counterpart in French Canada, where Louis Fréchette, who died in 1908, long held the seat of honor as one of the greatest poets in French literature outside France. His *Fleurs boréales* was crowned by the French Academy, and contains some beautiful poems. Fréchette's work, like that of his rival, W. Chapman, is full of a passionate sense of nationality, and in their songs, as in those of the Irish, is heard the plaint of a conquered but undefeated people. The atmosphere of the North, the crisp snows and the mighty forests, are as integral a part of their poetic landscape as the mist and bogland of the Irish poets, and these bring an unaccustomed note into French poetry, so highly civilized and sophisticated and polished. Here is nature as she is seen in the wilds, with a fiercer beauty than the mellow, formal charm of the eighteenth-century landscape-gardening which seems to be the background of so much French poetry.

In the early enthusiasm over *Maria Chapdelaine* there was a salute to the first really fine piece of prose to come out of French Canada. The author was unknown, but in time it was discovered that, though the story came from Canada, Louis Hémon was not a French Canadian. He was a Breton who had gone off to Canada and had written his book out of his first-hand experiences on the farms. His sister describes him as a silent man who "fled from the world and loved solitude and meditation," and this trait, together with the evidence of his book, indicate in him a certain resemblance to J. M. Synge. Like the latter in the Aran Islands, Louis Hémon in Canada learned how to observe and listen, and thus his notation of the Canadian-French idiom is wonderfully effective, for he knows just how far it can be used and how it can give a color and tang to the speech of the people, and he does not allow unconscious barbarisms to spoil his writing, as do so many of the Canadian-French authors. He has done for the speech of French Canada what Synge did for the Irish; he has brought it into literature.

After he had despatched the manuscript of *Maria Chapdelaine* to France, the author started off to tramp across country from St. John's Lake where the book was written. His plan was to follow on foot the route of the Canadian Pacific Railway. At a curve in the line neither he nor his companion heard the approaching train and both were run over and killed. When the letter accepting his story was returned to Paris, marked "dead," there was nobody to whom it could be sent, nor any known source from which information could be obtained concerning the mysterious author. So the story was published in a newspaper, where the father of Louis Hémon first learned of its existence. He wrote to explain the relationship and thus the facts were obtained concerning this supposedly Canadian-French novelist. In Canada, however, the loss of this promising writer, at the age of thirty-three, has been mourned as a loss to the literature of French Canada. A white marble monument has been erected on the spot where he was killed, and in 1919 a commemorative stone was placed at Peribonka, near St. John's Lake, on the farm where he wrote *Maria Chapdelaine*. The Geographical Society of Quebec has renamed two lakes, Lake Hémon and Lake Chapdelaine, in honor of the author who has given French-Canadian literature its first novel to transcend the limits of what has hitherto been a mere by-path of modern letters.

HYPHENATED POETS

HYPHENATED POETS

THE bond of sympathy uniting America and France is curiously affirmed by the preponderance of Americans in what may be termed the Foreign Legion of modern French literature. These naturalized French men of letters are happy exceptions to the rule whose stigma attaches to the word hyphenation, for the Franco-American writers have invariably refused to divest themselves of their American citizenship. If Francis Vielé-Griffin had been willing to add political to literary naturalization he would now share with Henri de Régnier the honor of representing the Symbolist movement in the French Academy. As it is, since the death, in 1916, of his compatriot, Stuart Merrill, he remains the most distinguished member of that group of foreigners, Roumanian, Greek, and even German, who have made a name in the French world of letters. Greece can point to Papadiamantopoulos, whose fame was established in Paris under the now familiar name of Jean Moréas; Roumania is responsible for quite a contingent of *femmes de lettres*, notably Hélène Vacaresco and the Comtesse de Noailles. These are the two most popular successors of Demetrios Bolintineano, whose *Brises d'Orient*, as far back as 1866, brought the Eastern rampart of Latin culture to the notice of France, and earned for him the title of "Roumanian Lamartine." But the American contribution to French literature equals in quantity, and surpasses in quality, that of Roumania, in spite of the latter's racial affinities.

Unlike his compatriots, Francis Vielé-Griffin, Renée Vivien and John Antoine Nau, Stuart Merrill did not altogether abandon the land of his birth. He was born in Hempstead, L. I., in 1863, and in 1887, when his first book, *Les Gammes*, appeared in Paris, he was a student at Columbia University. During this period he contributed critical articles to the *Times* and *Evening Post*, and in 1890, the year of his return to Paris, he published *Pastels in Prose*. This charming little volume of prose poems, Merrill's only book in English, consisted of translations from the younger French writers, many of the Symbolist generation, with whom he had been in contact while in Paris. Probably this work was the first introduction to an English-speaking public of Ephraïm Mikhaël, Pierre Quillard, and Henri de Régnier, to quote some names subsequently associated with the movement of which Merill was an exponent.

His student years in New York saw Merrill converted to socialism, and were devoted to revolutionary propaganda rather than to law, the ostensible subject of his studies at Columbia. He even sold Socialist papers in the streets, but when he returned to France these socialistic activities to some extent ceased. However they left their imprint upon his work; Merrill became the poet of "revolution," in the sense that Whitman was, and he showed all his life a constant bias in favor of those in revolt against society. His verse is tinged with a sadness springing from a sense of latent revolt, but it is only rarely that he allows his social iconoclasm to manifest itself openly, as in *Le Vagabond*, that fine poem which closes his last volume, *Une Voix dans la Foule*:

> "O vagabond, j'entends, dans ta chanson sonore
> L'écroulement des tours des villes de la nuit
> Ou l'incendie, ici et là, rougeoie et bruit,
> Et l'éclat des clairons rouges de la révolte
> Annonçant au soleil la nombreuse récolte
> Dont se rassasieront les pauvres de jadis."

Here one feels all the revolutionary ardor of the poet as he broods over life, finding in the tramp who passes the symbol of that freedom which comes to those who live in contact with nature, who have cast off the bonds of respectability. Yet, in contrast with Whitman, Merrill was rather conservative in his conception of poetry.

Educated at the Lycée Condorcet with René Ghil, Quillard, and Georges Vanor, he founded with them the short-lived journal *Le Fou*, and collaborated in *La Basoche*, *Le Décadent*, and all the various reviews in which the Symbolists essayed their strength, until finally *Le Mercure de France* served to crystallize the new movement.

Stuart Merrill was a contributor to the *Mercure* from the start, and has been consequently identified with the Symbolist group of which it became the centre. It must be said, however, that neither the form nor the content of his verse supplies any ground for the complaints and abuse showered upon the Symbolists. Compared with most of his friends, he showed a legitimate respect for the traditions of French poetry, and his verse presents fewer divergencies from the accepted formulæ than that of Vielé-Griffin. In this respect Merrill resembles Henri de Régnier, whose admission to the Academy was regarded as the final consecration of the Symbolist school.

If Poe had been as great a poet as his disrepute might have indicated him, he would offer the nearest parallel in American literature to the poetry of Stuart Merrill. The note of similarity is not so pronounced in *Poèmes* 1887-1897, the volume in which were collected his three early collections of more markedly Symbolist verse, *Les Gammes*, *Les Fastes*, and *Petits Poèmes d'Automne*. In these, as befitted a young poet *chez Vanier*, the claims of the then "new poetry" had to be accentuated. But his second volume, *Les Quatre Saisons*, and also *Une Voix dans la Foule*, supply numerous examples of that imagination which one feels in Poe, even when he fails adequately to express it. *La Mystérieuse Chanson* and *Les Poings à la Porte* might be cited to show how *The Raven* can be translated into terms of the purest poetry. The length of these poems makes quotation impossible, but the following verses, taken from the manuscript of an unpublished poem, may serve to illustrate a characteristic aspect of Merrill's imagination:

LA DANSE DANS LE CIMETIÈRE

Dansons au soleil, ô ma Joie,
Sur les tombes de la Mort !
Ta bouche est la grenade en proie
Aux désirs des abeilles d'or.

Pour mes chansons et pour ta danse
Il ne faudra ni le cri
Des pipeaux fous, ni la cadence
Des lyres dans le bois fleuri;

Mais seulement ta plainte, ô brise
Qui dans les cyprès t'endors,
Et le silence sans surprise
Du sommeil eternel des morts !

In spite of a certain *macabre* element in his work, however, Merrill has always emphasized the æsthetic duty of the poet. His rejection of current social conventions did not leave him without a well-defined morality. The true reformist spirit of the socialist is back of the conviction that "modern society is an ill-made poem which we must correct. In the etymological sense of the word a poet is always and everywhere a poet, and his duty is to try to bring some beauty into the world." This conviction not only inspired Stuart Merrill to write some of the most delicate and musical verses of his generation, it impelled him to take an active part in every enterprise which tended to raise the intellectual and spiritual level of the masses.

In a group of literary exquisites, whose thoughts were turned toward essentially abstract beauty, it was the distinction of this American to represent the union of life and art. Perhaps no happier illustration could be found of that native desire for the practical application of ideas than this atavistic manifestation of Americanism.

The most recent names in the list of American writers are those of Renée Vivien and Natalie Clifford Barney. Renée Vivien was the pseudonym of Pauline Tarn, who died a few years ago. Between 1901 and 1909 she published more than a dozen volumes, both prose and verse, and her premature death was deeply regretted. This slender, fair young woman revealed her Anglo-American race in every feature, and her life in the English-speaking colony of Paris, where she formed most of her ties, seemed to belie the poetess of *Evocations* and *Flambeaux Eteints*.

Her literary personality found expression only in the purest melodies of the French tongue, in those passionate verses whose intensity of emotion caused her to be described as "the new Sappho." A species of intuition, strengthened by the experiences of her own peculiar temperament, enabled her to translate, paraphrase, and complete the thought of the Greek singer whose spiritual descendant she was and whose amorous temperament was hers. Her version of Sappho in 1903 attracted considerable attention on this score, and confirms a relationship suggested by her first volume, *Etudes et Préludes*, published in 1901.

Mention should be made of John Antoine Nau, of

San Francisco, whose fame as a novelist has over-shadowed that of the poet since 1905, when *Force Ennemie* received the prize of the Goncourt Academy. But it is more interesting to consider for a moment the poet who alone represents a most creditable variety of "hyphenated American," since the death of Stuart Merrill. Francis Vielé-Griffin was born in Norfolk, Va., in 1864, while his father, General Egbert Louis Vielé, was quartered there, in charge of the Federal forces. In a novel published a few years ago, *Eve Dorre*, his sister has related, with the poetic license of fiction, the circumstances of Vielé-Griffin's childhood in Paris. After the Franco-Prussian War the family settled in France, the country from which their Huguenot ancestors fled in the seventeenth century, and, while one brother, Hermann K. Vielé, returned to make a name as an American novelist, the other became celebrated as a French poet.

His first book, *Cueille d'Avril*, was published in 1886, one year before Merrill's *Les Gammes*, and in rapid succession there followed the inevitable privately printed *plaquettes*, and the little books of verse with Vanier's imprint—the traditional procedure in young Symbolist circles. This early work was first collected in 1895 and published by the *Mercure de France* as *Poèmes et Poésies*. Since that date all his important works have been issued by the same publisher, *La Clarté de Vie*, *Phocas le Jardinier*, *La Légende Ailée de Wieland le Forgeron*, *Plus Loin*, and *Voix d'Ionie*.

As may be seen, Vielé-Griffin is a more prolific writer than was Stuart Merrill, whose work is contained in three volumes. From the beginning he threw himself whole-heartedly into the Symbolist movement, having founded with Henri de Régnier and Paul Adam *Les Entretiens Politiques et Littéraires*, that famous review whose red cover was the symbol of a literary revolution. Vielé-Griffin soon became one of the greatest exponents of *vers libre*, fortifying theory by the remarkable workmanship of his own verse.

It is perhaps more than a mere coincidence that the land of Walt Whitman should have given birth to this poet who participated so ardently in the movement which was to liberate the technic of French verse. As time went on, others made concessions to the precise regularities of poetic tradition, but Vielé-Griffin has been consistently intransigeant. Indeed, it is probable that the theory of "free verse" captured the imagination of his generation largely because of his translations of Whitman.

Vielé-Griffin is a *vers-libriste* rather than a Symbolist, and his claim to consideration must be based largely upon the influence of his work in this connection. He did not decide to break away from the metrical conventions on intellectual or theoretical grounds, but turned to free verse in a perfectly instinctive manner:

> "Le rythme de sa voix est ma seule métrique,
> Et son pas alterne ma rime nuancée."

He has a Whitmanesque breadth of inspiration, a deep feeling for nature, whose immensities and beauties he has sung in rhythms which recall those of Whitman. Such poems as *Etire-toi la vie*, *La Moisson*, and the numerous pictures of his beloved Touraine which Vielé-Griffin has given us, indicate his sensitiveness toward natural beauty. All his poetry has been a hymn to creation, the expression of a simple joy in living. Yet he is not devoid of subtlety.

Except for his translations from Swinburne and Whitman, Vielé-Griffin has placed on record no evidence of his affiliations with the English language.

He is, nevertheless, a truly "hyphenated" American in the best sense of the word, for he has remained true to his United States citizenship. Had he been willing to become politically, as well as intellectually, a naturalized Frenchman, he might have been honored with a seat in the Academy, but when his candidature was put forward he refused to comply with that condition precedent of Academic immortality.

His Americanism, however, has been most effectively demonstrated in his contribution to French literature, which owes to him its first acquaintance with the great genius of *vers libre*. Others have completed the work of translating Whitman; the technical qualities of the latter's work have exercised a profound revolution in French poetry, but the advantage of innovation and early practical example lay with Vielé-Griffin. He is, therefore, primarily responsible for the evolution of contemporary verse both in his native and his adopted country.

By a literary reversion America is now relearning from France the lesson which she originally imparted through the intermediary of Vielé-Griffin. Yet, as if to emphasize the biblical dictum concerning prophets, neither he nor Stuart Merrill has received much consideration at the hands of those who interpret French poetry in this country, and whose constant preoccupations are the latest literary fads of Paris. On the contrary, the American æsthete and his friends in London delight rather in a strange literature of miscegenation, a hybrid written in anglicized French by French writers whose knowledge of English is shaky and by English and American authors whose French should never have been allowed to pass the vigilant eye of their governess. The difference between the Franco-American poets of the last generation and those of to-day, is one which throws an interesting light upon the evolution of contemporary literature.

T. S. Eliot is the most prominent example of a tendency which might be illustrated by reference to many lesser-known contributors to the clique reviews of London, New York, and Paris. Mr. Eliot is described by one of his chief coryphæi, Richard Aldington, as "a distinguished American poet and critic," and he warns us very truculently that we must not criticise Mr. Eliot but bow before his linguistic, critical, and poetic achievements. As a poet and the author of *The Waste Land*, T. S. Eliot has provided me with a vast amount of innocent amusement; he is as superb a *farceur* as Guillaume Apollinaire. As a critic and the author of *The Sacred Wood*, he is one of the most orthodox and dry-as-dust of the younger pedants; his æsthetic theory bears no relation whatever to his practice. As the editor of *The Criterion*, he produces one of the handsomest and best literary reviews in England, again without any reference to the kind of writing in which he himself indulges to the admiration of his friends. But all these activities have one merit in common—they are in English, a language which Mr. Eliot knows and understands.

Unfortunately, it is also his pleasure to write in French, and here one is compelled to descend from the level at which differences of literary opinion are legitimate to that elementary stage where errors of grammar, syntax, and idiom are involved. One cannot discuss T. S. Eliot's French "poetry" until one has corrected his French. Apart from typographical errors, with which his verses in that language are freely disfigured from one edition to another, his mutilation of the French language is serious beyond question. In a poem highly cherished by the initiated, *Mélange adultère de tout*, one encounters at the outset a typical blunder made by tyros in French. The idiom "*se payer la tête de quelqu'un*" becomes "*vous me paierez bien la tête*" instead of "*vous vous paierez bien ma tête.*" Beginners in French usually make this mistake when using reflexive verbs, and Mr. Eliot makes it again in another poem, *Dans le restaurant*, where he writes "*de quel droit payes-tu des expériences,*" when he means "*de quel droit te payes-tu des expériences.*" In the same poem "*il fera temps pluvieux*" reveals the tyro once more misled by the false analogy of the simple phrase "*il fait beau temps,*" for in this case he should have said "*il fera un temps pluvieux.*" The first-mentioned poem, which excites the particular enthusiasm of Mr. Aldington, closes with the lines,

> "On montrera mon cénotaphe
> Aux côtes brûlantes de Mozambique,"

which evidently are an attempt to say "my cenotaph will be pointed out on the burning shores of Mozambique." What Mr. Eliot actually says is that the cenotaph will be pointed out *to* the burning shores, for "*aux côtes*" is not French for "*sur les côtes.*" Similarly "*pierres écroulantes*" should be "*pierres croulantes,*" for "*écrouler*" is a reflexive verb and must be "*s'écrouler.*" The reverse error occurs in "*on relève les draps pour mieux égratigner,*" where the reflexive form, "*s'égratigner,*" is required. "*Jambes molles tout gonflées*" should be "*toutes gonflées.*" There is even literal and unidiomatic translation from English, such as "*rediger un bilan*" instead of "*dresser un bilan.*"

In brief, where Stuart Merrill and Vielé-Griffin mastered French and contributed to modern French literature, their successors contribute neither to that literature nor their own. The laws of the French language are beyond the range of the vituperation which is the lot of all who protest against this butchery of language by a little group of provincial cosmo-politans, who misunderstand each other in two languages and are masters of none. It is not a question of doubtful points of phrasing or of the slightly exotic flavor which a language may have when written by a foreigner. Joseph Conrad has been criticized on that score, but had he written English like T. S. Eliot's French, making the equivalent blunders, he would have said, "There were ten minutes that he was holding himself on the door regarding the sun couching itself"; but I do not think any responsible adult would argue that this was good English for, "He had been standing at the door for ten minutes watching the sun go down." There are crimes and crimes!

INDEX

INDEX

INDEX

329